The Psychological Roots
of religious belief

The *Psychological Roots*
of religious belief

Searching for Angels and the Parent-God

M. D. Faber

Prometheus Books

59 John Glenn Drive
Amherst, New York 14228-2197

Published 2004 by Prometheus Books

Inquiries should be addressed to
Prometheus Books
59 John Glenn Drive
Amherst, New York 14228–2197
VOICE: 716–691–0133, ext. 207
FAX: 716–564–2711
WWW.PROMETHEUSBOOKS.COM

08 07 06 05 04   5 4 3 2 1

Library of Congress Cataloging-in-Publication Data

Faber, M. D. (Mel D.)
    The psychological roots of religious belief : searching for angels and the parent-god / M. D. Faber.
        p. cm.
    Includes bibliographical references and index.
    ISBN 1–59102–267–3 (hardcover : alk. paper)
    1. Psychology, Religious. I. Title.

BL51.F295 2004
200'.1'9—dc22

                                                        2004014877

Printed in the United States of America on acid-free paper

For Maxwell Joseph Faber

Contents

Preface

I regard what follows as a modest contribution to the emerging field of "neurotheology," as Eugene G. D'Aquili, Andrew B. Newberg, and Vince Rause express it in their volume, *Why God Won't Go Away*. Curious creatures that we are, we want to know all about the nature of our nature, including of course our evolutionally advanced mind-brains, which mediate our experience in the world. What might the growth and structure of the mind-brain have to do with our belief in a deity, in angels, or in the supernatural generally and also with our sense that such entities are actually there for us under certain conditions, such as prayer? I attempt to offer a few suggestions on this matter from a specific psychological angle that focuses on the first years of life, on the parent-child relationship, and particularly on how that relationship gets memorialized, or internalized, into the perceptual apparatus to influence or even govern our behavior, including our religious enactments. My guiding assumptions throughout have been, first, that formal descriptions of the way the mind-brain works become especially rich when they are tied directly to people's interpersonal relations and, secondly, that all religious experience has a developmental, psychological history that must be included in the picture if one wants to understand what's going on. I am hoping the reader, whether or not she subscribes to my psychodynamic theoretical perspective, will find the book elic-

iting fresh, perhaps crucial thoughts on the role of religious consciousness in our lives. As for the ultimate questions religion may pose—Why
are we here? What is life's meaning? Where did the universe come
from?—I leave them alone. This is not because I'm uninterested in such
issues; they just don't have anything to do with the kind of book I am
writing. The reader who yearns for this sort of engagement would do
well to seek out an expert in the upper regions, that is to say, a theologian or religious philosopher, not a hardheaded, psychological investigator plugging away down here.

I've had lots of help and encouragement along the way from a
variety of individuals, but mostly from the members of my family, whose
names I always delight in mentioning: Rebecca, Jared, Paula, Ethan,
Maxwell, Paul, and Arlene. I might have done this without them, but it
wouldn't have been easy. I extend to them a naturalistic blessing as well
as my heartfelt thanks. As for intellectual guidance proper, I am
indebted overwhelmingly to clinical psychoanalytic observation from
its inception to the present day, and in especial to the writings of D. W.
Winnicott, Marion Milner, and Margaret Mahler. I could cite other
names, of course, but these are the pivotal ones. I want also to mention
the staff of the library at the University of California, Irvine, whose
patience and assistance made the task much more pleasant, and much
more doable, than it would otherwise have been. Finally, I am grateful
to Ms. Bonnie Johnson for her extremely proficient production of the
final version of the manuscript and to Mr. Benjamin Keller of
Prometheus Books for his outstanding editorial assistance.

1.
Introduction

ANGEL: FROM THE GREEK ANGELOS,
MEANING 'MESSENGER'

Angels are indeed messengers, with extraordinary things to tell us, but they do not come from the supernatural realm, from God, from what we sometimes call "the beyond." They come from the human mind, including its unconscious component, and *only* from there. Thus they tell us about ourselves. They tell us about the motives that drive us to create a world of spirits and to indulge in rituals, or enactments, which magically empower and sustain us as we go about our business on the planet. My purpose in what follows is to develop this thesis in meticulous detail, to offer the reader a wide variety of materials through which the essential nature of angelic beings will emerge, along with—and this is my ultimate goal—the underlying psychological quality of religious beliefs and practices. In short, I will utilize my examination of angels as I work to construct a naturalistic view of religious experience. Naturalism is defined as a theory denying that an object or event has a supernatural significance and suggesting that scientific laws are adequate to account for all phenomena. I am not suggesting in the previous three sentences, of course, that I plan to explain the whole of religious experience, both past and present, as it has flourished in the world. Indeed, such experience is so variegated, so ancient, so boundless, as it were, that only a madman would set out to explain the whole of it. My intention is simply to offer enough to fashion a reasonably thorough and coherent picture, one that discloses, if not everything, then numerous crucial, central features, the proverbial pith of the matter.

THEORETICAL ALTERNATIVES

I offer a naturalistic view of religious experience not as a refutation of supernaturalism but as an alternative to it. We are dealing, truth be told, with subjective states, with emotions, with what depth psychology calls "affect" in its effort to wed unconscious developmental factors from the past to the individual's current feelings or inclinations. The materials that arise from this non-Cartesian world of perceptual, mind-body experience will of necessity be "soft," or elusive, both in relation to our examples and the conclusions we draw from them. The person who attempts to prove (or disprove) the naturalistic nature of religious experience in a manner similar to that which he would use to prove (or disprove) the heliocentric theory of the solar system or the molecular theory of chemical bonding will fall flat on his face. This does not mean that I won't try to establish my argument in a powerful, utterly convincing way. It does not mean that I won't proceed as if I had the answers, as if I were laying the matter bare, for every intelligent individual to see. Quite the contrary, I will strive to build an airtight case. At the same time, I realize that supernaturalists everywhere are just as convinced of their views as I am of mine. When the dust settles, the reader will simply make up his mind as to which explanation is more credible, the naturalistic or the supernaturalistic one, as I present them of course.

To express the matter from another angle, were someone to ask me how I *know* that God or some such supernatural entity is not behind everything in the world, including angels, I would reply at once, *I don't know*. I know only that religious matters, including angels, can be reasonably, competently, satisfactorily explained down to the nuances themselves by the psychological approaches and analyses that I will bring to bear in the pages to follow. When it comes to the *ultimate* questions, when I am asked to explain the origins of everything, the universe and all that dwells within it no less, I simply shrug my shoulders in total ignorance. How am I supposed to know such things, and what rational person would *expect* me to know them? While I do have a way of explaining the religious materials in front of my nose, I have no way whatsoever of explaining what occurred in the deepest past, what triggered the beginning (if there was one) or the event to which scientists currently refer as the big bang—that is, unless I adopt the religious perspective myself and thereby defeat the whole purpose of my discussion. Let me assure the reader, were I somehow able to *know* the answers to the ultimate questions, I would not be writing this book; I would not be troubling myself about angels, of all things. I would be attending to other matters worthy of an omniscient, godlike being, ruling the earth, for example.

My success here depends overwhelmingly on what we can think of as fine-grained work. Again and again I will subject my quotations, my examples, my data from the religious realm to intense, close, even delicate probing along specific theoretical lines set forth in subsequent sections where I offer the reader a psychodynamic model of human development with special emphasis on the first years of life, the years during which the seeds of religious belief are sown. Ultimately, I am looking for connections between religious belief as it emerges through narrative, precept, metaphor, and symbol, and psychological proposition as it emerges through clinical, therapeutic practice, through recent neuropsychological investigations of the human mind-brain and through related anthropological study of magical behavior. From the meticulous, fine-grained application of analytical insight to religious expression, and from that alone, the meaning of the book will emanate. In this way, the book depends entirely on the reader being struck by the details of the analysis, by the unmistakable, even amazing correspondences between the religious and psychological materials I bring to bear. This must occur many times, over scores of pages, until the argument in all its complexity is finally established.

It is time now to put forward a brief, preliminary statement of the book's overall contention, or thesis. Remember as you read the next few paragraphs that I am not writing a historical or cross-cultural treatise. My analysis explores only the current or relatively recent Western religious scene, the past one hundred years or so. Nor do I plan to deal in depth with group or congregational practices. The emphasis throughout will be upon individual, subjective experiences including above all the intensely emotional or "powerful" kind, which dominate the sources I employ. That such experiences can and do occur frequently in congregational settings or in the presence of other people should be obvious enough.

2.

The Basic Biological Situation

Our human lives are perceptual and emotional continuities. While it is mistaken to reduce the present to the past, it is also mistaken to divorce the past from the present. The soil, the ground, from which religious experience arises is the early period of our existence in the world, the period during which the child and the parent are locked in elemental care-giving, care-receiving interactions, or in what I choose to call henceforth, the basic biological situation. Here are a few specifics. The child is hungry; the child cries out. Then what happens? The caregiver appears to nourish and to soothe. The child is frightened; the child cries out. Then what happens? The caregiver arrives to reassure and to placate. The child is wet and uncomfortable; the child cries out. Then what happens? The caregiver appears with dry garments and ministering hands. The child is injured; the child cries out. What then? The caregiver comes forward to examine, and kiss, and "make better." Over and over again, dozens of times each day, hundreds of times each week, thousands of times each month, for years, the little one asks and the big one, the care-giving, all-powerful parent, sees to it that the little one receives. (The biblical formula for the heartfelt prayer that summons one's guardian angel to one's side is "ask and ye shall receive" [Mark 11:24].) Accordingly, life's early stages are characterized by what we can think of as a continuous biological rhythm of expressive need

17

and timely care, an endless series of crises and rescues, of asking and receiving, and in every instance it is a helpless, dependent little one who expresses the need, who does the asking, and it is a nourishing, succoring, protective big one who performs the requested, required ministrations. One would be hard-pressed to discover within the realm of nature another example of physiological and emotional conditioning to compare with this one in both depth and duration. Let's bear in mind that the basic biological situation is quite literally "a matter of life and death." The child is utterly dependent upon the all-powerful provider for his very survival.* A newly born zebra is up and running (sometimes for its life) a few minutes after emerging from its mother's womb; by contrast, the human infant has no resource but his cry for many, many months after his appearance on the planet. In this way, what happens early on is destined to "imprint" itself upon the child's developing *brain*, to forge permanent, specialized, synaptic connections at the root of the child's perceptual existence. But more of that in a moment.

AFFECTIVE ATTACHMENT

The little one's drive, or urge, to attach himself to the parent, indeed to elicit from the parent his life-giving nourishment, is sustained and strengthened by *affect*, a motive to action that is *felt* and not merely apprehended as an end. The basic biological situation is not a mechanical process but a living, emotional symbiosis streaked with powerful, dynamic feelings in both directions, with what we generally and informally call "love," and also with anxiety because care-giving and care-receiving are far from perfect and often encounter delay and even some sharp dissatisfaction. As it turns out, anxiety, delay, and dissatisfaction only increase the presence of positive affect as needs are finally met,

---

* Although this book refers to the child in the child-parent relationship with masculine pronouns, this is only a grammatical convenience, to differentiate him from the parent in question, which in most cases is the mother. Unless otherwise indicated, it should be understood that female children undergo the same developmental processes as male children.

provided that discomfort does not become severe or unbearable. Thus the child's instinctual endowment is not simply linked to affect; it is physiologically dependent upon affect for its successful, efficacious expression. Silvan Tomkins puts it this way in his monumental volume *Affect, Imagery, Consciousness*: "In our view, the primary motivational system is the affective system, and the biological drives have motivational impact only when amplified by the affective system." And again, "The drive system is . . . secondary to the affect system. Much of the motivational power of the drive system is borrowed from the affect system, which is ordinarily activated concurrently as an amplifier for the drive signal." It is affect that "guarantees" the motivational power of drives.[1] As human beings, and from the inception of our lives, we are in the world feelingly, perceive the world feelingly, interact with others feelingly, inhabit our minds and our bodies feelingly. The upshot? There is a tight, dynamic connection between what Tomkins calls the affect system and the appearance of the internalized "presence" or "object"[2] within the individual's psychological reality.

INTERNALIZATION AND IMPRINTING

As the parent-child relationship develops over time it is steadily, unremittingly *internalized* by the growing youngster, not in some vague, metaphorical way, mind you, but emotionally, affectively, organically, even *neurally* until it becomes the foundation of his budding perceptual existence. For a psychology of religion, this is of the utmost importance. The caregiver is taken psychically inside and set up as an internalized presence, or object, which is integrally connected to, indeed which is inseparable from, the emerging self. The early interaction becomes imprinted on the brain. What occurs as little one and big one revolve around each other like twin stars results in the establishment of actual neural pathways within the recesses of our chief perceptual organ (Hebb's famous principle: repeated behaviors strengthen synaptic connections). When we look within and discover what we take to be the self, our self, we discover not only a *relationship*, we discover not only a oneness which is ultimately a twoness, but we *respond affectively* to our inward perception in a manner that mnemonically recalls (among other things, of course) our early interaction with our primary provider. This holds for the entire course of our lives. As William Wordsworth poetically renders the matter in a famous line of verse from "My Heart Leaps Up," "The child is the father of the man." Thus we are physiologically, genetically, normally endowed with both a capacity and a predisposition to process current information along neural pathways that harbor our previous experience, including our experience of the basic biological situation, our experience of being a helpless, dependent little one in the care and protection of an all-powerful parent. "We cannot separate our memories of the ongoing events of our lives from what has happened to us previously," writes Daniel Schacter in his celebrated volume *Searching for Memory*.[3] Daniel Siegel expresses it this way in his equally celebrated book, *The Developing Mind*: "The mind emerges from the substance of the brain as it is shaped by interpersonal relationships." And again, "At birth, the infant's brain is the most undifferentiated organ in the body. Genes and early experience shape the way neurons connect to one another and thus form specialized circuits that give rise to mental processes." And finally, "Experiences early in life have a tremendously important impact on the developing mind."[4] The point is, when an individual suddenly, spontaneously senses the inward or outwardly hovering presence of an empathetic "supernatural" entity, or when he accedes with strong emotion to the idea that a benign divinity resides within or watches over him, he is recontacting, or relocating, the benign internalization, the benign inward *relationship*, upon which his life and well-being have been founded. He makes contact easily with the supernatural domain because in a manner of speaking *he has been there all along*. He has been living with or in the company of powerful, unseen, life-sustaining presences since he commenced the process of mind-body internalization, of interactional, physiological *imprinting*, as it naturally and persistently arose from his *affective interaction* with the all-powerful provider, the big one who appeared over and over again, ten thousand times, to rescue him from hunger and distress and to respond to his emotional and interpersonal needs, to his deep affective drive for *attachment*. The "mystery" of

tive symbiosis to the quasi-religious objects through whom he has maintained his primal, life-sustaining attachments. He knows exactly how to play the perceptual game that organized religion now asks him to play, and he is only too happy to idealize the internalized caregiver, or object, into a state of projective perfection, into an entity of perfect love and care, at the prompting of his mentors, and in the pleasurable excitement of removing whatever imperfections may have attended his actual early experience. The shortcomings his caregivers may have evinced as they participated in the basic biological situation the child can now erase as he luxuriates in the psychic possession of a flawless, loving, masterful Deity (this will vary qualitatively from one religion to another, from Jesus to Allah to the God of the Jews, as we shall see). Moreover, when religious narrative arrives upon the scene, the developing child's susceptibility to "priming" is *unqualified*. Implicit memories of symbiotic and postsymbiotic states fall into comfortable affective alignment with the religious messages of the cultural domain. The child's unconscious mind resonates to religious narrative *before* his rational faculties have ripened, *before* he can see and critically evaluate what it is that asks for his perceptual assent. Thus he is ready, mentally and emotionally ready, for the religious world that comes to embrace him, to offer him its alluring stories of supernatural guidance and eternal provision. The "hallucinatory sense of unity" will continue unabated.

NOTES

1. Silvan Tomkins, *Affect, Imagery, Consciousness*, vol. 1 (New York: Springer, 1962), pp. 6, 22, 24.

2. The term *object* is used customarily in psychology because the infant has yet to perceive the caretaker, usually the mother, as a separate, full-fledged *person* in the way we normally intend the term. *Object* is a linguistic attempt to render the phenomenology of the infant's perception.

3. Daniel Schacter, *Searching for Memory: The Brain, the Mind, the Past* (New York: Basic Books, 1996), p. 5.

4. Daniel Siegel, *The Developing Mind: Toward a Neurobiology of Interpersonal Experience* (New York: Guilford Press, 1999), pp. 1, 14.

5. Schacter, *Searching for Memory*, pp. 174, 10.

6. Ibid., pp. 167, 60.

7. Siegel, *The Developing Mind*, pp. 24, 29, 30.

8. Erik Erikson, *Insight and Responsibility* (New York: W. W. Norton, 1964), p. 153.

9. Erik Erikson, *Young Man Luther* (New York: W. W. Norton, 1958), p. 264.

10. Joan W. Anderson, *Where Angels Walk* (New York: Ballantine Books, 1993), pp. 81–82.

11. Erikson, *Young Man Luther*, p. 264.

3.

Credulity and
the Skeptical Tradition

That supernatural entities, including the gods and spirits of the religious realm, are human fabrications with no basis in reality is an idea as old as the hills. It turns up in ancient India, China, Greece, and Rome, and it appears sporadically in various regions of the world throughout the course of history.[1] However, it is only during the past five centuries, in the scientific societies of the West, that what we may term "a projection theory of religion" achieves widespread influence,[2] largely through the work of powerful thinkers such as Michel Eyquem de Montaigne, Denis Diderot, Thomas Hobbes, David Hume, Ludwig Feuerbach, Karl Marx, and Friedrich Nietzsche. "Religion is the dream of the human mind," writes Feuerbach in 1841,[3] echoing the skeptical conclusions of the Enlightenment. "God is dead," pronounces Nietzsche in 1882,[4] expressing succinctly the doubt and disbelief that have flourished on the Continent for more than three hundred years. In this way, when Sigmund Freud in 1927 pens what we may regard as a cornerstone of the modern psychology of religion, namely *The Future of an Illusion*, he is working within a well-established tradition, especially in the German-speaking world. While there are no direct references to Feuerbach in Freud's corpus, we can hardly doubt that Freud knew Feuerbach's notorious book, with its depictions of religion as a "dream" and theology as an "illusion."[5] As for the profundity of Nietzsche's influence on Freud—there really is no other way to express the matter—it is by now an uncontested fact. What is fresh and vital about Freud's projection theory is his approach to the origin and nature of projection. The religious world does not arise from projection in some diffuse general sense; it arises, in significant measure, from projection as it is rooted in the individual's early experience, the years during which parental ministrations protect the neonate and the child from both the dangers of the external world and from the anxieties that perforce attend the condition of helplessness, of absolute dependency. At their foundation, religious projections are unconscious.

"Religious ideas," writes Freud, "are illusions, fulfillments of the oldest, strongest, and most urgent wishes of mankind."[6] He goes on:

> The secret of their strength lies in the strength of these wishes. . . . The terrifying impression of helplessness in childhood aroused the need for protection—for protection through love—which was provided by the father; and the recognition that this helplessness lasts throughout life made it necessary to cling to the existence of a father, but this time a more powerful one. Thus the benevolent rule of a divine Providence allays our fear of the dangers of life; the establishment of a moral world-order ensures the fulfillment of the demands of justice; . . . and the prolongation of earthly existence in a future life provides the local and temporal framework in which these wish-fulfillments shall take place. (pp. 47–48)

In this way, when individuals confront the overwhelming powers of nature, as well as the imperfections of society and the tragedies of personal loss, they "fall back upon" an "infantile model" (p. 31) and cling to the notion that "over each one of us there watches a benevolent Providence which is only seemingly stern and which will not suffer us to become a plaything of the over-mighty and pitiless forces of nature" (p. 26). Indeed, nature itself is "humanized" (p. 22) through mankind's projective "longing" for the "father" and for "the gods" (p. 24). It boils down, then, to our helplessness at life's inception and to our helplessness throughout life's course: "When the growing individual finds that he is destined to remain a child forever, that he can never do without protection against strange superior powers, he lends those powers the features belonging to the figure of the father; he creates for himself the gods whom he dreads, whom he seeks to propitiate, and whom he nevertheless trusts with his own protection." In this "precisely" is "the formation of religion" (p. 35).

We might note here Freud's sensitivity to religion's adaptive, "emotional value" (p. 86), his recognition of the soothing, comforting role religion plays in the world—something Freud's critics generally ignore when they present his position. "Life is hard to bear," states Freud (p. 21), and without "religious ideas" would not be "tolerable" for many individuals (p. 28). Nor is Freud unaware of the mother's role in all this, although he gives the mother short shrift in his analysis as a whole: "The mother, who satisfies the child's hunger, becomes its first love-object and certainly also its first protection against all the undefined dangers which threaten it in the external world—its first protection against anxiety, we may say" (p. 34). However, in spite of religion's consolatory powers and soothing, adaptational functions, it is, finally, regressive, infantile, irrational—the product of "ignorance and intellectual weakness" (p. 70). Religion bears witness, Freud asserts, to humanity's fixation on "wishful illusions," to its present state of "blissful, hallucinatory confusion," to its "disavowal of reality" (p. 71). In a famous, perhaps provocative figure, Freud maintains that religion is "the universal obsessional neurosis of humanity" (ibid.). And what of the future? It is not without hope: "most . . . infantile neuroses are overcome spontaneously in the course of growing up," writes Freud, and "this is especially true of the obsessional neuroses" (p. 70). Thus, "a turning-away from religion" is "bound to occur" sooner or later "with the fatal inevitability of a process of growth" (p. 71). As a matter of fact, "we [now] find ourselves . . . in the middle of that phase of development" (ibid.). God may not be dead, as Nietzsche affirmed, but he is surely dying according to Freud. "Men cannot remain children forever" (p. 81). Freud had other interesting and controversial things to say about religious matters in such books as *Civilization and Its Discontents* and *Moses and Monotheism*, but it is *The Future of an Illusion* that has left an indelible mark on the modern psychology of religion.

REVISIONS, INCLUDING
A PIVOTAL CHANGE OF COURSE

Much of this moves us in the right direction—above all, Freud's insistence upon rooting religious beliefs and practices biologically in the "helplessness" of "childhood," in the "need for protection through love," and in the projection of that childhood need onto the gods, or God. We may consider such views to be commonplace today, at least among psychologically oriented skeptics, but in the early twentieth century they contained groundbreaking, revolutionary insight. At the same time, however, several facets of Freud's critical thinking require substantial revision, undertaken here both to indicate what I regard as noteworthy misrenderings of human behavior and to deepen and enrich the brief summary of our thesis proffered in the previous section.

I will set aside Freud's view of religion as "the universal obsessional neurosis of humanity," or the panhuman psychological malaise. There may be some sense in which this is so, and obviously during certain historical periods and in some individual instances religion does appear to be a self-persecuting, anxiety-laden sickness, at least in Western culture. Yet the overall picture, especially today, fails to support this view. When Freud describes religion as a "blissful hallucinatory confusion" he comes much nearer the mark, particularly in reference to religious faith itself, as we'll eventually see. No question the religious realm is obsessional, persistently urging participation upon its practitioners who frequently cannot survive apart from it. But then, eating and sleeping and making love and just plain enjoying oneself are also in a loose, informal sense obsessional. When it comes to religion, I believe Freud's word is more aptly used in this soft, metaphorical manner.

Nor will I offer the father here as the primary figure in the realm of religious "illusions." On the contrary, I find the maternal figure, or the maternal "object," to recall the terminology of our earlier summary, residing at the foundation, at the relational core from which the symbols of religion arise and flourish. By the time the father emerges as Deity in consciousness and ritual, He harbors within the complexity of His image the structuring, formative pre-Oedipal years during the course of which the person's primary internalizations develop. The projective Father-God inherits the longings, the conflicts, the anxieties, the joys and exaltations—in a word, the goodness and the badness—of life's initial stages. Accordingly, the maternal object resides in the figure of the paternal Almighty and is always perceived there unconsciously by the worshiper. To put it somewhat differently, when development leads normally toward separation from the primary caregiver and the establishment of ego boundaries for the child, the father and his projection into the Father-God are there to catch and to hold the growing individual. Indeed, unless development leads away from the mother, particularly for young males,[7] we are apt to get deep and lasting disturbance, distorted perception, inner turmoil, actual or emotional incest. Such disturbance within the spiritual realm is often acted out in occultism or wizardry or shamanism where the self-absorbed, all-powerful magician reflects the omnipotence and primary narcissism characteristic of the first relationship, as we'll also eventually see.

To grow up and become persons we must reach the Oedipal level; we must find our way to the Father-God. However—and this is the point—we do not leave the maternal object behind when we do so. The whole of infantile life, the whole of early childhood, is absorbed into our religious wishing, at the center of which is the urge to join with the Almighty and hence to recapture (among other things) the sensation of inviolable security, or symbiosis. Thus, when we worship, when we indulge our "religious ideas," we worship and indulge "from" the infant, "from" the child, as well as "from" the adolescent and adult. When we sense the presence of God, we sense Him "from" the infant and child within, as well as "from" the wishes and needs of the adult. This means of course that we behave religiously "from" the stage in which infant and child interact primarily with the maternal figure. It means that our religious life reaches all the way down to the infant and the child of the endopsychic world in whom reside our implicit, unconscious memories of the early symbiotic interactions. When Freud turns to the religious realm in *Civilization and Its Discontents* and writes that "religious needs" are ultimately derived from the "infant's helplessness" and from the "longing for the father" aroused by such helplessness; and when he declares further that this causal scheme appears "incontrovertible" because he "cannot think of any need in childhood as strong as the need for a father's protection," he obliges us to ask, where is the mother in all of this, and where are those feelings tied to the child's interaction with the mother?[8] Is not the need for symbiosis, union, or a close, protective relationship with the mothering figure as strong as the need for a father's protection, and is not the problem of separation from the parents, and especially from the mother, one of, if not the, key problems of childhood? It is almost astonishing that Freud could so neglect this aspect of human development in his analysis of the origin of religious needs and, ultimately, of the cultural configurations that arise from them. Feminist literature usually calls this Freud's patriarchal bias or patriarchal distortion of our psychological development. There will be no such bias, no such distortion here.

We come now to the pivotal items in this revision. When Freud describes "religious ideas" as the "fulfillments of the oldest, strongest and most urgent wishes of mankind," and goes on to pinpoint "the secret of their strength" in "the strength of these wishes,"[9] he prompts us to maintain the following: the strength of religious ideas is linked not only to the wish for protection and care—a powerful incentive, to be sure— it is linked also, and more fundamentally, to the *unconscious associative confirmation of religious ideas* that arises from the nature of the early period and in particular from the manner in which the caregiver is internalized into the perceptual system, indeed, neurally imprinted on the brain itself, such that "religious ideas" both reflect and deepen the inward affective experience of the individual to whom such ideas are presented. As we saw in our summary, the growing individual is perceptually, even epistemologically ready to accept the spiritual realm, the supernatural domain, the "religious idea" with its reassuring suggestions of parental ministration and protection, because in a manner of speaking he has been there all along; for some considerable time he has been harboring and indulging himself in similar "ideas" that have yet to be transformed into what we may think of as religious ideas proper (explicit theism). The trigger for the full-scale projection of inward animistic contents onto the external world is powerfully facilitated not merely by the wishful desire *that* the religious idea be so, but by an inner perceptual experience that says through implicit memory, it *is* in fact so. Accordingly, *it is not the wish that goads the projection; it is the budding mental and emotional structure that goads the wish.* There is an unconscious perceptual bias in human beings to experience the self in *relationship* because the self and the world are engendered and developed in and through the first, indelible relationship that comprises the basic biological situation. What Freud calls "reality" comes into being through precisely this primal, life-giving, life-sustaining interaction. Some other, some presence, is *there.* We can sense it. We can feel it. That is how we apprehend the externality in which we initially discover ourselves. From such a developmental, perceptual position it is not difficult to proceed to a "religious idea" that is but another version of the originative, inward, perceptual experience we share. How can the chief "religious idea"—that there exists an invisible caregiver who lovingly watches over one and to whom one is firmly attached—be disputed when the inner world of the internalizing person is structured psychologically, indeed neurally, in a manner that tells him in no uncertain terms, this is the case? By the time an individual has passed through the transitional stage of development (Winnicott) during the course of which he has interacted lovingly with imaginary companions, projective versions of the very internal presences upon which his emotive-perceptual existence has been founded, it is quite enough to tell him simply, "God loves you," to awaken within him a profound, associative, inward confirmation of this cardinal "religious idea." Simply calling a church or a temple a place of love and protection, and then going into it worshipfully, is sufficient to awaken confirmational religious assent. The individual doesn't need to *wish* anything; he *knows.* He merely *transfers* (in the unconscious, psychological sense) his early, affective perceptions to later, more complexified invisible entities such as gods, angels, saints, and holy spirits. We can imagine the worshiper thinking to himself, "Of course there exists an invisible spiritual being who loves and watches over me; I am experiencing such a one within me right now, just as I have experienced such a one as far back as I can remember." (Eventually we'll come to the crucial role of infantile amnesia in religious experience.) Here, then, is the "strength" of "religious ideas": they awaken neural pathways in the brain of the practitioner, well-established, responsive, synaptic connections that are loaded with confirmational emotion or affect that affirms the existence of God. The supernatural, we might say, slides smoothly into human perception. Thus the question arises, if God is rooted firmly in neural connections and in alluringly worded religious narratives, then how is it that some of us cease to believe, or never come to believe fully in the first place? The answer emerges immediately: other neural connections arise as we mature, and other kinds of narrative are existent in the world. What else?

When taken together, such observations oblige us to rethink Freud's contention that "religious ideas" comprise a "distortion of reality"; for surely if such ideas echo perceptually the very heart of the individual's early experience, the very core of his interactional development in the world, the very center of his mind's internalizing activity, they can hardly be said to "distort" anything, unless one makes up his mind beforehand as to what precisely "reality" consists in and then banishes any and all antithetical features to some hinterland of putative "distortions," which is not only what Freud has done in *The Future of an Illusion* but is also what some current skeptical writers are still doing in their books and papers.[10] Modern philosophy has chastised us roundly, and correctly, when it comes to our predetermining wherein "reality" consists. While we must not collapse into mere relativism on this score, as the soft-mindedness of New Age thinking, for example, has done in recent years, we must also not arbitrarily elevate some theory-laden "objectivity" or "factuality" as the final criterion for deciding what is and what is not "true" about the universe.

Recent clinical work on dissociation enables us to grasp exactly what is at issue here. Dissociation, observes Gary Whitmer, involves "those states of simultaneous knowing and not knowing" in which perceptions are "accurate and fully conscious" yet "have no credibility to the subject," who not only "constructs [his] self-knowledge in interaction with another" but "relegates to another" the job of "interpreting [his] experience." While the subject "registers" his "sensations," it is the other who "names" and classifies them. In this way, what the dissociative person recognizes as himself is actually "determined" by another human being.[11] Whitmer offers us in illustration a married professional patient dubbed Mrs. F, who was raped by her father as a child and who has endeavored to remove herself from the event. During "moments of remembering," writes Whitmer (p. 808), she "felt herself to be outside her body in time and space, frightened, and scarcely able to move." She experienced "a constant struggle" to talk about past occurrences that she could not name. She even suffered from a "bladder infection" that she appeared not to recognize in spite of the constant, considerable pain. Accordingly, Mrs. F was in a "state of dissociation" (p. 809). She felt "like a stranger to herself" as her life took on a "me-but-not-me quality" (ibid.). The aim of Whitmer's intervention with Mrs. F, needless to say, is to resolve the "dissociation," to foster integration as opposed to inner division, to guide the woman toward a full, honest knowledge of herself, toward an undistorted, unclouded perception of her motives and conduct. Whitmer writes that "dissociation at its core is an impairment in the subject's ability to represent his or her own experience" (p. 812). If personhood is to be achieved, not merely for this patient but for people generally, it is the subject and not the other who must serve as the "interpreter" of his existence. We come now to a watershed: there is one time in our lives when a salubrious self-determination of our experience does not and cannot occur, when our normal, healthy mental structure depends and must depend on our relationship with another, and that time is precisely the early one in which our interactions with the caregiver actually shape, actually determine, the basic nature of our minds. The first "self-structure" turns out to be "interpersonal" (p. 815).

Whitmer notes that during infancy and early childhood, or "before the child understands the representational nature of ideas and feelings," what the mother presents to her offspring comprises his "reality" (p. 819). Because the neonate inhabits what is sometimes called the presubjective realm of psychic equivalency, wherein perception and interpretation are "identical processes" and sensorial experience is "unmediated" by cognitional awareness, the parent or the adult who "responds to the child" provides him with a "medium" in which he can perceive his experiential world "in tangible form." Thus it is "the mother's words, gestures, and emotional expression" that guide the newcomer "to his own mind" (ibid.). By "finding an image of himself in his mother's mind," by seeing his idea or fantasy represented in the caregiver's mentality, the child is able to create and to structure his own thought processes, his own selfhood, and to discover his way toward his own unique participation in the world (p. 820). Obviously this is a crucial, even dangerous period for the infant-child, one that can lead to perceptual distortion and affective disturbance. But in the vast majority of instances, where mothering is "good enough" to foster normal development, the early period provides the budding individual with a secure foundation for his emerging identity. What we must bear in mind above all as we approach the realm of religion is that the representation of self and world that emerges here does not constitute merely "one view among many." Rather, the early foundational experience "has the impact of singular truth" and is adopted by the child as the very core of the self. The caregiver's impact on her offspring actually triggers the sensation of "me." The child cannot at this stage say to the parent, "You misunderstand me," because no "me" exists "apart from the parent's understanding." Thus the "reality" of the caregiver does not become *a* "reality" for the child; it becomes *the only* "reality," the only "place" in which he has *existence*. As for dissociation, it constitutes, as Whitmer sees it, the "pathological form" of this presubjective mode of relating to another person (ibid.).

We may begin to grasp in earnest, now, the decisive, all-important role of infantile amnesia in the onset and advent of religious belief. As the child finds his way toward the supernatural divine, he discovers a sphere that bears a striking, uncanny resemblance to the experiential world in which he has been dwelling right along through his presubjective interactions with the caregiver, the ultimate source of his most persistent and powerful implicit memories, the ultimate source of his perceptual, affective core, his selfhood, his psychological structure, his very "me-ness." To put it another way, the religious realm into which the child gradually enters *mirrors* unconsciously, associatively, perceptually, and affectively the presubjective "reality" that the child has been internalizing and installing neurally as the basis of his gradually emerging identity. The religious realm, in two words, *corresponds implicitly* to the child's mind. It is a realm that contains at its center an invisible parental presence who supports and sustains the child, *who gives him his existence*, his being (the "Creator"). This is exactly what the child has internalized to this point, as he verges upon his symbolic, verbal representations. *He contains*, as microcosm, an invisible, creative, parental presence, or "object," as the psychological lingo has it, that holds him sustainingly in and through a primal, foundational, structural bond, the rocklike support of the religious literature, dependable, unfailing, always there. It is a realm that contains an invisible parental presence who *loves* the child, who grapples him unto Himself in an affective, life-giving, life-enhancing symbiosis. This is exactly what the child harbors within: the invisible, loving, care-giving presence of the early period, the one who adored him and whom he adored as only the gushing, spontaneous infant-child can adore. It is a realm that contains a powerful, indeed an omnipotent parental figure devoted in large measure to protecting the child, to shielding him from harm, to "watching over" him. Again, this is exactly what the child harbors within his developing mind: an awareness of the parent's all-powerful, protective presence, the parent's capacity to do everything, and in particular, to do all those things the relatively helpless child cannot do by himself. Not only has the child internalized such a one, such a "mighty fortress," he has for many early months and years identified with, or "introjected," the parent's omnipotent quality. As it turns out, such omnipotence was partially and reluctantly relinquished as the child came to recognize during his third and fourth years the limitations of his capacity to control the world; but now, through religious narrative, such omnipotence can be partially regained, recouped, through a vicarious, fantasy-level participation in the Almighty's mightiness. The child can once more identify himself with a limitless, omnipotent protector. Still again, the religious realm *guides* the child, tells him yes in response to certain activities and certain behaviors, and tells him no in response to other interests and inclinations, thus echoing the primal yes and no that found their way interactionally to the child's mind during the phase in which the child's every move was subject to the parent's administration. All of this, divine creation, divine support, divine love, divine omnipotence, divine protection, divine guidance, may be subsumed under the general notion of infantile *attachment* to an internalized, all-powerful parental presence.

Accordingly, what the child is capable of projecting, of externalizing psychically as he enters the representational, verbal, symbolic stage of his development, and what the realm of religion extends to him through its "reality," its monotheistic narrative at the center of which resides the invisible, supernatural Almighty—these two perceptual realms, or worlds, now begin to touch and to ignite. The child affirms the religious realm because, like the presubjective realm he has internalized and transmuted into his self-structure, it has "the impact of singular truth" at the *unconscious* level of implicit recollection. Because the child cannot *see* the naturalistic, psychological, developmental *connection* between his own mind-brain, his own internal world, and the transcendent, supramundane narrative to which he is now increasingly exposed at the conscious level, he is impelled to accept the truth claims of the religious institutions that surround him "out there" in the wider world. Implicit memory validates cultural myth. The perceptual, affective nature of the child's inward domain is predisposed unconsciously to affirm the culture's religious stories, to say yes to the supernatural landscape that looms. On the inside, the child can *feel* the accuracy of religion's macrocosmic depictions. As the old expression has it, he's "been there, done that" already. To view the matter from the "hard" neuropsychological perspective, we might say that the child's mind-brain, primed and grooved by his presubjective interactions, *maps* his early experience onto the religious narrative he encounters. As Gerald Edelman would express it, the child's emerging supernatural world, his newly discovered "present" reality, is not only perceived, it is also "remembered," just as all his subsequent "presents" will be remembered as his mind-brain processes information according to "programs" it already "knows."[12] What we have here is a perfect or nearly perfect neurologic, affective correspondence or fit, one that does not require proof because it has the inward ring of truth, the veracious impact of the child's very selfhood which has been molded by his presubjective, interpersonal dealings with his loving caregiver, the dealings that provide the mnemonic "stuff" of his implicit recollection. And indeed, if those dealings contained maltreatments or even abuses of some sort, the child's reentering process, his remapping of the early "data," is flexible enough to transform imperfection into wished-for ideal, the flawed god of the nursery into the wondrous God of religious doctrine. When the religious world dawns, it discloses a perfection that anyone of any age might detect and crave immediately. The mighty Jehovah, the mighty Allah, the mighty Jesus—all of them will love you and protect you and guide you: what joyful tidings!

Similar unconscious recognition occurs as the child is introduced gradually to religious ritual and in particular to religion's cardinal ritualistic enactment: prayer. With an eye to the individual, subjective variety of prayer, we note the child (and later of course the adult) going to his knees, adopting a worshipful, dependent attitude, bowing or perhaps prostrating himself, taking his legs away, manifesting submission and helplessness—the chief prerequisites for successful supplication, as we'll see in a later section. We note also the prayerful requests for assistance, for succor, protection, and nourishment (one's "daily bread"), as well as the expressions of gratitude and love. To proceed at once to the heart of the matter, we note the supplicator acting out an unerring metaphorical version of the basic biological situation, the primal symbiotic attachment, in which the helpless, dependent little one calls on the omnipotent big one for physical and emotional sustenance, for the continuation and the enhancement of life. Thousands upon thousands of times, for years, the child has experienced and internalized this arrangement, this condition, this *state*, and now as he moves toward the religious domain, he is instructed to recreate it again and again through prayer. The upshot is clear: religion's chief ritual, its essential rite, its *sine qua non*, is designed to foster in the supplicator—regardless of his age or circumstance—an implicit, state-dependent memory of the parent-child relationship from which his self-structure, his identity, his existence initially arose. Prayer returns the pray-er unconsciously to the internalized root of his being and thus triggers a sense of God's loving presence that has "the impact of singular truth." Just *doing this* is enough to awaken the old feelings of dependency, connection, and care. Just doing this is enough to arouse the oldest and most persistent implicit memory that we retain at the affective, neurological level. One has only to *ask* in order to *receive*. One has only to ask in order to make contact with a loving, supportive presence on the "other side," a loving, supportive being from the putative supernatural sphere. Of course the supplicator knows that his Lord is present: he can *feel* the Lord within by virtue of his having internalized into his mind-brain the daily, hourly, moment-to-moment presence of his loving, all-powerful, care-giving provider during the weeks, months, and years of the early period. What we can only term a massive affective and neuronic conditioning has prepared him psychically for the uncanny sensation of the Almighty's engendering closeness. It is in this naturalistic, psychological way, and in this way alone, that prayer is able to "prove" the presence of God, the "miracle" of His caring, responsive existence. Thus religion turns out once again to comprise a fresh neural "mapping" onto a well-established neural and affective "reality." It derives its attractive power, its validity as a "supernatural" enterprise, from precisely the realm of implicit, state-dependent memory, from precisely the condition of infantile amnesia that loads the potential practitioner up with protoreligious beliefs and sentiments that he cannot cognitively locate, let alone fathom. The way is open for the projection of purely inward materials (one's religious "convictions") onto the external world, as well as for the establishment of religion's timeless, official "mysteries": it is the "innocent" who "see." It is the "child" who apprehends the deepest religious truths and who possesses thereby the key to the kingdom of heaven. What this means to the psychological investigator with his obligation to remain within the naturalistic bounds of human growth and development may be expressed as follows: when we allow the unconscious forces of infantile amnesia to determine the quality of our religious faith, we discover our way smoothly and happily to symbiotic union with our projective version of the internalized parent. For the "innocent," for the "children," God is *there*. It hardly needs to be added that billions of "innocent children" currently inhabit the earth.

The external, explicit supports for religious belief, the aspects of religion with which we are all thoroughly familiar, are tied integrally to the unconscious, implicit foundation and make religion's doctrinal, supernatural claims overwhelmingly persuasive. Obviously such claims take on a life of their own, but their lifeblood flows afresh as each generation internalizes and subsequently projects its primal interactions with the care-giving parent. Doctrine would be empty of meaning were it not unconsciously grounded in the basic biological situation of dependency, succor, and love. Indeed, as we have just seen, the presubjective period primes the young religionist affectively and neurologically for the transcendent rituals and narratives to which he is now regularly exposed. Religious attachment is reattachment. Religious presentations re-present the past through the workings of implicit, state-dependent memory. The child listened to the parent's verbalizations and took his direction and comfort from them. Now he listens to the Omnipotent's "word," directly as it is proffered in His book or indirectly as it is explained by His official, authoritative interpreters—the priest, the pastor, the rabbi, the mullah, each in his distinctive and sometimes splendid trappings. The young worshiper is told to sit still and pay attention. He sees his parents doing exactly what he is told to do. He sees hundreds, perhaps thousands of others similarly busying themselves with holy books and supplications, reading, pondering, mumbling, discussing, standing up and sitting down on command, bowing, swaying, stretching themselves out upon the ground. In the company of his parents, who also instruct him, he gazes at temples, churches, mosques; stained glass, gigantic columns, mandalic domes. He hears chanted calls to prayer; harmonic, mesmeric hymns; sonorous sermons and pronouncements. He is swept along in processions, swept up in festivals, kissed and congratulated for his loyal participation. What child could resist, particularly with ritual and narrative, including above all the rite of supplication and the story of the loving Parent-God, continually echoing, or mirroring, the unconscious shape of his own experience as it transpired during the years that precede the advent of symbolic enactments and expressions? The variations from culture to culture and from child to child are of course notable, as Robert Coles makes clear in his spectacular volume *The Spiritual Life of Children*; yet the underlying neural, affective, causative factors apply generally, worldwide, across the centuries, down to the present day. We are, as many have observed, a theological animal.[13]

The point arises: is not the "map" of the early period only the first in a series of religious maps, a series that is characterized by increasing moral and theological complexity that mirrors our development over the years, indeed over an entire life span? I reply as follows: assuredly this is so. However, all the religious maps that are devised and entered with time's passage are based upon the first one, which reflects the early period. The initial, unconscious, internalized experience with the loving, care-giving provider holds the primal, "eternal" source of religion's affective power, the primal, foundational source of its compelling, persistent appeal, its mystery, its resistance to logic and reason. The initial map in the depths of the mind is the powerhouse. To dislodge it, deconstruct it, destroy it in one way or another is quite simply to lose the living power of one's faith, to dry up religiously, to abandon the holy, life-giving waters in which the "children" and the "innocent" bathe their minds and spirits. Religion thrives when its adherents remain in close touch with the infantile level of their development, preserving their early, projective realities, their implicit memories of primal symbiosis, of magical asking and magical receiving from the omnipotent parental creator and provider. Although one can grow religiously, there is no growing out of the infantile stage. Bear in mind, I am not writing about deism here, or rational arguments concerning the ultimate origin of the universe. I am writing about emotional, heartfelt belief in an anthropomorphic, supernatural God (and His angelic extensions) Who is concerned with and responsive to the idiosyncratic wishes and needs of individual worshipers. Precisely this kind of belief is a natural, projective outgrowth of implicitly recollected parental ministrations in infancy. Were we loved parentally in the beginning? Well, we still are. The beginning is now. It is always now in *that* sense where religion is concerned. We are never without a parent unless we choose to be by rejecting the existence of a loving, supernatural Provider. If we are "theological animals," then we are such because our "theology" fits in smoothly with our "adult" perception of the universe around us. What after all can interfere with the belief in a supernatural system that does not require a single empirical fact to substantiate its claims and that is felt to be true at the deepest inward level by those who fervently wish it to be so? For the minority of unbelievers, of course, the religious "program" is irrelevant, or perhaps unengaging, because it has been replaced by other "programs," by other neural, perceptual connections, by other narratives, by other theoretical outlooks and conclusions. To put the matter crudely, the religious continue to be emotionally and intellectually susceptible to facets of the mind-brain to which the nonreligious are susceptible no longer.

ENTER (BRIEFLY) WILLIAM JAMES

What is undoubtedly the most influential, and readable, discussion of these experiential, religious problems was penned about one hundred years ago by William James. I am referring to *The Varieties of Religious Experience*,[14] which, at this very hour, still serves as a bible for millions of individuals who regularly move into the divine, supernatural sphere through rumination, meditation, mystical feelings, and above all prayer—for James "the very soul and essence of religion" (p. 416). James admits readily that we have no scientific, empirical evidence in support of religious belief. He asserts that religion is integrally bound up with the "subconscious" mind (p. 74). He is impressed by the powerful, utterly convincing nature of heartfelt religious experience, and he is sensitive to the genuine psychological and physical benefits that flow toward those who believe. (Religion alone was able to mitigate James's severe, persistent depression.) In a famous *mot* James holds that religion doesn't work because it's true, but is true because it works. He calls this his pragmatic criterion. Although James knows his conclusions about the nature of religious experience will not sit well with his learned colleagues in America and Europe, he goes ahead with those conclusions just the same: religious experience, all things considered, is best ascribed to *something* supernatural, "transmundane energies" he writes in one place (p. 467), and in another, simply "God" (ibid.). It is the religious person's vivid, immediate sensation of the Lord's *presence*, of His *being there*, that compelled James more than anything else toward his final, affirmative view.

Let's look a little further into this. Faith, for James, is not merely a mentalistic, intellectual, or even an emotional position adopted by the believer after inwardly debating the theological issues. On the contrary, it is a "biological state" by which the believer "lives," a biological state that reaches into his "subconscious" region (ibid.). As James gets into the meat of his discussion he relies not on the word "faith" but on the expression "faith-state" (p. 452), and he offers compelling declarations of God's "presence" in illustration of his meaning. One of James's subjects maintains in the "hallucinatory" perceptual mode to which we've been referring, "God is more real to me than any thought or thing or person. . . . I talk to Him as a companion in prayer and praise, and our communion is delightful. He answers me again and again, often in words so clearly spoken that it seems my outer ear must have carried the tone, but generally in strong mental impressions. Usually a text of Scripture unfolds some new view of Him and His love for me, and care for my safety. I could give hundreds of instances. . . . That He is mine and I am His never leaves me" (pp. 70–71). Another informant asserts, "I feel as if God [is] with me, on the right side of me, singing and reading the Psalms with me. . . . And then I feel as if I could sit beside Him, and put my arms around Him, kiss Him, etc." (p. 71). Still another states that the imagined absence of his "communion" with God "would be chaos. I cannot conceive of life without its presence" (p. 70). James remarks in the face of these powerful testimonials (his treatise contains dozens of them), "our impulsive belief is . . . always what set up the original body of truth, and our philosophy is but its showy verbalized translation. The immediate assurance is the deep thing in us, the argument is but a surface exhibition. Instinct leads, intelligence does but follow. If a person feels the presence of a living God after the fashion shown by my quotations, your critical arguments . . . will vainly set themselves to change his faith. Please observe, however, that I do not yet say that it is *better* that the subconscious and non-rational should thus hold primacy in the religious realm. I confine myself to simply pointing out that they do so hold it as a matter of fact" (p. 74). Of overwhelming significance to my purpose here is the "fact" that in all of this, in the postulation of a biologically based faith-state, in the citing of testimonials wherein the believer feels affectively attached to his loving Creator, in the insistence on the instinctual and the subconscious as the foundational designers of the religious realm, James has not a single developmental observation to offer us in clarification of "religious experience." There is nothing here, absolutely nothing, on life's first years, on the way in which religious belief takes shape interpersonally among humans from the time of infancy and childhood, through adolescence, and into adulthood, our "state" of "maturity." James's religious subjects appear before us fully grown, without a history, without a progressive, sequential "evolution" through which we might come to understand the subconscious, instinctual forces that underlie their outlook on the spiritual, supernatural sphere. Mind you, I am not *faulting* James for this: he lived and wrote on the cusp of modern psychology; his wonderful book was penned shortly before we began to view human "experience" from a historical, interpersonal, developmental angle—or at least just as the study of infancy and childhood was beginning to come into its own. A scant three decades after James's demise Piaget and his colleagues made headway in Switzerland, and the psychoanalytic study of the child commenced in earnest in Britain and the United States. Accordingly, as I view the matter, it was *both* the vivid, uncanny sensation of God's "presence" on the practitioner's part *and* the inability to spy a natural, developmental cause for such an event that ultimately impelled James to believe something "supernatural" must be going on, to find "transmundane energies," even God Himself, in the fabric of "religious experience." Whether or not James took this direction because it served his own emotional requirements, whether or not *The Varieties of Religious Experience* is an argument of personal hope on the part of a severely depressed psychologist who wanted religion to be "true," is certainly a fascinating issue, and one to which I cannot address myself here.

When we wed James's observations on "religious experience" to our own developmental perspective, including above all the recent neuropsychological investigation of memory as it extends itself across the life span, we can see the degree to which the "faith-state" is tied to internalized interactions with the caregiver of the early period, the maternal provider through whom the individual's very selfhood germinates both biologically and psychologically. We can see that implicit recollections of affective *states*, triggered by retrieval cues in the environment, have the capacity to restore the *presence* of the maternal figure at the "subconscious" levels of perception. The remarkable, mysterious, uncanny aspect of our "creation" is this: the nurturing parent of the early period is *not* explicitly recalled by us as grown-ups in spite of the fact that she governed the quality of our inner world and mapped out the initial course of our existence. The "biological faith-state" by which we "live" is, then, a "state" with a developmental history that can be aroused by present events, including the wish for symbiotic merger. People "get religion" not through their "religious experience" as such but through their early internalized experience with the biological parent, the experience upon which religion *operates* to construct its mythic, ritualistic edifice. When we sense the Creator within us and acknowledge with gratitude His delicious love and care, we don't know whence such "experience" derives because we cannot *find* explicitly the foundational strata of our lives. We attribute to the outside what is happening on the inside, always, and without exception.

NOTES

1. Ninian Smart, *The Religious Experience of Mankind* (New York: Scribner's, 1969), p. 499.

2. John R. Hinnells, ed., *The Penguin Dictionary of Religions* (London: Penguin Books, 1995), p. 392.

3. Ludwig Feuerbach, *The Essence of Christianity*, trans. George Eliot (1841; Amherst, NY: Prometheus Books, 1989), p. xix.

4. Friedrich Nietzsche, *The Gay Science* (1882; New York: Vintage, 1974), p. 125.

5. Feuerbach, *The Essence of Christianity*, pp. xviii, xix.

6. Sigmund Freud, *The Future of an Illusion*, trans. J. Strachey (1927; New York: W. W. Norton, 1964), p. 27. Page numbers for the other Freud quotes in this section are included in the text.

7. See Carol Gilligan, *In a Different Voice: Psychological Theory and Women's Development* (Cambridge, MA: Harvard University Press, 1982), pp. 7–10.

8. Sigmund Freud, *Civilization and Its Discontents*, trans. J. Strachey (1930; New York: W. W. Norton, 1961), p. 20.

9. Freud, *The Future of an Illusion*, p. 47.

10. For an excellent example, see John F. Schumaker, *The Corruption of Reality: A Unified Theory of Religion, Hypnosis, and Psychopathology* (Amherst, NY: Prometheus Books, 1995).

11. Gary Whitmer, "On the Nature of Dissociation," *Psychoanalytic Quarterly* 70 (2001): 807. Page numbers for the other Whitmer quotes in this section are included in the text.

12. Gerald Edelman, *The Remembered Present: A Biological Theory of Consciousness* (New York: Basic Books, 1989), pp. 98–108.

13. See Robert Coles, *The Spiritual Life of Children* (Boston: Houghton Mifflin, 1990), pp. 203–302; Otto Rank, *Psychology and the Soul*, trans. W. Turner (New York: A. S. Barnes, 1950), pp. 192–95.

14. William James, *The Varieties of Religious Experience* (1902; New York: Library of America, 1987). Page numbers for the individual James quotes in this section are included in the text.

4.

The Early Period

Because the world of infancy and childhood is not an easy one to capture discursively, because as adults we run the risk of ascribing to the very young aims and motives at work in us rather than in them,[1] I would prefer to explore the religious realm psychologically without also exploring life's early period; but alas, there is just no hope of getting at the truth that way. Religious behavior is an outgrowth, a development, in a special sense an expression of this period with its symbiotic attachments, its blissful transformations, its powerful, persistent anxieties, attunements, frustrations, and fears. Indeed, if psychoanalytic psychology has made a lasting and valuable contribution to the understanding of religious conduct, it is in precisely this area. Focusing momentarily on the originator, we must point out that even Freud's opponents in the matter of spirituality, even those who ultimately disagree with his outlook, acknowledge the correctness of rooting the psychological study of religion in the ground where human existence commences. Although Freud's view of religion as a regression to "the earliest psychic strata" demands "rethinking," writes W. W. Meissner, although it is loaded with Freud's "prejudices" and "inner conflicts," it nevertheless brings us by virtue of Freud's "genius" to the "interface of man's religious life with his psychological life in a more poignant and telling way than ever before in human history."[2] In spite of several misemphases and outright errors, maintains Ana-Maria Rizzuto, Freud's view of "God" is "essentially correct" and constitutes a "major contribution" to our "understanding of man," and in particular "of man's lifelong use of early imagos and object representations."[3] Thus we really have no choice. Our business in what follows must be to indicate the "early imagos" and "object representations" that constitute the foundational "strata" of religious belief. An additional issue arises at this juncture.

As everyone knows, for the past thirty or forty years psychoanalysis as theory and therapy has been attacked by a variety of philosophical skeptics, from Adolf Grünbaum to Frederick Crews, from Richard Webster to Frank Cioffi. It has also been partially superseded by biological and pharmacological approaches.[4] Why then does psychoanalysis continue to "live" and to live vigorously, as John Horgan expresses it in *The Scientific American*? Horgan replies, "One explanation may be that [Freud's work], in spite of its flaws, still represents a compelling framework within which to ponder our mysterious selves." Another may be that "psychotherapists of all stripes still tend to share two of Freud's core beliefs: One is that our behavior, thoughts and emotions stem from unconscious fears and desires, often rooted in childhood experiences. The other is that with the help of a trained therapist, we can understand the source of our troubles and thereby obtain some relief."[5] Yet there may be just a tad more to it than that, for as the aforementioned skeptic Webster, whose major work is titled *Why Freud Was Wrong*, puts it, psychoanalysis "has every claim to be regarded as richer and more original than any other single intellectual tradition in the twentieth century."[6] While psychoanalysis may sometimes get it wrong in the "details," writes Daniel Liechty (echoing Ernest Becker), it still "claims a hold on us because it is so close to the truth we all experience. Even the least introspective among us knows that we are anxiety-ridden creatures whose conscious will is fooled and distorted by unconscious forces. If Freud was wrong on any or all of the details, he continues to fascinate because he looked at this condition and did not turn away into the pious platitudes of philosophy or religion. . . . His place will always be one of respect amongst those who also did not look away."[7] In all of this, by the way, I am not suggesting that the philosophical skeptics, Grünbaum,

Crews, Cioffi, and others, continue to hold sway in professional circles. On the contrary, their arguments against psychoanalysis have been effectively countered, even refuted, by several writers, including most notably Donald Levy, whose landmark work, *Freud among the Philosophers*, deals in depth with the major attackers and concludes as follows: "Psychoanalysis is amply equipped to respond to the philosophical criticism that has been mounted against it thus far. No good philosophical arguments against it have been produced, and much empirical evidence supports it. It is no wonder that psychoanalysis has been experienced, from different viewpoints, as a radical shift in human thought, and that many have treated it as an advance in our self-understanding—precisely the extension or unfolding of individual subjectivity that it claims to be."[8] However, it is not in regard solely to philosophical issues that psychoanalysis has lately experienced a vindication of its approach to human behavior. On the contrary, striking evidence of its accuracy and value emerges from the burgeoning field of neuroscience, a field that bears directly upon our discussion to come. Writing in a recent issue of *The Scientific American*, the cover of which announces in bold type, "Science Revives Freud," Mark Solms contends that modern biological descriptions of the brain may "fit together best" when "integrated by psychological theories Freud sketched a century ago." Solms continues in a number of pivotal sentences,

> Neuroscience has shown that the major brain structures essential for forming conscious (explicit) memories are not functional during the first two years of life, providing an elegant explanation of what Freud called infantile amnesia. As Freud surmised, it is not that we forget our earliest memories; we simply cannot recall them to consciousness. But this inability does not preclude them from affecting adult feelings and behavior. One would be hard-pressed to find a developmental neurobiologist who does not agree that early experiences, especially between mother and infant, influence the pattern of brain connections in ways that fundamentally shape our future personality and mental health. Yet none of these experiences can be consciously remembered. It is becoming increasingly clear that a good deal of our mental activity is unconsciously motivated.[9]

Mindful of the the pitfalls, then, and with the endorsements of Levy and Solms ringing in our ears, let us begin to indicate precisely the direction from which will flow our analytical view of religious experience.

Regardless of the geographical location and the nature of familial organization, the conflict between separation and merger not only dominates the life of the infant but extends itself far beyond infancy and childhood into the life of the adolescent and adult. It revolves around the struggle to become an autonomous, separate person, differentiated and distinct, and at the same time, to retain one's connection to significant others—either the actual parents or their later substitutes in a protean variety of shapes and forms. For the human creature (as I indicated in the previous paragraph), two of life's most powerful needs are, paradoxically, to be joined and to be separate, to be related and to be independent, to be autonomous and to be connected, and it is precisely this paradoxical and in some sense contradictory thrust in human growth and development, this antithetical, two-sided inclination of people, that makes human behavior so problematical, so maddeningly difficult to see and to fathom, and that brings so much confusion to the lives of individuals and societies. Ethel Person, in her wonderful book *Dreams of Love and Fateful Encounters*, renders the matter this way: "Without self-will there can be no psychological separation. But neither is there any highly individuated self. The self is delineated only through separation, but the sense of being separated proves impossible to bear. The solitary self feels cut off, alone, without resources. The solitary self feels impelled to merge with a new object."[10] What Person has captured, if I may be permitted to indicate the issue still again, is that the two needs, to be separate and joined, independent and connected, are from a deep psychological angle one need neither side of which finds expression without engaging the other, like a crab going backward and forward at the same time. When the desire for merger is felt, it typically engages the need to be separate, and the need to be separate engages the wish to be connected, joined. While it is easy to write about the matter, to employ such terms as alogical, paradoxical, and antithetical, it can be most unpleasant to experience the actual conflict when it occurs, along with the inner confusion that it often engenders. I would suggest, in fact, that we have here a major source of human stress.

From the many psychological accounts of infancy and childhood, I choose what is generally regarded as the most methodologically sophisticated, accurate, and helpful—namely, Margaret Mahler's *Psychological Birth of the Human Infant*.[11] A child psychiatrist and pediatrician working with normal children in a specially constructed facility in New York City during the 1950s and 1960s, Mahler (with her associates) places the accent immediately on the struggle between separation and union. We take for granted, she reminds us, our experience of ourselves as both fully "in" and fully separate from the "world out there" (p. 3). Our consciousness of ourselves as distinct, differentiated entities and our concomitant absorption into the external environment, without an awareness of self, are the polarities between which we move with varying ease, and with varying degrees of alternation or simultaneity. Yet the establishment of such consciousness, such ordinary, taken-for-granted awareness, is a slowly unfolding process that is not coincident in time with our biological emergence from the womb. It is tied closely and developmentally to our dawning experience of our bodies as separate in space and belonging only to us, and to our dawning experience of the primary love object as also separate in space, as having an existence of its own. Moreover, the struggle to achieve this "individuation" reverberates throughout the course of our lives: "It is never finished; it remains always active; new phases of the life cycle find new derivatives of the earliest processes still at work" (ibid.). As we shall see, the realms of religion and magic are designed in large measure to address the endless transformations of these "early processes."

What must be stressed in particular here is the strength of both sides of the polarity. Children, with every move toward maturation, are confronted with the threat of "object loss," with traumatic situations involving separation from the caregiver. Thus they are constantly tempted to draw back, to regress, to move toward the object and the old relation as opposed to *away* from the object and the anticipated future, the new reality. At the same time, the normally endowed child strives mightily to emerge from his early fusion (we could say confusion) with the mother, to escape and to grow. His individuation consists precisely of those developmental achievements, those increasing motor and mental accomplishments, that begin to mark his separate existence, his separate identity as a separate being. The ambivalent impulses toward and away from the object, the great urge to differentiate and at the same time stay connected, are in Mahler's words, forever intertwined (p. 4), although they may proceed divergently, one or the other lagging behind or leaping ahead during a given period.

Mahler makes plain that this process is not merely one of many equally important processes that transpire during the early time. On the contrary, the achievement of separation constitutes the very core of the self (p. 4), the foundation of one's identity and being as a person. Yet this foundation can be gained (and here is the echo of a paradox again) only if the parent gives to the child a persistent, uninterrupted feeling of connection, of union—a tie that encourages the very breaking of it. This delicate balancing act is never perfect, and Mahler emphasizes throughout the course of her study that old conflicts over separation, old, unresolved issues of identity and bodily boundaries, can be reawakened or even remain active throughout the course of one's existence, at any or all stages of the life cycle. What appears to be a struggle for connection or distinctness in the now of one's experience can be the flare up of the ancient struggle in which one's self began to emerge from the orbit of the *magna mater*. We will shortly be exploring the degree to which this last observation sheds light on one facet of religion in which the practitioner longs to be absorbed into the supernatural body of the Deity.

By separation, then, Mahler does not mean primarily the physical separation of the baby in space or the distance from the caregiver, the kind of separation we associate, for example, with the work of John Bowlby. What Mahler has in mind is an inward or intrapsychic separation from both the mother and her extension, the world. The gradual development of this subjective awareness, this inward perception of the self and the other, leads eventually to clear, distinct inner representations of a "self" that is distinguished from "external objects." It is precisely this sense of being a separate individual that psychotic children are unable to achieve.

Similarly, when Mahler uses the term *symbiosis*, the accent is not upon a behavioral state but an inward condition, a feature of primitive emotional life wherein the differentiation between the self and the mother has not occurred, or where a regression to an undifferentiated state has occurred. This does not necessarily require the presence of the mother; it can be based on primitive images of oneness, or on a denial of perceptions that postulate separation. Thus for Mahler, identity during the early period does not refer to the child having a sense of who he is; it refers to the child having a sense that he is (p. 8). Indeed, the sense that he is can be regarded as the first step in the process of an unfolding individuality. The achievement of separation-individuation is a kind of "second birth," a "hatching" (p. 9) from the symbiotic mother-infant "membrane" in which the child is originally contained.

THE STAGES OF DEVELOPMENT

Mahler calls the earliest stage of development "autistic." The infant "spends most of his day in a half-sleeping, half-waking state" (p. 41). He awakens mainly to feed and falls to sleep again when he is satisfied, or relieved of tensions. "Physiological rather than psychological processes are dominant," and the period as a whole is "best seen" in physiological terms. There is nothing abnormal about this "autism," as Mahler employs the term. The baby simply lacks awareness of the mother as a ministering agent and of himself as the object of her ministrations.[12]

From the second month on, however, the baby increasingly feels the presence of the mother, and it is just this sense of the caretaker (or the "need-satisfying object") being there that marks the inception of the normal symbiotic phase, which reaches a peak of intensity at about six to nine months. The most remarkable feature of this phase (and one that will be of great significance for us when we turn to angels) is contained in Mahler's point that the infant "behaves and functions as though he and his mother were an omnipotent system—a dual unity with one common boundary" (p. 44). The symbiotic infant participates emotionally and perceptually in a kind of delusional or hallucinatory fusion with the omnipotent mothering figure. Later in infancy and childhood, and indeed later in life at all stages when we experience severe stress, "this is the mechanism to which the ego regresses."

In this way, when the autistic phase subsides, or, to use the metaphors characteristic of Mahler's treatise, when the "autistic shell" has "cracked" and the child can no longer "keep out external stimuli," a "second protective, yet selective and receptive shield" begins to develop in the form of the "symbiotic orbit," the mother and the child's dual unity. While the normal autistic phase serves postnatal physiological growth and homeostasis, the normal symbiotic phase marks the all-important human capacity to bring the mother into a psychic fusion that comprises "the primal soil from which all subsequent relationships form" (p. 48). We commence our existence as people in the illusion that the other (who appears to be omnipotent) is a part of the self. Although the mother is actually out there, ministering to the child, she is perceived by the latter to be a facet of his own organism, his own primitive ego. What the mother "magically" accomplishes in the way of care—the production of milk, the provision of warmth, the sensation of security—the baby omnipotently attributes to the mother and to himself. At the emotional, preverbal level, he declares, in effect, "I am not separate from my symbiotic partner; my partner and I are one. Whatever my partner appears to possess and to do, I possess and do as well. Whatever power my partner has, I also have. We are one, one omnipotent indestructible unit, twin stars revolving around each other in a single orbit of emotion and will." As Winnicott unforgettably expresses it, the feeling of omnipotence is so strong in the infant (and so persistently clung to in the growing child when the dual unity of the symbiotic stage begins to break down) that it is "nearly a fact."[13]

What this means, of course, is that the decline of symbiosis, or the increasing awareness of separation on the part of the child, will be experienced as a loss of self. If union with mother means wholeness, then disunion will mean less than wholeness. As Mahler phrases it elsewhere, the cessation of the symbiotic phase marks the "loss of a part of [one's] ego."[14] Let us examine Mahler's account of this original human trauma (the expulsion from paradise), and let us bear in mind as we proceed, first, that the transition from symbiosis to individuation is a multifaceted, complex process that consumes the first three years of life and, second, that for many, many people the loss of omnipotent merger and the narcissistic gratification that goes with it is never entirely accepted at the deep, unconscious level. I am not suggesting that the infant's growing abilities and independence fail to provide him with satisfaction; to be sure, they do, and Mahler is careful to emphasize both sides of the equation—the drive to remain with and to relinquish the mother. I am suggesting only that the movement away is attended by powerful anxiety and by the irrational wish to have it both ways: separateness and symbiotic union. Also, as one would suspect, the babies in Mahler's study often differ dramatically in their developmental inclinations and capacities, but more of that later.

SEPARATION UNDER WAY

What Mahler terms the "first subphase" of "differentiation" occurs "at the peak of symbiosis," when the infant is about six months old. During his more frequent periods of wakefulness, the field of his attention gradually expands "through the coming into being of outwardly directed perceptual activity" (p. 53). No longer is the "symbiotic orbit" the exclusive focus of his limited, yet evolving "sensorium." In addition, the baby's attention gradually combines with "a growing store of memories of mother's comings and goings, of good and bad experiences" that compose the mnemonic core of what psychology calls the "good" and the "bad" object. The infant is more alert, more goal-directed, and his attendants begin to talk of his "hatching," of his emergence from the "autistic shell."

As the seventh month approaches, "there are definite signs that the baby is beginning to differentiate his own body" from that of his mother (p. 54). "Tentative experimentation at individuation" can be observed in such behavior as "pulling at the mother's hair, ears, or nose, putting food into the mother's mouth, and straining his body away from mother in order to have a better look at her, to scan her and the environment. This is in contrast to simply moulding into mother when held." The infant's growing visual and motor powers help him to "draw his body together" (p. 55) and to commence the construction of his own, separate ego on the basis of this bodily awareness and sensation. At times, the baby even begins to move away from the mother's enveloping arms, to resist the passive "lap babyhood" which marks the earliest months of life. As he does this, however, he constantly "checks back" to mother with his eyes. He is becoming interested in mother as "mother" and compares her with "other" people and things. He discovers what belongs and what does not belong to the mother's body—a brooch, eyeglasses, a comb. He is starting to discriminate, in short, between the mother and all that which is different from or similar to her.

This incipient individuation on the baby's part is accompanied by considerable anxiety, the most striking manifestation of which occurs in the presence of strangers. Like so much else in the area of separation-union, "stranger anxiety" evinces two distinct yet interrelated aspects. On the one hand, strangers fascinate the infant, who, in Mahler's words, shows great "eagerness to find out about them" (p. 56). On the other hand, strangers terrify the infant by reminding him of the other-than-mother world, the world of separation, the world that appears as symbiosis and dual unity fade. After pointing out that babies vary in their susceptibility to stranger anxiety (and other anxiety as well), Mahler offers us the example of Peter, who at eight months reacts initially with wonder and curiosity to a stranger's mild overtures for his attention. Yet, two minutes later, although he is close to his mother, even leaning against her leg, Peter bursts into tears as the stranger touches his hair (p. 57). Such is the emotional turbulence that accompanies the onset of individuation during the first subphase.

INCREASING AUTONOMY, PERSISTENT AMBIVALENCE

Mahler divides the second subphase into the early practicing period and the practicing subphase proper. During the former, the ten- to eleven-month infant becomes more and more deeply absorbed in his expanding mental and physical universe. He begins rapidly to distinguish his own body from his mother's, to actively establish a specific (as opposed to symbiotic) bond with her, and to indulge his autonomous, independent interests while in close proximity to her. In a word, he begins to transfer his absorption in mother to the world around him. He explores the objects in his vicinity—toys, bottles, blankets—with his eyes, hands, and mouth; his growing locomotor capacity widens his environment. Not only does he have a "more active role in determining closeness and distance to mother," but the "modalities that up to now were used to explore the relatively familiar" suddenly transport him to a new reality. There is more to see, to hear, to touch (p. 66).

Yet in all of this, Mahler is careful to point out, the mother is "still the center of the child's universe" (ibid.). His experience of his "new world" is subtly "related" to her, and his excursions into the other-than-mother realm are often followed by periods of intense clinging and a refusal to separate. For an interval the baby is absorbed in some external object and seems oblivious to mother's presence; a moment later he jumps up and rushes to her side expressing his need for physical proximity. Again and again he displays a desire for "emotional refueling" (p. 69), that is to say, for a dose of maternal supplies—hugging, stroking, chatting—after a period of independent activity. What Mahler's children (and all children) want—and we come here to a crucial utterance—is to "move away independently" from the mother and, at the same time, to "remain connected to her" (p. 70).

The practicing subphase proper (eleven to fifteen months) marks the high point of the child's move toward a separate existence. Not only does he experience a dramatic spurt in cognitive development, he also achieves what Mahler calls "the greatest step in human individuation," his upright locomotion (p. 71). These "precious months" of increasing powers and skills constitute "the child's love affair with the world": the "plane of his vision changes; . . . he finds unexpected and changing perspectives. . . . The world is the junior toddler's oyster. . . . Narcissism is at its peak. . . . The chief characteristic of this period is the child's great narcissistic investment in his own functions, his own body, and the objectives of his expanding reality" (ibid.). Adding to the exhilaration, notes Mahler, is the child's "elated escape from fusion with, from engulfment by, mother." Here is the movement away in its most striking biological and psychological expression.

Yet even here, in the midst of this great expansion, this "love affair with the world," the paradoxical, ambivalent aspect of human development rears its head as mightily as ever in the form of deep-seated, pervasive anxiety. "The course of true love never did run smooth," observes Shakespeare, and the words would seem to apply to our earliest developmental experiences. The child's rapidly expanding ego functions bring with them both the threat of "object loss" and the fear of being "reengulfed" by the mother. One minute he expresses a need for "checking back," for "emotional refueling," for knowing exactly the mother's whereabouts; the next minute he forcibly removes himself from mother's caressing arms in an effort to assert his capacity for active, independent functioning. Sometimes the baby runs away to make sure mother wants to catch him up; yet when she does, he shows resentment at being held and stroked.

Even the enormous step of upright locomotion and the increase in perception that it brings to the child holds both sides of the dual unity equation. It is the need for mother's emotional support at the instant he learns to walk that Mahler captures unforgettably: "The child walks alone with his eyes fixed on his mother's face, not on the difficulties in his way. . . . In the very same moment that he is emphasizing his need for her, he is proving that he can do without her." In this way, the toddler "feels the pull of separation from his mother at the same time he asserts his individuation. It is a mixed experience, the child demonstrating that he can and cannot do without, his mother" (p. 73). As for the mother's physical absence during this period (she may be working, ill, etc.), it typically sparks sadness or even depression in the infant. The "symbiotic mothering half" of the "self" is "missed" during the very subphase that is most obviously filled with the joys of separation (p. 74).

UNDENIABLY ALONE

The entire separation-individuation process culminates at approximately thirty months in what Mahler terms "the rapprochement subphase," the period during which the infant perceives with growing clarity and certainty that he and mother are separate beings, that the old symbiosis and the narcissistic gratifications (including omnipotence) that go with it are illusory, that he is physically and psychically alone. Here is Mahler's powerful description of this watershed in a person's life: "With the acquisition of primitive skills and perceptual cognitive faculties there has been an increasingly clear differentiation, a separation, between the intrapsychic representation of the object and the self-representation. At the very height of mastery, toward the end of the practicing period, it had already begun to dawn on the junior toddler that the world is not his oyster, that he must cope with it more or less on his own, very often as a relatively helpless, small, and separate individual, unable to command relief or assistance merely by feeling the need for it or by giving voice to that need [i.e., omnipotence]" (p. 78). We may note parenthetically at this juncture that much magical and religious activity is designed to deny precisely this momentous event—and not only deny it but bring about its reversal through just those mechanisms that Mahler mentions here, namely, "mere feeling" (wishing) and "giving voice" (prayers and invocations). Needless to say, we will eventually explore these denials and reversals in great depth.

With the erosion of symbiosis, the "fear of losing the love of the object" (ibid.), as opposed to losing the object, makes itself felt increasingly in the child. Up to this point (the rapprochement subphase) the object and the self have been more or less psychically indistinguishable. Now, as differentiation occurs in earnest, the object's love becomes the focus of the child's attention. This does not mean that the original anxiety over loss of the object as a part of the self disappears. It means only that an additional, more conscious or even cognitive anxiety has been superimposed upon the original, primal dread. Accordingly, the toddler begins to demand the mother's constant attention. He is deeply preoccupied with her whereabouts. He expresses enormous anger and anxiety at her leave-taking and anguish at being left behind. He clings to mother, seeks her lap, and may begin to show a dependent interest in maternal substitutes. In a thousand ways he attempts to coerce the mother into fulfilling his wishes. He tries at times to be magnificently separate, omnipotent, rejecting: he will gain the mother's love and attention by showing her the proverbial "cold shoulder." At other times he plays the helpless baby. For weeks on end his wooing of mother alternates sharply with his expressions of resentment and outrage (p. 97).

How do the mothers react to all this? "Some cannot accept the child's demandingness; others are unable to face the child's gradual separation, the fact that the child can no longer be regarded as part of her" (p. 78). Yet, whatever the relational dynamics happen to be, they cannot stop the process: "No matter how insistently the toddler tries to coerce the mother, she and he can no longer function effectively as a dual unit— that is to say, the child can no longer maintain his delusion of parental omnipotence, which he still at times expects will restore the symbiotic status quo." The child must "gradually and painfully give up the delusion of his own grandeur, often by way of dramatic fights with mother—less so, it seemed to us, with father. This is the crossroads of what we term the rapprochement crisis" (p. 79). Mahler observes in a sentence at which we prick up our ears as we ponder the meaning of the supernatural that "many uniquely human problems and dilemmas" that are "sometimes never completely resolved during the entire life cycle" have their origin here, during the end of symbiosis and the onset of separation (p. 100).

RESOLVING THE DILEMMA

The resolution of the rapprochement crisis comes about in a variety of ways, the description of which concludes the first half of Mahler's study. As the child experiences a growing capacity to be alone, his clamoring for omnipotent control starts to diminish. He shows less separation anxiety, fewer alternating demands for closeness and autonomy. Not only does he begin to understand empathetically what his mother is going through, which allows him to "unify the good and bad objects into one whole representation" (p. 110), but he begins to identify with the problems and struggles of the youngsters around him. In this way, he begins to turn to other people, and in many instances to his own father, in his effort to satisfy his needs. And with the wholesale emergence of gender differences, the child starts to participate in those activities that are peculiar to his or her sex.

Equally important, the child's capacity for verbalization and symbolization begins to lead him toward the cultural realm, toward an endless variety of substitutive, or, in Winnicott's famous expression, "transitional" objects that characteristically take the form of "blankies," storybooks, toys, pets, and so on, and that exist somewhere "between the child's fantasies and reality," in what Winnicott calls "transitional space."[15] We might say that the child's growing ability to incorporate the world into his burgeoning ego leads him to a series of new internalizations, new inward presences, which are appropriate to his age and to the problems he confronts. He is beginning to live with his own thoughts and with the companions of his inner world. This is what we usually mean by "being alone."

In the majority of cases and generally for all normal children, such developments culminate in the establishment of what Mahler calls "object constancy," and with it, the inception of an individuated life. By "object constancy" Mahler has in mind "the presence of a reliable internal image that remains relatively stable irrespective of the state of instinctual need or inner discomfort. On the basis of this achievement, temporary separation can be lengthened and better tolerated" (p. 110). This is the necessary step, the vital inward accomplishment, that permits further growth, further individuation, and further ego strength in the preschooler and eventually in the schoolchild.

Mahler devotes the second half of her treatise to several lengthy case histories in which we see children struggling from normal autism and symbiosis to separation and individuation. She strives in these sections to illustrate her theoretical position at the clinical level, the level from which the theoretical materials originally arose, of course. As she does this, Mahler makes clear something that she stresses in many places in part 1, namely that it is the combination of a particular caretaker interacting with a particular child that ultimately shapes the child's emerging character in terms of both conscious and unconscious processes. Projections pass not only from the baby to the mother but from the mother to the baby as well. "It seemed that the ability to cope with separateness, as well as with actual physical separation," declares Mahler, "was dependent in each case on the history of the mother-child relationship, as well as on its present state. We found it hard to pinpoint just what it was in the individual cases that produced more anxiety in some and an ability to cope in others. Each child had established by this time his own characteristic ways of coping" (p. 103). Thus, when we look at the whole picture, we spy an element of mystery, a unique, intangible quality that pertains to each mother-infant bond and that can never be fully explained by observers or indeed by the mother and infant who are involved in the relationship. What occurs early on is not strictly an enigma but it has its enigmatic aspect, and we must always bear this in mind. Human behavior finally escapes whatever logical space we try to fit it into. Reality happens from the inside and can never be perfectly reconstructed.

As I suggested on several occasions in the context, the struggle for and against separation extends itself powerfully not only into the ritualistic behaviors of religion but into the nature and development of our perceptual lives generally, including the whole of culture. Although it may appear a bit strange to express the matter thus, our ordinary consciousness in the widest, most all-inclusive sense is inextricably bound up with the early struggle over separation and cannot be grasped apart from it. We must remember as we proceed that what Mahler describes in the final paragraphs of her theoretical section is the passing of the rapprochement crises, not the passing of the separation-union conflict. Indeed, it is the position of this book, and has been from the outset, that this conflict never ceases, that it so forcefully shapes and directs our conduct as to gain a place among the central conflicts of our experience as a form of life.

As Mahler herself observes (p. 115), a "sound image" of the maternal figure does not mean that the old longing for merger stops, that the fear of reengulfment goes away, that anxiety, ambivalence, and splitting suddenly vanish, along with feelings of omnipotence and narcissistic grandiosity; it does not mean that the primal terrors of rejection and loss miraculously disappear forever. The establishment of a sound maternal image simply means that the little person can stumble ahead still loaded with the great, absorbing issues of the early time, still loaded with the stress that attends the erosion of symbiosis, still wishing contradictorily for both merger and differentiation, and still smarting from the collapse of dual unity. What occurs as the infant undergoes separation has been described by Rizzuto as a "life-long mourning process that triggers an endless search for replacement."[16] To express the matter from a different yet crucially related angle, the passing of the rapprochement crisis simply means that one is now in a position to act out among others this basic human dilemma, this rooted, unconscious issue as it manifests itself projectively at the levels of both individual and group conduct. It means that one can now seek for omnipotence, fusion, and narcissistic gratification in the wider world. In a manner of speaking, one is loose. The old cliché that we are all more or less neurotic hopefully emerges with fresh clarity at this juncture.

The dynamic, shaping influence of implicit memory on religious belief may also emerge with fresh clarity here. As we peruse Mahler's work and come to appreciate the intensity and the complexity of the neonate's initial encounter with the world, we have the impression that the little one is passing through a veritable lifetime of emotional and physical experience, a lifetime of potent, interpersonal events. Yet the whole extended episode, incredibly, is destined to go mnemonically underground, to discover a brain-based pathway to the land of "infantile amnesia"! Make no mistake, this is not because babies can't remember things. On the contrary, they have strong memorial capacities almost from the outset. It is because ongoing mnemonic, neural developments (mainly language), along with a host of emerging tasks and requirements, come sharply to the fore as infancy gives way to childhood and gradually relinquishes its hold upon the mind. As I have been suggesting all along, we have in this remarkable situation the living seed of the "faith-state," of the believer's hallucinatory, heartfelt conviction that his invisible, mysterious, "transmundane" Parent-God is *there*. Not only does the will to believe, to accept the veracity of religious narrative, push upward ineluctably toward consciousness from an inward source one affectively recognizes yet cannot directly detect, but the narrative's wishful, alluring core holds the promise of *attachment* to a loving provider, to a Spirit through Whom one may lessen the pain of precisely the *separation* just described by Mahler. For most human beings the combination is irresistible, and its effects persist with varying degrees of intensity throughout the course of the life cycle.

Let's deepen and enrich Mahler's findings, then, by concentrating further on the early period, this time with ordinary consciousness itself as the focus.

NOTES

1. See Suzanne Kirschner, *The Religious and Romantic Origins of Psychoanalysis: Individuation and Integration in Post-Freudian Theory* (Cambridge: Cambridge University Press, 1996), pp. 10–13.

2. W. W. Meissner, *Psychoanalysis and Religious Experience* (New Haven, CT: Yale University Press, 1984), pp. vii–viii.

3. Ana-Maria Rizzuto, *The Birth of the Living God* (Chicago: University of Chicago Press, 1979), p. 28.

4. Nathan G. Hale Jr., *The Rise and Crisis of Psychoanalysis in the United States: Freud and the Americans, 1917–1985*, vol. 2 (New York: Oxford University Press, 1995).

5. John Horgan, "Why Freud Isn't Dead," *Scientific American* 282 (December 1996): 106–11.

6. Richard Webster, *Why Freud Was Wrong: Sin, Science, and Psychoanalysis* (New York: Basic Books, 1995), p. 8.

7. Daniel Liechty, "Freud and the Question of Pseudoscience," *Ernest Becker Foundation Newsletter*, no. 6 (1999): 7.

8. Donald Levy, *Freud among the Philosophers: The Psychoanalytic Unconscious and Its Philosophical Critics* (New Haven, CT: Yale University Press, 1996), p. 172.

9. Mark Solms, "Freud Returns," *Scientific American* 290 (May 2004): 82–89.

10. Ethel Person, *Dreams of Love and Fateful Encounters* (London: Penguin, 1990).

11. Margaret Mahler, Fred Pine, and Anni Bergman, *The Psychological Birth of the Human Infant* (New York: Basic Books, 1975). In this chapter, all page numbers in parentheses in the text refer to this source.

12. See note 2 in chap. 1 for more on this use of *object*.

13. D. W. Winnicott, *Playing and Reality* (London: Penguin, 1971), p. 13.

14. Margaret Mahler and Manuel Furer, *On Human Symbiosis and the Vicissitudes of Individuation* (New York: International Universities Press, 1968), p. 9.

15. Winnicott, *Playing and Reality*, p. 188.

16. Rizzuto, *The Birth of the Living God*, p. 49.

5.

Construction of
the Inner Realm

From the inception of our existence we internalize the world; we take experiential events into our emerging mind-body, and we do this fully, deeply, and finally at the level of ganglionic-synaptic development itself. If the reader is wondering why the early period is so crucial, so all-determining for our later lives, this is where the answer begins to emerge, in the psychodynamics of human internalization. "Mind is born early in life," writes Jose Delgado, "as an infant is attracted to sources of comfort and repelled by sources of distress."[1] Even when we are thinking logically as adults, even when we are indulging in the "pure reason" that we associate with philosophers such as Descartes and Kant, the legacy of our early years is there, humming beneath the surface, as it were. If one can think of the multifaceted human ego as a group of actors standing on a stage, one will understand "pure reason" as a mental request that everyone move out of the way so that "reason" may preside at the center. The cooperative members of the cast may do this, but they do not leave the stage, and they influence "reason" by their continued presence there. The living organism, in other words, always perceives the world with the whole mind, as opposed to thinking about it with only a part of the mind. Perception, not thinking, is primary. This also holds for regression. I mean, when adults regress amid crisis, or when they become involved in childlike activities, they do not generally regress altogether. Parts or aspects of the personality remain at appropriately mature levels. Again, perception as a whole, not thinking, is primary.[2]

Of the powerful internalizing that we do toward the beginning, that which involves the caretaker (usually the mother) is of enormous significance. As developmental psychologists express it, the object (this term is used, remember, because the caretaker is not yet perceived by the baby as a person) "enters the infant's dawning psyche" as the deep internalization of life's earliest phase, and she "persists there as a presence, later to become an image" during the period in which verbalization begins. This interplay between mother and infant is "directly involved in the shaping of the infant's personality." Intuitive or feeling perception "begins with maximal intensity at birth as the baby becomes subject in a structuring way to the maternal attitude."[3] So intense, so pervasive, and so basic is this interaction between mother and child that we would do well to regard the mother herself not as a distinct entity but as a kind of organ of the baby. It is in the growth of this unique union, or in the evolution of this unique "biological state,"[4] that we find the nucleus of human identity.

THE MIRROR

The genesis and the formation of the self derive from the baby's initial mirroring experience with the mother. For the past few decades this remarkable aspect of our origins has been studied intensively and has come to be regarded as a central feature of our development. The investigations of René Spitz and his associates during the 1950s and 1960s established at the clinical level the baby's inclination to concentrate on the mother's face—and in particular on her eyes—during periods of feeding.[5] For three or perhaps four months the nursing infant does not look at the mother's breast (or at the bottle held close to her breast) but at her face. "From the moment the mother comes into the room to the end of nursing he stares at her face." What is especially interesting in this regard is the connection between such primal gazing and the mouth, or "oral cavity."

While the child takes into his mouth and body his physical nourishment, he takes into his dawning awareness or his "visceral brain" the emotional, psychological materials that he discovers in the face, eyes, and bodily attitude of the mother. It is often remarked that the first ego is a body ego and that our later life is influenced at the perceptual level by the foundational experiences our bodies undergo as consciousness awakens. We have here a compelling instance of how this works. When Spitz calls the "oral cavity" in its conjunction with the mother's body "the cradle of human perception," he reminds us that sucking in and spitting out are the first, the most basic, and the most persistent perceptual behaviors among humans. They underlie at the bodily level our subsequent rejections and acceptances, our subsequent negations and celebrations, of experience.

Although Spitz established the baby's inclination to stare at the mother's face, notes H. M. Southwood,[6] whose discussion I will follow closely here, he did not state that mother and infant spend considerable time looking at each other, nor did he contend that such looking, along with the mother initiating the infant's facial expressions and sounds, provided the means for the baby to regard the mother's face and sounds as his own. An inborn tendency on the part of the infant prompts him to seek out his mother's gaze and to do so regularly and for extended periods. The mother, because of tendencies developed during the course of her relationship with her own mother, sets about exploiting this mutual face-gazing activity. As the eye-to-eye contact becomes frequent, and easily observed by the investigator, the mother's inclination to continually change her facial expression, as well as the quality of her vocalizing, emerges with striking clarity. Usually she smiles and nods and coos; sometimes in response to an infant frown she frowns. In virtually every instance the mother's facial and vocal behavior comprises an imitation of the baby's.

Thus, as the mother descends to the infant's level, she provides him with a particular kind of human reflection. She does not simply give the baby back his own self; she reinforces a portion of the baby's behavior in comparison with another portion. She gives the baby back not merely a part of what he is doing but something of her own in addition. In individual development, "the precursor of the mirror is the mother's face."[7] The upshot may be stated as follows: the kind of behavior we connect with the ego or the perceptual apparatus derives in large measure from the behavior of the mother. Not only does she trigger the ego's formation, she determines the kind of stimuli to which the child will attend, including the stimuli that will eventually come through language.

Our mental makeup, then, is shaped by those with whom we entered into "object relations" during the early phases of our development. Our earliest "objects" become dynamic parts of our personality structure and continue to influence us in all that we do long after the specific persons who were the aim of our internalizing tendency have ceased to be. By the time we have reached adulthood there exists within us an inner world, a kind of psychic universe that is inhabited by the "objects" that have entered us, or more properly, that we have taken into ourselves along our maturational way. We live in two worlds, from the beginning, and our perceptual life must be regarded as a function of the interaction of these worlds, which continually impinge upon one another.

THE DARK SIDE OF THE MIRROR: SPLITTING

We are beginning to understand the psychological direction from which our ordinary consciousness arises. To do this more fully, however, we must grasp the two-sided, or "split," nature of our early, foundational experience, something that Mahler touched upon during the course of her investigations.

On the one hand, many of the representational units that the baby takes in contribute to his contentment. The mother gives him a positive, nurturing introduction to existence. She soothes him, reassures him, delights him; she develops his confidence, his enthusiasm, his "joy in life." In a word, she triggers his participation in "good" materials. On the other the hand, many of the units that are assimilated by the growing child are disruptive, or, in a very special sense, negative in quality.

As the child goes about building up his good maternal representation, as he gradually enlarges those aspects of the caretaker that will serve as the perceptual basis for his positive participation in the world, he confronts of necessity the imperfections of the symbiotic relationship in which he is involved. No matter how solicitous the mother is, the infant is fated to undergo tension, frustration, discomfort, and even a certain amount of pain. Such experiences mobilize anxiety. Indeed, very young infants display identical patterns of anxious behavior when they are in contact with the caretaker during a period in which she is tense, angry, disquieted, or anxious herself. Repeated, inescapable exposure to inconsistent conduct prompts the developing baby to split the care-taker into a "good" and a "bad" object and to internalize these objects into a part or aspect of his perceiving self. The collection of people each of us harbors within, carries about, and projects into our reality reaches back in every instance to the first pair of our personifications: the good mother and the bad or evil mother. With the passage of time these early, primitive personifications get transmuted into the good me, the bad me, and the ambiguous, dreadful not-me.[8]

We must remember here that the mother's inconsistency is a grave, disruptive event for the child, that it corresponds to his worst imaginings and fears. The postponement of gratification from his mother's supplies constitutes for the infant a trauma, and residues of the infant's reaction to this trauma can be found in the psychology of later years. Because he is simply not able to integrate the mother's two sides, her "bad" and "good" aspects, the infant attempts to coordinate them by splitting and then dealing with the splits. He declares, in effect, "Mother is not bad. There just happens to be this bad mother who appears once in a while. She and Mother are not really the same person, for Mother is always good and will never hurt and disappoint. I am obliged to interact with both Mother and the other one." Only later, when the child achieves object constancy, will he be able to accept goodness and badness in the same person.[9]

Thus threats to our narcissistic integrity, to our primitive emotional and bodily self-esteem, exist from the inception of our psychic lives and stem from the interaction of the child's wishes and needs with the demands and frustrations of the external world. Such narcissistic wounds may evoke feelings of depression and a growing sense of perplexity, which is frequently answered with aggressive behavior. The infant's mere inability to influence, predict, or comprehend an event that he expected on the basis of his previous experience to be able to control or understand is registered as trauma. Because the infant's thought, the whole of his primitive mentation, is tied inextricably to the mother, her mere absence through temporary departure can leave the infant with the terrible feeling that he is empty, empty in his mind and emotions. We may have here the deep origin and most basic, enduring expression of the feeling that one is "losing one's mind." We also now realize that the parent's very power over the life and death of the child is perceived as threatening and is internalized to become part of everyone's susceptibility to nightmare, everyone's residual paranoia. Odd as it may sound to express it this way, merely being born human is a major source of stress. In the words of Michael Eigen, "Fragmentation and division are as much a part of our starting point as union and continuity."[10]

The Jungian researches of Erich Neumann are helpful on this score. The symbolism of the "Terrible Mother," he writes, "draws its images from the inside"; that is, the "bad object" appears in fantastic, ghastly forms that do not originate in the environment. Whether we are in "Egypt or India, Mexico or Etruria, Bali or Rome," we confront the "archetypal" expression of these intrapsychic "monsters." In the tales and myths of "all peoples, ages, and countries," as well as in our own nightmares, "witches, vampires, ghouls and spectres assail us, all terrifyingly alike."[11] It is the internalizing of this bad object that explains our emotional fear of death. At issue here is not death as the adult conceives it, but a threat of a quality and magnitude beyond the adult's imagination. We get a glimpse of it in states of panic and in the momentary probe into infancy that some individuals experience during the course of psychotherapy.[12] Thus the struggle between the forces of life and death, which is inherent in the biologically precarious infantile condition, becomes involved in the infant's response to the mother that protects and satisfies and to the mother that frustrates and deprives. Where the fear of death is concerned, it is the uncertain ties to the living world at all ages that shake us more than the awareness of biological cessation.[13]

What I am maintaining is that we cannot understand the complex symbol that death constitutes for the human creature, or the powerful role of death-consciousness in the impulse toward religious belief, if we exclude from the discussion the primal anxiety of the early period. "When a child has a fear of dying," writes Mary Shaw, "it often translates into an extreme fear of being separated from his mother."[14] Because the mother's impact on the child is preverbal, because her presence is internalized before higher conceptualization begins, it is very, very difficult to subject our split foundations to reason. True, as Mahler points out, there is a diminution of splitting during the rapprochement subphase, when the child becomes more empathetic to the mother's position. But as I have suggested, this marks only a diminution (sometimes a temporary one) that permits the rapprochement crisis to pass. It does not even begin to mean that the human tendency to split has ceased. On the contrary, our anxious obsession with death, as well as our dangerous indulgence in rigid, dichotomous views of the world, with the good guys over here and the bad guys over there, is rooted largely in the primitive splitting of the early time, which leaves perdurable traces on our normal perception.

EARLY EXCITEMENT, EARLY AFFECT

I want to reemphasize here that the parent-child interactions of the early period must not be viewed as primarily cognitive events. In the words of Daniel Stern, to whose *Interpersonal World of the Infant* I now turn, "they mainly involve affect and excitement" and become part of the infant's effort "to order the world by seeking invariants."[15] When the preverbal, inward Representation of such Interaction becomes Generalized into what Stern calls a RIG, the infant's "sense of a core self" (p. 90), or what we call the "ego" in previous sections, is well upon its developmental way. "Affects," writes Stern, "are excellent self-variants because of their relative fixity" (p. 89), which means, of course, that affects are a central part of mirroring. By creating a "continuity of experience" (p. 90), and in particular a "continuity of affective experience" (p. 93), the RIG provides the baby with the psychic, emotional foundation of his subsequent perceptual interactions with the world. As I earlier observed in my references to Silvan Tomkins, we see the world "feelingly."

Thus mirroring in its early stages (we'll come to the later stages very soon) comprises for Stern a "mediation" in which the caregiver "greatly influences the infant's sense of wonder and avidity for exploration" (p. 103). It is "only the feeling state" that belongs to the nascent self, that is a "self-invariant," and "merger experiences" become simply "a way of being with someone" (p. 109). The infant lays down over and over again the memory of specific affective episodes; he develops RIGs; and he becomes susceptible to subsequent experiences that recall the foundational ones. Later affective exchanges reactivate the original exchanges; they "pack the wallop of the original lived experience in the form of an active memory" (p. 110). This is the essence of the infant's affective world.

EVOKED COMPANIONS

Employing terminology that will help us enormously in understanding religious experience, Stern calls these active memories "evoked companions" (p. 116) and suggests that they constitute what psychology usually refers to as internalized relationships. "For instance," Stern writes in an effort to let us know exactly what he has in mind, "if a six-month-old, when alone, encounters a rattle and manages to grasp it and shake it so that it makes a sound, the initial pleasure may quickly become extreme delight and exuberance, expressed in smiling, vocalizing, and general body wriggling. The extreme delight and exuberance is not the only result of successful mastery, but also the historical result of similar past moments in the presence of a delight-and-exuberance-enhancing (regulating) other" (p. 113). It is partly a "social response," but in this instance it takes place in a "nonsocial situation." At such times, the original pleasure born of mastery acts as a "retrieval cue" and activates the RIG, resulting in an "imagined interaction with an evoked companion" which includes of course the "shared and mutually induced delight" about the mastery.

Equally crucial for our grasp of religious belief is Stern's observation that evoked companions "never disappear." They "lie dormant throughout life," and while they are always retrievable, "their degree of activation is variable" (p. 116). Stern writes, "Various evoked companions will be almost constant companions in everyday life. Is it not so for adults when they are not occupied with tasks? How much time each day do we spend in imagined interactions that are either memories, or the fantasied practice of upcoming events, or daydreams?" (p. 118). Robert Rogers comments on these materials, "The seemingly unaccountable experience by an adult of strong emotion, such as love or anger, as a response to a relatively trivial situation involving a comparative stranger might be accounted for by assuming that an 'evoked companion' has suddenly been mobilized, however unconsciously. Where else could all that affect come from?" Thus "attachment is the internalized representation of repetitive interactions with caregivers." What is internalized in the earliest representations "is not simply the infant's own action, nor the environments' response, but the dynamic interplay between the two."[16] Can anyone fail to spy here the manner in which these citations touch upon, indeed mesh with, our earlier discussion of separation anxiety as presented in Mahler?

Many individual and group behaviors and beliefs, particularly those that occur in the religious or spiritual realm, are designed unconsciously to address the problem of separation (and/or other psychological problems) by offering practitioners experiences that evoke companions. Such experiences grant the solace of companionship to those who are struggling in the after-separation-world, those whose aloneness, self-alienation, or persistent separation anxiety prime them to respond to an unseen universe of powerful forces and beings to which they are ostensibly connected. Indeed, many of the figures at the heart of religious ritual (e.g., God the Father, the Son, Mary, guardian angels) may be regarded in significant measure as projective, psychological expressions, or complex, multilayered symbolifications, of those longed-for inward companions associated originally with the dynamic affects included in the dual unity situation, the baby's delicious, regulating, invariant, and internalized encounters with the care-giving figures of the early period.

AFFECT ATTUNEMENT

What Stern calls "the next quantum leap in the sense of self" occurs when the infant discovers that he "has a mind and that other people have minds as well" (p. 124). Here we come to the first of two direct, foundational precursors of religious communion.

At about nine months, infants come gradually upon "the momentous realization" that subjective experiences are "potentially shareable with someone else." The infant "must arrive at a theory not only of separate minds but of interfaceable separate minds" (ibid.). This is not, of course, a "theory" in the usual sense, but a "working notion that says something like, what is going on in my mind may be similar enough to what is going on in your mind that we can somehow communicate this without words and thereby experience intersubjectivity" (p. 125). Now, intersubjective relatedness, or the "new organizing subjective perspective about the self," is built upon a foundation of "core relatedness," the sharing of affective states. Stern dubs this empathetic responsiveness between caregiver and child "affect attunement," observing that it constitutes what is meant when clinicians speak of parental mirroring (p. 138).

After presenting a wealth of clinical evidence for the existence of affect attunement, Stern observes in a crucial passage, "Strict imitation won't do. . . . The parent must be able to read the infant's feeling state from the infant's overt behavior, must perform in some way to the infant's, and the infant must be able to read this parental response as having to do with his own original feeling" (p. 139). Parent and infant are engaged in what we can term telepathic or clairvoyant exchanges; they manifest a kind of ESP in regard to affective states and affective wishes—what they want to happen as they interact on this intimate, feeling level. Stern writes, "Infants . . . appear to have an innate general capacity, which can be called *amodal* perception, to take information received in one sensory modality and somehow translate it into another sensory modality. We don't know how they accomplish this task" (p. 51). He continues, "The information is probably not experienced as belonging to any one particular sensory mode. More likely it transcends mode or channel and exists in some supra-modal form. . . .

It involves an encoding into a still mysterious, amodal representation." And again, what "the infant experiences are not sights and sounds and touches and namable objects, but rather shapes, intensities, and temporal patterns—the more 'global' qualities of experience" (ibid.). And finally, "the experience of finding a cross-modal match . . . would feel like a correspondence or imbuing of present experience with something prior or familiar. Present experience would feel related in some way to experience from elsewhere" (pp. 52–53). Here we have a realistic, psychological source (through state-dependent or implicit memory) of what many consider to be the supernatural level upon which religious communion transpires. Moreover—and perhaps of equal importance—the essence of affect attunement between parent and child resides in its synchronous nature, in its happily timed interactive quality. Parent and offspring are affectively in synch. The parent knows intuitively, telepathically, clairvoyantly the affective meaning of the infant's signals, and the parent provides response in a timely fashion, magically echoing or mirroring the infant's inner world as the infant makes that world manifest. Conversely, the infant strives to engage the parent affectively in time to gratify his (the infant's) surging affect. Synchronous rapport, in short, is the pith of preverbal existence, and "transaction" takes place, says Stern, only when such "conditions" are met (p. 139). Just as evoked companions never disappear, just as they lie dormant throughout life waiting to be activated, so affect attunements become deeply internalized, providing the emergent self with a foundational legacy of feeling that is sought over and over again in subsequent years. Indeed, it is "attuning" with "vitality" that permits us as humans to *be* with one another in the sense of "sharing likely inner experiences" on a continuous basis (p. 157). Here is a memorable consequence: when we discover (or rediscover) an attunement, an evoked companion, an energetic, affective fix, we often feel transformed.

THE TRANSFORMATIONAL OBJECT

Guiding us toward the psychological core of spiritual thinking, toward the essence of its interrelations with the early period, Christopher Bollas observes in *The Shadow of the Object* that the infant's experience of his first object, "the mother," is fundamentally transformative in character: "It is undeniable that as the infant's other self, the mother transforms the baby's internal and external environment. . . . [She] is less significant and identifiable as an object than as a process that is identified with cumulative internal and external transformation."[17] Just as evoked companionship and affect attunement never disappear, so this feature of early existence "lives on in certain forms of object-seeking in adult life." The object is sought for its "function as a signifier of transformation." The quest is not to possess the object but to "surrender to it as a medium that alters the self," that promises to "transform the self" (p. 14). It is an old refrain: having met you, or found Jesus, or joined the party, or started meditating, I'm changed. In significant measure, and in psychological terms, the refrain translates into something like this: I've rediscovered (through unconscious memory) the transformational essence of the early period, of dual unity, of mirroring. My new connection reunites me with a transforming internalized caretaker and thus diminishes my sense of separation. I am restored to the delicious symbiosis I once knew directly.

This conception of the maternal figure as transformational is supported by the overriding fact that she regularly alters the baby's environment to meet his need; she "actually transforms his world" (p. 15). The infant identifies his own emerging capacities of motility, perception, and integration with the presence of the mother, and the failure of the mother to provide a facilitating environment can result in the ego's collapse. With the infant's creation of the transitional object (upon which I'll expand in a moment), the transformational process is "displaced from the mother-environment, where it originated, into countless subjective objects." The transitional phase is "heir to the transformational period." Not only can the infant play with the illusion of his omnipotence, he can experience the "freedom of metaphor" (ibid.).

In a section titled "The Search for the Transformational Object in Adult Life," Bollas declares that psychology has failed to take notice of the "wide-ranging collective search for an object that is identified with the metamorphosis of the self" (ibid.). For example, in religious faith, when a person believes in the Deity's potential to transform the environment, he "sustains the terms of the earliest object tie within a mythic structure." Such knowledge is "symbiotic" (p. 16), writes Bollas, touching implicitly on the theme of separation in Mahler. The symbiotic knowledge "coexists alongside other forms of knowing." Aesthetic objects, too, frequently elicit transformational response from the individual, who may feel a "deep subjective rapport" with a painting, poem, song, symphony, or landscape and experience "an uncanny fusion" with the item, an event that "re-evokes an ego state that prevailed during early psychic life" (ibid.). Such occasions are "less noteworthy as transformational accomplishments" than they are for their "uncanny quality," the sense of being reminded of something "never cognitively apprehended but existentially known." They draw forth a sense of "fusion" that is the individual's recollection of the transformational object. Thus, as psychological categories, transformation and separation are integrally related once again.

As I just suggested and wish to reemphasize here, the search for symbolic equivalents to the transformational object, and the experience with which it is identified, continues throughout the life cycle. We develop faith in a God whose absence is held ironically to be "as important a test of man's being as his presence" (p. 17). We visit the theater, the museum, the landscape of our choice, to "search for aesthetic experience." We may imagine the self "as the transformational facilitator," and we may invest ourselves with abilities to change the environment that are not only "impossible" but, upon reflection, "embarrassing." In such daydreams the self as transformational object is somewhere in the future, and even meditative planning about the future is often a "kind of psychic prayer for the arrival of the transformational object," a "secular second coming" of a relation experienced in the earliest period of life (ibid.).

How does such transformation look during the early period? What are its phenomenological features? Here we reach the second direct, foundational precursor of religious communion, and in particular of divine intervention: God "answering" one's supplication. If the child is in "distress," writes Bollas, the "resolution of discomfort is achieved by the apparition-like presence of mother," who arrives in a timely, synchronous manner to remove the "distress" (p. 33). Not only is the "pain of hunger" transformed "by mother's milk" into an experience of "fullness," but the transformation is accomplished synchronously, as the hungry child makes his needs known. Bollas calls this a "primary transformation": emptiness, agony, and anger become fullness and contentment. Over and over again during life's initial stages parent and offspring are joined in such ministering, synchronous encounters. The child is injured; the child cries out. Then what happens? The parent appears to soothe and "make better." The child is wet and uncomfortable; the child starts to squall. Then what happens? The parent appears with dry garments and ministering hands. In this way, the early period of maternal care comprises an endless series of "answered prayers." The big one, like a guardian angel, hovers over the little one and ministers to the little one's needs just as they arise. Of particular fascination here is the close, even inextricable connection between maternal care and the development of the time sense.

The essentials of the matter are captured in a seminal paper by Peter Hartocollis. "As tension eases," he writes, "and the mother is not yet there, the 'good object' image or representation emerges protectively in fantasy and unites with the self-image in a need-fulfilling hallucinatory experience; but if the mother's arrival is further delayed, it begins to fade away rapidly. As the infant tries to hold onto it and unpleasure increases, the uncertain 'good' object begins to turn into a 'bad' one. It is the effort to hold onto the 'good' object and expel the 'bad' one that . . . creates the ability to anticipate the future."[18] Eventually what Hartocollis calls "object constancy" develops in the maturing child; the early hallucinatory process is replaced by the ability to anticipate the fulfillment of a need. As the fused "good" and "bad" maternal figures are set up within as the scaffolding for normal character development, a relatively trustful tendency to believe in good outcomes is projected onto the environment, which begins to be experienced as continuous, as possessing the attribute of duration. Accordingly, the good object is in large measure good time, or synchronous attention and care. The bad object is, by contrast, delay and neglect. When we experience divine interventions in the now of our existence as adults, they are magical, powerful, "numinous," and convincing to the extent that they recall unconsciously the timely ministrations of the good, attentive parent. Indeed, such interventions can occur in the first place only because people tend to compartmentalize or "split" the parental object into its "good" and "bad" components, and people do this precisely as a consequence of the temporal side of their early care.

Let's turn now to Winnicott's depictions of the manner in which the province of "illusion" arises in the life of the individual. Our development from the early period of helplessness to the attainment of separation and autonomy has a magical and in some sense paradoxical aspect to it. It is bound up integrally with mothering, with substitute objects, and with that "intermediate area" in which substitution finds its full, phenomenological expression, namely play. In the words of Winnicott, the "good-enough mother" begins by adapting almost completely to the "infant's needs." As time goes on, "she adapts less and less completely . . . according to the infant's growing ability to deal with her failure" through his own experience. If all goes well, the infant can actually "gain" from his "frustration" by developing his own idiosyncratic style of relative independence. What is essential is that the mother give the baby, through her good-enough care, the illusion that "there is an external reality that corresponds to the infant's own capacity to create." It is precisely within this area of creativity that the infant will begin to make his transition away from the maternal figure by finding, or discovering, "transitional objects"—blankets, teddy bears, story books— which afford him the "magical" or "illusory" belief that he is moving toward, or staying with, the caretaker at the same time that he is moving away from her or giving her up. Because the transitional object is discovered in the real world it has a kind of objectivity, or facticity; because the child projects into it his own idiosyncratic wishes and needs, it also takes on a subjective cast. It is both found and created. Such magic, such illusion, such creativity provides the child with his primary link to the cultural realm, to the religious and artistic symbols that constitute the shared, illusory reality of grown-ups. "The matter of illusion," declares Winnicott, "is one that belongs inherently to human beings and that no individual finally solves for himself or herself." The "task of reality-acceptance is never completed. . . . No human being is free from the strain of relating inner and outer reality." It is the "inter- mediate area of experience" including art and religion that provides "relief from the strain" and that is "in direct continuity with the play area of the small child who is lost in play."[19] In this way, "there is a direct development from transitional phenomena to playing, and from playing to shared playing, and from this to cultural experiences."[20]

In order to "get the idea of playing," Winnicott goes on, it is "helpful to think of the preoccupation that characterizes the playing of the young child. The content does not matter. What matters is the near-withdrawal state, akin to the concentration of older children and adults." Playing "involves the body," is "inherently exciting," and transpires amid the experience of a "non-purposive state" that is marked above all by "relaxation." It is "only in playing," Winnicott concludes, that the "child or adult is free to be creative" and that the world he inhabits becomes "invested with a first-time-ever quality."[21] Thus the good-enough mother permits the growing child to participate playfully in the first objects of his cultural experience and hence to find a method of separating from the parental figure while, paradoxically, maintaining the connection to that figure all in the same psychological moment.

I want to enrich these seminal notions with a citation or two from other psychological authors. Of the transitional object itself Phyllis Greenacre writes, "It represents not only the mother's breast and body but the total maternal environment as it is experienced in combination with sensations from the infant's body. It serves as a support and convoy during that period of rapid growth which necessitates increasing separa- tion from the mother." We should also note that during this period "speech is in the process of formation."[22] Indeed, the creation and exploitation of the transitional realm derives from the same psychological impetus that lies behind the creation of the symbolic universe in general and the religious universe in particular. The driving need is to internalize the environment, to grip the external world, and thus to answer the problem of loss with the kind of psychological mastery or control that Geza Roheim terms "dual-unity," the state of having the object at the symbolic level and of relinquishing the object at the level of reality.[23] To express the matter from another, related angle, because the infant's attachment is there before the other is experienced as other, the growing awareness of the caretaker as a "differentiated being" is itself "experienced as a loss." True, there is an "objective" gain in "cognitive comprehension" as this process transpires. At the same time, however, there is the awareness that "certain treasured sensations are not part of the self but can come and go."[24] Accordingly, the presence of the early powerful attachment both facilitates and complicates our movement away from the mother, our growth as separate, differentiated creatures. It facilitates by providing us with a stable, loving internalization, a good object that endures and that leads us toward positive attachment to other people and toward the objects of culture (art and religion). It complicates because the experience of loss "permanently endows the relationship to the mother with painful undercurrents and sets up a developmental pathway that can be traversed in both directions," that is, toward progression and selfhood on the one hand, or toward regression, hostility, and pathogenic absorption in the objects of the past on the other.[25] Here is the "dichotomous human condition," the "forward maturational pulls" and the "neurotic backward attractions" that all of us experience to one degree or another at various times in our lives.[26] If we strive to exist "authentically," to look bravely and honestly at the truth of our relations with others and with ourselves, we have a reasonably good chance, as Rona Bank expresses it in a recent paper on Winnicott, to know how it feels to be "humanly alive."[27]

Let me sum the whole matter up from a slightly different angle. The Winnicottian moment of illusion, the foundation of religious belief, is specifically the moment of timely maternal ministration, the moment in which the maternal object transforms the infant's world, changing anxiety into security, discomfort into satisfaction. When the helpless little one cries out (protoprayer) the omnipotent, caring big one (protodeity) arrives to succor and to reassure. Remember, during life's first years this happens over and over again, thousands of times, and establishes for the child through simple conditioning the essential nature of reality. Accordingly, religious faith is the adult's wishful, willful insistence (based on experience) that the attentive caregiver of the early period is still there watching over one, that one's cry (prayer) can still beget the wished-for, loving, interventional response. To turn the coin over, religious faith is the wishful, willful denial that separation has occurred, that the caring maternal object, the ministering angel as it were, is gone, that ego boundaries differentiate the big one and the little one. What William James calls the faith-state (see chap. 3) arises unconsciously from precisely this early object relation, which is deeply internalized into the perceptual system.

Again, the wondrous sense of God's presence, or the remarkable coincidence that one regards as a blessing (sometimes the synchronous result of supplication), is essentially the product of implicit memory, the wishful, unconscious resurgence of the period in which the original version of such events was the order of the day, the period during which the religious universe began to emerge from the powerful Winnicottian illusions. In this way, the inward certitude that arises from successful prayer or communion (one has "made contact") is an instance not of the supernatural but of the uncanny. It is as if the universe is still in the orbit of the believer's wish and will. What actually happened before appears to be happening again when it isn't "supposed to happen," when the caregiver and the child are separate from one another. Supernatural events and personages in the religious realm are the result of ego boundaries dissolving; indeed, the religious realm as a whole is unconsciously designed to accomplish such a dissolution. It permits the psychic remerger of parent and child. The "miracle" of faith resides here. Not only does one get the caregiver back, but one gets the caregiver back in an idealized form. One is not alone, and one has nothing to fear from a just and merciful God. We have in all this, needless to say, and ideal formula for mitigating the stresses of human existence.

THE WORD

Seventy years ago, the pioneering investigations of Soviet linguist Lev Vygotsky made clear that the development of language was not primarily a cognitive process (the orthodox view) but an interactive, social process loaded with emotional, bodily components from the preverbal period.[28] Because thought and speech develop in a parallel and reciprocal fashion, we must ultimately think of language as a dynamic system of meaning in which the emotional and the intellectual unite. The egocentric speech of the three-year-old does not disappear when the child reaches seven or eight. Instead of atrophying, such egocentric speech goes underground; that is, it turns into inner speech and forms the foundation of that inward babble which, joined to higher cognitive components, comes eventually to comprise a sizeable portion of our ordinary consciousness. In this way, the development of thinking is not from the individual to the social but from the social to the individual. The child starts conversing with himself as he has been doing with others.

As for the spoken word, it is initially a substitute for the gesture, for the bodily attitude and bodily expression that precede the verbalized sound. When the child says "mama," it is not merely the word that means, say, put me in the chair, but the child's whole behavior at that moment, his reaching out for the chair, trying to hold it, etc. In contrast to the egocentric speech that goes inward, verbalized speech goes outward; the child uses it as a method of pointing. It is the fusion of this inward speech and developing outward speech that finally emerges as human thought in its ordinary, basic expression.

We appreciate from this viewpoint the growing psychological realization, based explicitly on Vygotsky's work, that thinking is an unconscious process in the first instance.[29] Even our conscious speech, the psychological community has come to recognize, is pervaded by unconscious mechanisms to the degree that it is tied to our thinking.[30] This means that our thinking, our stream of consciousness itself in the most general, all-inclusive sense, is the source of those slips of the tongue on which Freud stumbled nearly a century ago.

With regard to the role of separation in all of this, we must note that symbol formation (or word formation) arises from the infant's shared experience with the mother.[31] The common act of "referential pointing" starts with the mother's invitation but soon leads to the child inviting the mother to join in the contemplation of some object. This marks the beginning of what psychologists call "intellectual stereoscopy," in which the objectification of the world is dependent on social interaction. The child names things to someone, and the loving feedback he receives becomes the incentive for naming further things. The whole idea of twoness and separateness arises from this mutuality. Thus the presence and absence of the mother and of important physical objects in the child's world play motivational roles in the development of representational thought.

In fact, the ability to recognize the mother, to conceptualize her as mother, is goaded into existence by the need to cope with her absence, or loss. The feeling of loss becomes the motive for "acquiring the capacity to represent absent objects or to represent objects regardless of their presence or absence." When the baby names the absent object, he predicates it on the basis of its former presence: thus, "mommy gone." The same act can predicate a future presence on a current absence. The ideas of "gone" and "mommy" are linked and placed in relation to one another.[32] The whole business of linguistic predication is thus associated with the problem of separation from the caretaker. Again, as the child links up "mommy" and "gone," he creates a dependent relationship between two ideas that substitutes for each idea's dependency on actual experience. This gives the child the power to recall the mother at will. Symbolic representation (as we saw in Winnicott's discussion of play) comes to provide a way back to the missing object of one's emotions.

Because the verbal representation of the thing is the culmination of the symbolic process, the word is the magical tie that reunites us with the all-important figure(s) of infancy and childhood. It is not merely that maternal stimulation during the time of language development is necessary for the fulfillment of the child's potential; our symbolic seeing is charged with the emotional energy that went into our life-and-death struggle to maintain our connection to the caregiver at the same time we were giving her up.

Through the early imperfections of mothering we learn to grip the world with our bodies, with our tense anticipation (the time sense). Through the crises of separation, which continue to transpire after the early period, we learn to grip the world with our minds, with our symbols, with our words. The mirror phase of infancy eventually gives way to the presentational mirror of a mind that has separation on its mind. The very running on of our thoughts in ordinary consciousness becomes a link to the figures of the past. To express the matter in terms that recall the context of our discussion explicitly, because the word becomes the child's chief tool for "matching mental states,"[33] the word also becomes the child's chief tool for preserving the "attunement" and "evoked companionship" from which Winnicottian "illusions" arise. Thus language as the means of approaching God harbors perforce the unconscious aims and wishes of the early period as they inform the supplications of the adult. In the universe of religious behavior, the word always reaches back to its primitive communicative origins.

NOTES

1. Jose Delgado, *Physical Control of the Mind* (New York: Harper and Row, 1971), p. 26.

2. See Harold Blum, "The Conceptual Development of Regression," *Psychoanalytic Study of the Child* 49 (1994): 73.

3. Joseph P. Rheingold, *The Fear of Being of Woman* (New York: Grune and Stratton, 1964), p. 30.

4. Winifred Gallagher, "Motherless Child," *Sciences* 32 (July 1992): 13.

5. René Spitz, *The First Relationship* (New York: International Universities Press, 1965), p. 81.

6. H. M. Southwood, "The Origin of Self-Awareness and Ego Behavior," *International Journal of Psychoanalysis* 66 (1973): 235–39.

7. D. W. Winnicott, *Playing and Reality* (London: Penguin, 1971), p. 130.

8. Rheingold, *The Fear of Being of Woman*, p. 164.

9. Rozsika Parker, *Mother Love/Mother Hate: The Power of Maternal Ambivalence* (New York: Basic Books, 1995), p. 174.

10. Michael Eigen, "Toward Bion's Starting Point," *International Journal of Psychoanalysis* 66 (1985): 329.

11. Erich Neumann, *The Great Mother*, trans. R. Manheim (Princeton, NJ: Princeton University Press, 1970), p. 148.

12. See Rheingold, *The Fear of Being of Woman*.

13. See Bernard Steinzor, "Death and the Construction of Reality," *Omega: Journal of Death and Dying* 9 (1979): 97–124.

14. Mary Shaw, *Your Anxious Child* (New York: Birch Lane Press, 1995), p. 141.

15. Daniel Stern, *The Interpersonal World of the Infant* (New York: Basic Books, 1985), pp. 74–75. Page numbers for the other Stern quotes in this and the following two sections are included in the text.

16. All Rogers quotations in this paragraph from Robert Rogers, *Self and Other: Object Relations in Psychoanalysis and Literature* (New York: New York University Press, 1991), p. 41.

17. Christopher Bollas, *The Shadow of the Object: Psychoanalysis of the Unthought-Known* (London: Free Association Books, 1987), pp. 13–14. Page numbers for the other Bollas quotes in this section are included in the text.

18. Peter Hartocollis, "Origins of Time," *Psychoanalytic Quarterly* 43 (1974): 247.

19. All quotations to this point in this paragraph from Winnicott, *Playing and Reality*, pp. 12–13.

20. Ibid., p. 51.

21. Ibid., pp. 51–52.

22. Phyllis Greenacre, "The Transitional Object and the Fetish," *Psychoanalytic Quarterly* 40 (1971): 384.

23. Geza Roheim, *Magic and Schizophrenia* (Bloomington: University of Indiana Press, 1955), p. 109.

24. Fred Pine, "On the Psychology of the Separation-Individuation Crisis," *International Journal of Psychoanalysis* 60 (1979): 226.

25. Ibid.

26. Peter Neubauer, "Preoedipal Objects and Object Primacy," *Psychoanalytic Study of the Child* (Yale) 40 (1985): 169.

27. Rona Bank, "Mythic Perspectives and Perspectives on Truth: Approaching Winnicott," *Psychoanalytic Review* 86 (1999): 131.

28. See Lev Vygotsky, *Thought and Language*, trans. E. Hanfman and G. Vakar (1934; Cambridge, MA: MIT Press, 1979).

29. See Michael Basch, "Psychoanalytic Interpretation and Cognitive Transformation," *International Journal of Psychoanalysis* 62 (1981): 151–74.

30. See François Roustang, *Dire Mastery: Discipleship from Freud to Lacan* (Baltimore: Johns Hopkins University Press, 1976).

31. See David Bleich, "New Considerations on the Infantile Acquisition of Language and Symbolic Thought," paper presented to the Psychological Center for the Study of the Arts, State University of New York at Buffalo, March 16, 1990, pp. 1–28.

32. Ibid.

33. Henry Plotkin, *Evolution in Mind: An Introduction to Evolutionary Psychology* (London: Penguin, 1997), p. 249.

6.

Brain, Mind, and Religion

O f overriding significance in this book is the extent to which the psychodynamic picture presented contextually has come to be supported in recent years by neurobiological investigations of the developing mind-brain. What occurs early on as the infant-child interacts with the parental provider is not registered, or internalized, in some vague, "psychological" way that may or may not be "there" depending upon how one chooses to "view" the matter. On the contrary, what we are calling "the basic biological situation" is registered physiologically, at the synaptic level itself, to become the neurobiological foundation of human perception in general and the essential inspiration of the religious realm in particular. Religious narrative and ritual, the human creature's distinctive planetary signature, spring directly from the interactive nurturing that dominates the early stages of our existence. "Human connections shape the neural connections from which the mind emerges," writes Daniel Siegel in *The Developing Mind*.[1] While the "structure" and the "function" of the "brain" are "directly shaped" by "interpersonal experience throughout life," such "shaping" is "most crucial during the early years of childhood" (p. 4). Different "patterns" of "child-parent attachment" are "associated" with differing "physiological responses" and with "ways of seeing the world." It is the "communication of emotion" that serves as the "primary means" by which such experiences of "attachment" mold "the developing mind" (ibid.). In this way, the "repeated patterns of children's interactions with their caregivers" (the basic biological situation of asking and receiving) become "remembered" in the "various modalities of memory" and "directly shape not just what children recall" but "how the representational processes develop. Behavior, emotion, perceptions, sensations, and models of others," Siegel notes, "are engrained by experiences that occur before children have autobiographical memorial processes available to them. These implicit elements of memory also later influence the structure of autobiographical narratives" (p. 5). For countless millions of human beings, needless to say, one's "autobiographical narrative" becomes interwoven inextricably with one's "religious narrative," the timeless, traditional, cross-cultural "myth" that captures the manner in which individuals "see the world" in the widest, most encompassing sense.

At the center of the spiritual "narratives" to which we are devoting ourselves here resides the image of a loving, care-giving Parent-God Who devotes Himself, among other things, to watching over His vulnerable, dependent children, the human flock He has engendered and for which He is ultimately responsible: "The Lord is my shepherd, I shall not want" (Psalm 23). A genuine understanding of religion resides in the conscious comprehension of the manner in which this "core narrative" or "core myth" is "wired" directly into and emanates directly from our human mind-brain as it unconsciously and wishfully projects the implicit memory of our early "attachment experience" into the "present" reality in which we discover ourselves. The religious narrative with the loving Parent-God at its center is the mnemonic *retrieval* of the early biological pattern of attachment through which we found or tried to find our emotional security and our physical safety in the world. The upshot: our religion becomes our ongoing attachment narrative designed to enhance our inward stability, our calmness, our happiness, our vitality, in our always dangerous and always unpredictable surroundings. It serves the straightforward evolutionary purpose of ensuring and increasing the effectiveness of our interactions with the environment by ensuring and increasing our inward psychological equilibrium, in reference particularly to our abhorrence of feeling isolated and alone, "separate" in the psychical sense we discovered in Mahler and others a few pages earlier. "God is love" means God inherits mnemonically, as a synaptically rooted projective entity, the primal love of the early time; He preserves our attachment to the "parental object" as we go off, inevitably, "on our own." The attachment patterns of the early period are "mapped" onto the religious narratives of an ever-receding future—the unknown. Thus the God we ostensibly "discover" at the cultural level turns out to be the "God" we unconsciously *remember* at the level of our internalizing brains.

To express the whole business a tad more technically, Siegel points out that "experience early in life" is "especially crucial in organizing the way the basic structures of the brain develop." The "brain's development" is an "experience-dependent process" in which "experience activates certain pathways in the brain, strengthening existing connections and creating new ones" (p. 13). As Donald Hebb has axiomatically and famously expressed the matter, "Neurons that fire together wire together" (quoted in Siegel, p. 26). What are "stored," observes Siegel, "are the probabilities of neurons' firing in a specific pattern—not actual things" (p. 27). Thus the "neural net" *remembers* even though the memory itself may not be consciously and explicitly brought to the illuminated center of the subject's focused attention. As for the neural "mechanisms" involved in our characteristic way of "encoding" our significant experiences into retrievable "packets" or "engrams," the "amygdala" is believed "to be involved with imparting the emotional significance" to objects and "linking" them to "other memory systems" initially "imparted by the hippocampus" but then "subserved by other complex cerebral pathways potentially involving many hundreds of thousands if not millions of synapses." Just as the "properties of objects" are "synthesized convergently by different pathways," we can "surmise that the historical and emotional significance of objects are likewise synthesized," yet also "edited, updated, and revised" based upon "new experiences." The more complex "associative experiential properties and cues" may be "attached to critical objects in the environment, such as parents, siblings, and even the concept of oneself" (p. 49). Our lives, then, are "filled with implicit influences, the origins and impacts of which we may or may not be aware" (ibid.). Affectively charged, "value-laden" memories are "made more likely to be reactivated" among the "myriad of infinite engrams laid down" as we move ahead. The early period is "encoded" in the brain, and our existence is "shaped" by the "reactivations of implicit memory, which lack a sense that something is being recalled. We simply enter these engrained states" and undergo them as "the reality of our present experience" (pp. 32–33). What James calls "the varieties of religious experience" offer us the most familiar, striking exemplifications of such neurally rooted "entrances" and such engrained, concealed "presences." Through an endless variety of retrieval cues, from supplications to oratorios, from stained-glass windows to sacred robes, from the interpersonal crises of divorce or illness or death, to the physical dangers lurking in proverbial foxholes, and on and on forever, we "enter" unconsciously the putative spiritual domain and experience the vital, sustaining, soothing attachment of our parental internalizations, as they were originally taken in and as they are modified and complexified by our continuous, wishful enhancements over time. The interpersonal origins of our mind-brain trigger the primal inclination to make the universe in which we abide interpersonal too. Let's get down to it further.

TOWARD THE ADVENT OF RELIGIOUS NARRATIVE: IMPLICIT MEMORY AND THE BASIC BIOLOGICAL SITUATION

"Specific brain systems are involved in the nonconscious effects of the past on the present," writes Daniel L. Schacter in *Searching for Memory*; "we cannot separate our memories of the ongoing events of our lives from what has happened to us previously." Our "encoded connections," or implicit memories, form "the foundation of our most strongly held beliefs."[2] Accordingly, as Siegel expresses it, "here-and-now perceptual biases" are "based on these nonconscious mental models," models that are "reactivated" when an individual is exposed to "retrieval cues" and thus "primed" for the return of encoded events (p. 30). The notion of "state-dependent memory" may also be used to disclose the essence of this synaptic configuration. "State-dependent memory," writes Siegel, "is a term referring to the way in which events encoded in particular mental states will be more likely to be recalled if a person is in a similar state in the future" (p. 105). He goes on: "This normal feature of memory is prominent throughout life and is particularly relevant to how being a parent can induce states resembling those of one's youth." Surely the perceptual, brain-encoded significance of the basic biological situation emerges sharply at this juncture. Over and again, thousands upon thousands of times, for *years*, the little one, the "youth," cries out for nourishment, for care, for love, and the big one, the "parent," responds (the perceptual ground for all subsequent asking and receiving, including the supplications of religion). As attachment deepens, so does the pain of separation for the child (and often for the parent as well). The newcomer must gradually relinquish the treasured symbiosis that constitutes the core of the first relationship. The "separation stage" as described in Mahler becomes for Siegel an "emotionally charged, value-laden memory" (p. 48) that (1) demands both attention and restorative resolution; that (2) leads eventually to Winnicott's "transitional stage," with its substitutes for the relinquished "object"; and that (3) extends itself forward into the religious realm with its providential, loving Parent-God at the center.

That our initial interactions with the caregiver are deeply internalized into the perceptual system can no longer be disputed: "From the first days of life," notes Siegel, "infants perceive the environment around them. Research has shown that infants are able to demonstrate recall for experiences in the form of behavioral, perceptual, and emotional learning" (p. 28). If infants are frightened by sounds associated with particular objects, for example, they will become agitated when subsequently shown the same objects. "These forms of memory are called 'implicit.' They are available early in life and, when retrieved, are not thought to carry with them the internal sensation that something is being recalled" (p. 29). Thus implicit memory involves "parts of the brain that do not require conscious processing" during both "encoding and retrieval." We "act, feel, and imagine" without recognizing "the influence of past experience" on "present reality" (ibid.). With "repeated experiences"—and here we have first and foremost the basic biological situation—the "infant's brain" is able to detect "similarities and differences" across experiential units and from such detections to make "summations," or "generalized representations," that become "encoded" in the brain. The result is the "mental model," or the "scheme," that is used to interpret the surrounding world and that serves as the "basic component" of the implicit memory system (pp. 29–30). For countless millions of people, as I've been suggesting, the chief "mental model" of the world in which they find themselves is embodied in precisely their religious narrative.

By the middle of life's third year, states Siegel, "a child has already begun to join caregivers in mutually constructed tales woven from their real-life events and imagining. The richness of self-knowledge and auto-biographical narratives appears to be mediated by the interpersonal dialogues in which caregivers co-construct narratives about external events and the internal, subjective experiences of the characters." In this way, "we can hypothesize that attachment experiences—that is, communication with parents and other caregivers—may directly enhance a child's capacity for autonoetic consciousness," or autonomous thought (p. 36). "Narrative enactments," then, "can be seen in the patterns of behavior, of relating, and of decision making that steer the course of an individual's life" (p. 63). Indeed, "our nonconscious mental models" themselves may be "revealed as narrative themes." Siegel does not have religious narrative explicitly in mind here, of course, but we do: it is the "narrative enactments" of religion that come to comprise for vast numbers of people the "patterns of behavior," of "relating," and of "decision making" that "steer the course of their lives." And it is the "non-conscious mental model" of the early parent-child interaction that reveals itself in the very core of the "religious narrative." As Siegel renders it for us, once again without focusing directly on the spiritual realm, "The central coherence-creating narrative process has a unifying quality that links otherwise disparate aspects of memory within the individual." Our "enactments" become the "behavioral manifestation" of the "core narrative process" that "links past, present and future" and that is "shaped" overwhelmingly by "our early life experiences" (ibid.). As we may now express the matter in the official religious language that sits atop, as it were, the implicit memories of the early period that serve as the underlying inspiration of the "narrative": our faithful indulgence in the Word reveals our creation, our present estate, and our end, all fashioned by our omnipotent Parent-God, upon whose ministrations and mercies we, his little children, entirely depend. That all of this applies "cross-culturally" only underscores the extent to which "categorical emotions" such as those tied to early attachment and separation, or to the basic biological situation, "have evolved into the specific, engrained patterns of activation" (p. 127) that reside at the heart of the religious narratives upon which we are concentrating here, namely the narratives of the major, present-day Western creeds.

ATTRACTOR STATE: THE STATE TOWARD WHICH A SYSTEM SPONTANEOUSLY SHIFTS

The neurobiological approach to an "attractor state"[3] helps us along nicely as we strive to disclose further the unconscious origin of the human creature's inclination to "people" the world with spirits, and in particular with a supernatural Parent-God. "Reinforced patterns" of "activation," writes Siegel, "are called 'attractor states.'" They consist in the "activity" of each "component" of a "system" at a "given point in time." As experience unfolds in the light of a person's "values," specific "brain states" become "more probable," and eventually more "engrained" within the activity of the "system" as a whole. It is "emotional response," observes Siegel, that serves as the system's building block and that ensures the "neural firing," or the "activation," of the concerted "state." As states become engrained through repeated expression and emotional intensity they become "more likely to be activated." And when a "state of mind" is continually and powerfully aroused, it is prone to configure into "a deeply engrained attractor state" (p. 218). Finally, declares Siegel in the crucial words upon which our line of reasoning rests, "Repeated states of activation at the critical early period of development shape the structure of neural circuits which then form the functional basis for enduring states of mind within the individual" (p. 219). Accordingly, what transpires between offspring and caregiver during the early period comes gradually to serve as not merely one neurobiological "state" among many but the central, enduring "attractor state" of our ongoing lives. The basic biological situation gives rise at the implicit, unconscious level to the perceptual, emotional "scheme" from which emanate our deepest emotional longings and perceptual inclinations. How could it be otherwise? For many crucial months and years our physical and mental survival depends entirely on the caregiver; thus the affective intensity of this "critical" early stage is colossal; we attach ourselves to our provider with utterly spontaneous, unabated ardor; nothing is held back; our needs for nourishment, for care, for love, are "activated" continuously, over and over again, thousands upon thousands of times, to become rooted synaptically in our brains; our emotional "values" are established in an indelible, permanent manner that seeks fulfillment forever after along lines that affectively recall the initial, primal interaction. In short, we internalize into our developing minds early on the instinct-driven, affective "pattern" that will govern our behavior as we relinquish the immediate familial unit and move into the wider world of culture, including of course culture's religious dimension. The "truth" of the religious narrative with the loving Parent-God at the center is confirmed implicitly, unconsciously through a primed, fully readied "attractor state" that resides at the foundation of our interpersonally sculpted, interpersonally wired brains. We are not simply attracted *to* the religious narrative to which we are eventually exposed; the system is completely dynamic: it is *we who also attract the narrative to ourselves*, yanking it in, absorbing it, mapping it onto the model, the scheme, upon which we've been relying all along. The attractor state within us is as eager for confirmation of its core perception as those who offer the narrative to us are eager for our acceptance of it and our entry into the flock.

It is not only religion, needless to say, but a wide variety of human participations that are linked firmly to the basic biological situation: our ongoing interpersonal relationships at both the individual and group level (spouse, family); our national loyalty and identification with "motherland" and "fatherland," including the "leader" or "chief";

our absorption in music, art, literature; and of course our inclination to make gods out of other institutions such as science or philosophy. However, because the spiritual or supernatural domain of religion is imponderable, invisible, entirely unsupported by what we term empirical criteria, because for millions of people everywhere mental and emotional stability depends significantly on religious ties, and finally because religion must compete with other emergent systems and brain states that come into play as an individual develops over time, religion's humble, worldly task is to reinforce, to strengthen, to deepen the participant's original, brain-based convictions through steady, even continuous exposure to ritual and to word from early childhood onward. The neurons that fired together and wired together to create the primal attractor state during the early period must be regularly activated in the proper devotional context to ensure the continuation of the supernatural attachment that emerged on initial exposure to official, sacred narrative. To put it another way, the worldly task of institutional religion is to provide the flock with the inspiration to continue its mapping of the primal, core experience of attachment to the parental figure onto the orthodox version of the substitute Parent-God. Unless this happens, both flock and earthly shepherds are apt to disappear. Accordingly, to employ a few familiar examples in illustration, when we hear the gospel choir on television singing, "Jesus came and found me / And put His arms around me," we detect the primal attractor state of union, with the biological caregiver humming along quietly beneath the mapped-on surface expression of the core fantasy. We detect the very same attractor state when we read the following, prototypical accounts of the Parent-God's mysterious appearance, or presence, in a variety of religious writings:

> I was sitting by myself beside the fireplace; I couldn't sleep very well during the previous nights; something just didn't seem right. I thought about my life and what it was like when I was a child. Then there was an odd sensation and I felt as if my heart had been embraced. The warmest experience I had ever felt touched me and I knew that God was there.[4]

During the night of September 9th, 1954, I awoke and looking out of my window saw what I took to be a luminous star which gradually came nearer, and appeared as a soft slightly blurred white light. I was seized with violent trembling, but I had no fear. I knew that what I felt was great awe. This was followed by a sense of overwhelming love, coming to me, and going out from me [i.e., the projection of the original, loving symbiosis], then of great compassion from the Outer Presence [implicit recollection of the original caregiver]. After that I had a sense of overpowering peace, and indescribable happiness.[5]

There was no sensible vision, but the room was filled by a Presence which in a strange way was both about me and within me. I was overwhelmingly possessed by Someone who was not myself, and yet I felt I was more myself than I had ever been [i.e., the internalized caregiver is both contained within and projected from the self].[6]

Behind the world—to use an almost inevitable spatial metaphor—there is apprehended to be an omnipotent, personal Will whose purpose toward mankind guarantees men's highest good and blessedness. The believer finds that he is at all times in the presence of this holy Will [i.e., the primal internalization of the omnipotent caregiver]. Again and again he realizes, either at the time or in retrospect, that in his dealings with the circumstances of his own life he is also having to do with a transcendent Creator who is the determiner of his destiny and the source of all good.[7]

Whether we are sitting in front of the television, or reading in the living room, or listening in church or temple or mosque to the sermon of the inspired theologian, we encounter in all such materials, and instances, the same psychodynamic process: the early, primal attractor state, wired into the brain, implicitly remembers its way into the current version of the longed-for attachment to the benign parental object, now projected into the transmundane Parent-God. It is Jesus over here, it is Allah over there, and it is Adonai over here again, and in all cases the magical "contact" is grounded entirely in those "categorical emotions" and those "evolved, engrained patterns of activation" to which we contextually referred and that we eventually singled out as the "attractor state" itself. As for the classic, generalized expression of the mysterious, uncanny quality of the unconscious attractor, it resides in the notion of the "Holy Ghost," the elusive, fleeting, airborne manifestation of the embodied, omnipotent Parent-Deity who lurks at the implicit levels of our fruitful, fantasizing mind-brains.[8]

ADDICTION
(WITH ANOTHER LOOK AT WILLIAM JAMES)

The prototypical citations at which we've just glanced underscore at least three items in our overall theoretical picture: the interpersonal, intrapsychic, and ultimately projective source of religious experience ("he was both about me and within me"); the uncanny, mysterious quality of sensations drifting toward consciousness from the realm of implicit memory ("something felt odd, strange; a blurred white light came closer"); and the powerful feelings of love and attachment that accompany activation of the attractor state ("I sensed compassion, love, blessedness, goodness"). Concentrating on the last item, we begin to spy the emotive source of Winifred Gallagher's observation that "mother and offspring live in a biological state that has much in common with addiction. When they are parted the infant does not just miss its mother; it experiences a physical and psychological withdrawal from a host of her sensory stimuli, not unlike the plight of a heroin addict who goes cold turkey."[9] The building block of the attractor state, as I've suggested in passing on a couple of occasions, is *affect*, or emotions, feelings of attachment and love that reach all the way down to the core of the developing self, or alternatively, to the neurobiological foundations of the developing mind-brain. As we enter the putative supernatural realm and spontaneously shift toward the basic biological situation, now outwardly projected in the "sacred" image of Parent-God and filial worshiper, we do so ardently, passionately, reverently, needfully, in search of our primal, foundational connection, our felicity, our security, our stability—in a word, our affective "fix." The gravitational power of religion emanates in significant measure from precisely this psychological direction. Thus religion is not, as Freud maintains, a neurotic obsession;[10] rather, it is a compelling emotional dependency that, when gratified, allows us to proceed more contentedly, more vigorously, and hence more efficaciously than we might otherwise do as we encounter an endless variety of social and psychological challenges, from the commonplace stresses and strains of everyday life in an anomic world to the traumatic experiences of illness, separation, danger, and death.

The "affect system," observes Silvan S. Tomkins, who offers us definitive insights here, "provides the primary motives of human beings. The human affect system is nicely matched in complexity both to the receptor, analyzer, storage and motor mechanisms within the organism and to a broad spectrum of environmental opportunities, challenges and demands from without."[11] And then, moving us by implication toward the link between religious belief and the basic biological situation, he writes, "To the extent to which human beings become addicted to specific satisfiers, either in the case of drives or affects, substitutability of objects declines. Just as an American may find non-American food not a completely satisfying substitute for the satisfaction of his hunger, so a lover may find there is no other love object than the beloved, a friend find there is no other friend quite like his oldest friend, a child find there are no substitute mothers and fathers" (pp. 140–41). Tomkins goes on: "As addiction to specific objects grows, substitutability therefore declines. To the extent to which the addiction is to the affect, however, rather than to its objects, there can be a growth of objects. I may be addicted to excitement in New York City or in travel. One is addiction to place, the other essentially to the affect of excitement which then dictates unceasing novelty" (p. 141). The uniqueness of religious attachment resides in its magical capacity to provide us with *both* a substitute object in the symbolic, externalized form of the Parent-God *and* the genuine, original article in the activation of the attractor state, including above all the *affect* that catalyzed the attractor state's development in the first instance. As we confront ideationally the notion of the Parent-God, or even see Him, we can and we do at the same instant implicitly and affectively recall the actual parent from whose neurally engrained internalization the Deity is ultimately fabricated. In a word, we *feed the object back into the Parent-God* and thus complete (or "close," as we'll see momentarily) the circle, or the system, through which we discover our security, our enjoyment, and our meaning in life. We're taken care of, and we get "hooked" on the feeling—which translates of course into our propensity to "believe in God," to find ourselves "embraced" by spiritual arms, moved by omnipotent "will," sheltered by heavenly "wings," attended by "holy ghosts." Because the entire affective, perceptual arrangement is engendered as much from within by ourselves as it is by the external institutions to which we are exposed, because the religious impulse is implicitly seeded in the land of infantile amnesia, because it springs from a psychological place to which we have no direct access, we actually experience uncanny, confirmational sensations as we are asked to trust in supernatural, doctrinal claims. It may well have been this combination of unconscious internalization, profound affective longing (or addiction), and state-dependent memory (jogged by supplicatory ritual) that finally spooked William James into believing some Presence was actually out there listening to his prayers.

Thus religion is a cunning, unconscious method of preserving the tie to the original object, the original "mother and father" as Tomkins expresses it, at the same time that we *relinquish* the original object, the original "mother and father," and attain thereby a measure of separation and autonomy in the environment in which we discover ourselves. We can play the game of life in two directions, staying put and moving on. We can get our old, affective "fix" on a regular basis through our connection to religious institutions whose duty is to prime us, and we can also move forward on our own, nonincestuously as it were, as we cope with our existence on the planet. Religion survives and flourishes, as I've been contending all along, not in spite of infantile amnesia but because of it. Holding us in addictive entrancement, religion is the magical, unassailable product of the primal attractor state forged during the critical early period of our lives. In the final analysis, we become addicted to an aspect of our own mind-brain. Let's move on now to the tie between religious addiction and perceptual feedback, something to which I alluded a few sentences earlier.

At the "heart of the matter," writes Tomkins—and we must of course think on the religious "matter" here—"is the *preference* based on the positive affect which the object evokes" (p. 264). What was "experienced," he continues, "was an 'unforgettable' mother bathed in the glow of the joy response. This experience plus the following response is . . . stored as a neurological program which, when later activated, will support a continued preference for this particular object" (p. 269). Now, this primal interactive arrangement, or "blueprint," states Tomkins crucially, can become so "strong" a "guiding activator" as "finally" to "stop the feedback mechanism" (p. 328). In other words, "after some experience" with the "enjoyment" of such "positive affect" it is "highly probable that the human being will conceive images, or purposes, to repeat such experience." Here is religion itself, from the emotional, psychological angle. Once the primal attractor state is in place, and once it is projectively transferred to the religious narrative with the joy-giving Parent-God at the center—once, in short, religion has given the practitioner the "image" to "repeat" his early "experience" of attachment to the caregiving "object"—he, the practitioner, can subsist in his addicted state for the rest of his earthly days. He has completed the feedback system that assures his well-being. Life, death, the world, the universe itself, can be "fed" into his religious "program" (or "mapped" onto his religious "blueprint") and he will remain emotionally intact, which means of course emotionally attached to the unconscious presence upon which he came to depend "in the beginning." The image of the Parent-God commands his affective, perceptual domain, and nothing could be more pleasing to him. Indeed, he is eager to look at his "blueprint" over and over again, in temple, or church, or mosque, or simply as he goes about his business. He has only to ask his own mind-brain for his "fix" in order to experience an addictive gratification.

That there is nothing dissociative or neurotic in all this Tomkins stresses by implication in a striking passage: "The claustral and preverbal complexes are not less important for human beings because of their origin in the earliest experience. They are not perverse nor infantile in the sense that they must be transcended by later experience. Their appeal at any age is perennial and human" (p. 426). And so it is with religion. One indulges because he is "human," because he wants to pre-serve his tie to the early, care-giving provider, and because he lacks the capacity to *see* what he is doing as he projects the object appetitively into the religious narrative to which he is exposed by virtue of his societal involvement. Who can blame him? Who can object to those prayers that reconnect him intrapsychically to the loving ministrations of his parental provider? As Tomkins notes, echoing our earlier approach to the under-lying psychodynamics of speech, and anticipating our analysis of suppli-catory ritual, soon to be fully developed, "Earliest speech is an attempt to commune, to deepen experienced communion rather than an attempt to communicate, in the sense of expressing personal message to the other. . . . Its aim is essentially no different than a tightening of clinging to the mother, by an infant who is already clinging. Speech never loses this earliest function" (p. 429). And in another place, again with explicit reference to matters of communion, "The fascination with speech begins in the arms of the mother, then becomes a critical vehicle of being together without body contact, and later is invested with every variety of the adult communion needs" (p. 440). As we will eventually see in con-siderable detail, the specific, doctrinal instructions for prayer in an explicitly religious context give striking, unmistakable support to Tomkins's assertions about "adult communion needs."

Surely we can appreciate at this juncture the accuracy of James's contention that religion's "end" as manifested in religion's quintessential action, namely prayer, is "not God, but life, more life, a larger, richer, more satisfying life."[12] Because we are writing from a psychological per-spective, however, we cannot allow "life" to hang there generally, and perhaps unprofessionally: it could mean anything. Within the psychody-namic model of religion we are developing, it, "life," means primarily, if not exclusively, the affective tie to the life-giving provider of the early time, the "internalized object" from whom our "life" emanates directly, joyously, addictively. It is this life-giving connection that we seek in our supplications as we projectively aim them at the spiritual Parent-God, the mysterious, implicitly remembered Presence of James's "transmun-dane" realm. Why else, after all, should the "collapse" of James's "faith-state" be a life-or-death matter?[13] Why else should the faith-state's dissolution frequently predicate one's psychological, emotional demise, or as James puts it, "anhedonia"[14]—the absence of "joy," of pleasure, of precisely that quality that, according to Tomkins, resides at the core of the neonate's attachment to the caregiver, to the maternal "object" who is "bathed in the glow of the joy response" (p. 429)? Joy, maintains Tomkins in another place, "promotes the formation of what we . . . call psychological addiction," a "class of complex affect organizations in which a particular psychological object . . . activates intense positive affect in the presence of the object, as well as in the absence of the object so long as the future presence of the object or past commerce with [it] is entertained in awareness" (p. 493), including of course the "awareness" that resides at the level of implicit recollection. Calling to mind not only James's "faith-state" but the whole issue of separation and attachment as developed in Mahler, Tomkins observes, "The absence of the object evokes strong negative affect which grows stronger as the object which is missed grows more and more positive, and the presence of the object evokes stronger and stronger positive affect as it reduces more and more intense negative affect which was evoked by the absence of the object" (p. 495). The "essential condition" here is that "the presence of the object is the unique activator of positive affect as well as the unique remedy for the absence of the object," a "condition," needless to say, which perfectly captures the affective quality of the care-giving provider. From precisely this addictive "syndrome," from precisely this psychological configuration of attachment and separation, spring the psychodynamics of religious narrative and rite.

We seek the joy, the security, the "life" of the first relationship upon which we are "hooked," and we abhor the "withdrawal" we are forced to experience as the primal symbiosis collapses. Because the "map" or "blueprint" of our early struggle is retained at the unconscious level, indeed, because our map or blueprint becomes neurally, synaptically configured into our primal, unconscious attractor state itself, we can enjoy through priming and through state-dependent memory our addictive tie to the object as we accede to the claims of religious narrative and rite simply by affirming our "faith," the "biological state" by which we "live." All who seek shall find, and in finding be soothed and comforted.

As I've maintained from the outset, however, such naturalistic analyses of religion and its Parent-God by no means resolve, or are intended to resolve, the ultimate theological questions. From my perspective, nothing can resolve them—that is, until we become omniscient gods our-selves. The entire psychological pattern I am working to depict here may have been conceived and initiated by a supernatural Almighty and Ulti-mate First Cause. He, the Omnipotent Himself, may have wisely and lov-ingly arranged the whole setup so as to make it possible for us to find Him in our unique human way, through our peculiar human psychology, with our large neocortexes, with our remarkable mind-brains as they are forged in our early relationships with other, God-manufactured humans. As Western theology and philosophy have reminded us for millennia, behind what moves may reside the Unmoved Mover.

COMMUNION AND THE SELF'S DUAL NATURE

A unified theoretical picture begins to emerge: the transformation and attunement on which we concentrated earlier are integral features of the attractor state and the affect on which we are concentrating now. The addictive joy of the early period flows freely when the caregiver trans-forms the newcomer's existence, over and over again, on thousands of occasions, through timely ministration to his needs, including of course his need for attachment and love. The attunement between mother and child that is both the prerequisite to and the product of such transforma-tional encounters comes gradually to form the heart of the attractor state itself. The change one experiences through his religious participation invariably recalls—sometimes dramatically as in sudden conversion, sometimes subduedly as in silent prayer—precisely this early, preverbal interaction, the bedrock of the spiritual realm. As one cries out, "Lord, I'm saved," or as one quietly communes with his Parent-God though scripture, he is restored to those primal episodes of transformation and attunement that eventually create, grain upon addictive grain, the psy-chological core of his religious leanings. Remember, we're talking mind-brain here. "Parental sensitivity to signals," writes Siegel, "is the essence of secure attachment and can inform us about how two people's 'being' with each other permits emotional communication and a sense of connection to be established at any age. In these transactions, the brain of one person and that of another are influencing each other in a form of co-regulation." Such "collaborative communication," Siegel continues, "allows minds to connect with each other. During childhood, such human connections allow for the creation of brain connections that are vital for the development of a child's capacity for self-regulation" (p. 70). This "initial sharing of mental experience," then, "lays the groundwork for the rest of mental development" (p. 200). Our "synaptic connections" themselves are "shaped" by these early "connectionist" events (p. 216). Accordingly, the attractor state as we have been depicting it in relation to religious experience arises directly from the transformational attunement that characterizes the basic biological situation. Emotionally, psychologically, physiologically, neurally, we are "produced" by the loving provider, in combination with our genetic makeup.

We may perceive here, I believe, the answer to a fascinating, fundamental question as follows: why do millions upon millions of people require a Parent-God to feel centered in *themselves*, to feel secure, attached, happy, joyous? Why cannot the self derive these emotional benefits simply by communing with itself, self to self, mind to mind, subjectivity to subjectivity? Why must a Parent-Deity *be* there at all? The solution goes like this: our foundational oneness (or selfhood, or integration) turns out to be a twoness, the twoness that characterizes our early development as we attune with our creative provider, the *one* who not only gives us life but who is fated to be internalized into our mind-brains at the synaptic level such that we cannot feel (or experience) ourselves without feeling (or experiencing) the other, who is *us*. To find the self is to find the other from whom the self originates and grows. Because the other is wired into our brains, because self and other are inextricable, synaptically connected at the neurobiological level, we tend psychologically to project the other "out," and to discover it "out there" (where it originally was) when we seek our deep connection with ourselves on the "inside," or "in here." We discover "us" when we discover "it." We just happen to be that kind of internalizing, projective creature. Our Parent-

God is a facet of our brain function, a facet that becomes integrally tied to our longing for security and attachment in ourselves. Thus our religious narratives and rituals with the Parent-God at the center (prayer and the Eucharist above all) continue the style of communion, or connection, that defines our attuned interaction with the "object," the internalized caregiver who turns our discomfort into pleasure, our anxiety into security, on a daily, hourly, moment-to-moment basis, for years, during the critical early period of our existence, that "life-or-death" stage when we depend as little ones entirely on the big ones, who are, or are supposed to be, "always there." *Of course* when we successfully commune with God we learn that He knows all about us already through His divine, telepathic powers. How could He *not* know? He's *us*! By splitting and projecting an aspect of ourselves outwardly we simply put ourselves in the psychological position to discover that aspect of ourselves again through our communion with the putative omniscient Almighty. *Of course* when we successfully commune with God we learn that He loves us unconditionally. How could He not? He's us, or that aspect of ourselves (our narcissism) which has internalized deeply the loving ministrations of the transformational caregiver. And so it goes projectively, unconsciously, addictively, and adaptively in a thousand similar emotional contexts inhabited by millions of individuals looking to enhance what James calls "life" by reactivating that core of early experience toward which everything religious or supernatural gravitates. The mind-brain leads and the mind-brain follows (the Lord is my shepherd), all at the same time. Perhaps the central illusion of the entire arrangement, the one with the greatest adaptational benefits to the believer, is the illusion that someone is *there*, that the believer is not alone, that a caring, protective Presence is with him as he goes his separate, mortal way upon the earth (and I will dwell in the house of the Lord forever).

NOTES

1. Daniel Siegel, *The Developing Mind: Toward a Neurobiology of Interpersonal Experience* (New York: Guilford Press, 1999), p. 2. Page numbers for the other Siegel quotes in this chapter are included in the text.

2. Daniel L. Schacter, *Searching for Memory: The Brain, the Mind, the Past* (New York: Basic Books, 1996), pp. 5, 4, 5, 7.

3. The definition of *attractor state* as given in the heading of this section appears in "Definitions," Folke Günther Web site, http://www.holon.se/folke/kurs/Definitions.shtml (accessed August 10, 2004).

4. Quoted in Richard H. Schlagel, *The Vanquished Gods: Science, Religion, and the Nature of Belief* (Amherst, NY: Prometheus Books, 2001), p. 302.

5. Quoted in William P. Alston, *Perceiving God: The Epistemology of Religious Experience* (Ithaca, NY: Cornell University Press, 1991), p. 18.

6. Quoted in Schlagel, *The Vanquished Gods*, p. 302.

7. Quoted in Alston, *Perceiving God*, p. 27.

8. Michael Persinger's clinical experiments at Laurentian University in Canada have attracted a good deal of attention over the past twenty years, and they should be mentioned here. Persinger attempts to find the "neuropsychological bases of God belief" by wiring up his subjects (students) and then stimulating their brains with electrical currents. The reported results indicate to Persinger that God may turn out to be nothing more nor less than a "temporal lobe transient." The problems with Persinger's approach are taken up in the final chapter of this book. See Michael Persinger, *The Neuropsychological Bases of God Belief* (Westport, CT: Praeger, 1987).

9. Winifred Gallagher, "Motherless Child," *Sciences* 32 (July 1992): 12.

10. Sigmund Freud, *The Future of an Illusion*, trans. J. Strachey (1927; New York: W. W. Norton, 1964), p. 71.

11. Silvan S. Tomkins, *Affect, Imagery, Consciousness*, vol. 1 (New York: Springer, 1962), pp. 111–12. Page numbers for the other Tomkins quotes in this section are included in the text.

12. William James, *The Varieties of Religious Experience* (1902; New York: Library of America, 1987), p. 452.

13. James, ibid., calls the "faith-state" a "biological condition *by which men live*" (emphasis added).

14. Ibid.

7.

Infantile Amnesia

That the decisive, determining source of our most powerful, compelling emotions as people should be inaccessible to our direct apprehension during the entire course of our lives can only be described as one of the most extraordinary and defining aspects of our fundamental humanity. For years as little ones we passionately and unceasingly interact with our caregivers; for years we depend on them for everything, including our very survival. Yet we cannot explicitly recall these events; we cannot "find" them mnemonically, no matter how long and how hard we try. As far as conscious perception of our emotional roots is concerned, the early period has simply vanished from view. This is not because infants and young children can't remember things. On the contrary, from nearly the beginning, and equally for both sexes, infantile memory is robust. "Studies on infant memory carried out at the University of Toronto," writes Richard Restak, "suggest that infants may remember more about events than, only a few years ago, the most optimistic researcher would have thought possible."[1] Nor is it solely in a "wide" or "general" sense that memory emerges as an integral feature of our early mental functioning, with past experience exerting an effect on current behavior. As Restak observes, infants remember in a fashion that makes plain their powerful "associative" capacities: mother's "face" goes with mother's "voice"; this particular "object" calls that particular "object" to mind; the baby is "storing information"; the "association tracts" in his developing mind-brain are open for business—toward the inception of his days and, of course, forever after.[2]

This associative bent on the baby's part is of the utmost importance when we take the word "object," as we must, in both a hard, physicalistic sense and in an internalizing, psychological sense that looks forward to the advent of religious conviction. Emmett Wilson Jr. writes, "Internal objects are lost if they are not subject to a permanent reconstruction, like a language that is no longer used. The [gravitation toward a] new person has the power, more or less lasting, to remodel these internal objects, and, for better or worse, to remodel the self and its structures."[3] We would add immediately that such emotional movement toward the "new person" applies fully and commandingly to the new "person" of the Parent-God, the spiritual One to Whom the newcomer is introduced as the primal, preverbal stage of experience melds inexorably into the stage of symbolic awareness and explicit, autobiographical memory. Indeed, it is the implicit, preverbal stage that is unconsciously projected into the emergent religious narrative such that the spiritual newcomer is impelled to grab hold of the supernatural Deity, at the prompting of his elders. The religious realm rears up its edifice of divine, supernatural "mystery" upon precisely this *unconscious association* made by the associatively robust mind-brain of the neophyte, who has already lost direct contact with his early experience.

Surely one cannot miss the associative, emotional connections at work here: the omnipotent parent controls and guides the child's life, as does the omnipotent Parent-God; the attentive caregiver shapes the child's character, introduces him to a brand-new world, as does the transformational Creator; the loving provider nourishes the child, protects him from danger, from harm, as does the benign Parent-Deity Who watches over the vulnerable members of His flock, leading them to green pastures, and even through the valley of the shadow of death; and on and on it goes through dozens of related, unconscious, emotional associations, as anyone can see. When Joseph Le Doux declares that "memories are more easily retrieved when the emotional state at the time of memory formation matches the state at the time of retrieval"[4] and thereby calls to mind the phenomenon of state-dependent memory on which our analysis of religious narrative and rite has been based from the outset, he captures for us vividly in the immediate context how the early period serves as a vast, inexhaustible emotional reservoir from which religion derives its affective power throughout an individual's lifetime. The "lost," unconscious realm of our early years can be and is "matched" endlessly, forever as it were, with the "stories" and the "practices" of the official doctrine. Indeed, as I've been suggesting, it is the humble, earthly duty of organized religion to see to it that such "matching" occurs regularly for all who are seeking attachment to the comforting Parent-God of their particular creed. From the psychological perspective we are developing we may reword the old scriptural promise "all who seek shall find" as follows: all who seek shall smoothly transfer their early, unconscious attachments and longings to the Parent-God of the mysterious, supernatural realm. After all, what we have here is one facet of the mind-brain mapping itself onto another, emergent facet, and neither more nor less than that. The prompted mind-brain will direct itself to locate the treasured parental internalization harbored within the mind-brain.

Let's look further into infantile amnesia now with an eye to distinguishing sharply the quality of early (or implicit) memory and later, autobiographical (or explicit) memory. The distinction will lead us nicely to a number of compelling realizations. "Infantile amnesia," writes Elizabeth Johnston, "refers to the general inability of people to remember specific events from the early years of their lives. On the basis of both free recall studies (What is your earliest memory?) and studies for memories of notable and datable early events (the birth of a sibling, hospitalization, the Kennedy assassination) psychologists have concluded that there are very few memories from before the age of 3 years. The average age of the earliest memory reported is 3½, with a small but consistent gender difference indicating that females reported earlier memories." Johnston goes on, "If people are asked to recall episodes from the entire life span the number reported before age 8 falls off sharply in comparison to other periods. This indicates that it is not the age of the memories per se that accounts for their relative paucity, rather it is the life period that they occur within (the earliest years) that is sparsely represented in long term autobiographical memory."[5] To apply accurately an understanding of memory to an understanding of religious belief, then, we must employ what investigators currently term a "dual memory system," which characterizes the nature of our memorial capacity from the inception to maturity. On the one hand, we have the "non-verbal, image-based system," with the following characteristics as presented in Johnston: "1) primitive; 2) present from birth; 3) addressable by situational or affective cues; 4) contains fragmentary information; 5) memories expressed through images, behaviors, or emotions; 6) learned routines; 7) generalized past experiences not linked to specific events; and 8) accessed through reinstatement." On the other hand, we have the "socially accessible system" as follows: "1) emerges slowly throughout the preschool years; 2) addressable through intentional retrieval efforts; 3) personally experienced events; 4) encoded in narrative form; 5) actively thought about or processed; 6) can be accessed and recounted in response to social demands; 7) contains information specific to time and place; 8) develops with the acquisition of language."[6] When we put these "systems" together, of course, we begin to perceive the whole mind-brain at work— not merely in some general, theoretical sense that floats about in the realm of pure ideas, but in relation to specifically the substance and the expression of religious belief. We perceive the image-based nature of the creed, the depictions of sacred materials contained in sacred texts and sacred objects (and He parted the Red Sea; and He walked upon the waters; the Madonna cradled the dying Jesus in her arms; Muhammad flew up to heaven on a horse). We perceive the endless affective cues in an endless variety of ritual contexts (let us kneel in our helplessness before our Almighty Creator); the memories contained in emotions and behaviors (your heavenly Father loves you; bow your heads humbly in recognition of His blessings, in gratitude for your daily bread, which He provides); the learned routines that come to constitute a sizeable portion of one's religious life (the ceremonies of the service, the holiday celebrations, the garb); the generalized past experiences not linked to specific events (this accident is tragic, but we cannot fathom fully the ways of our loving God [any more than we could fathom what our parents were doing early on]); the access through reinstatement (let us open our Bibles once again and read of His wondrous works). One might continue in a similar vein forever. Indeed, even those aspects of religion about which we "think" discursively, even those aspects that are intentional, conscious, accessed in response to social demand, are themselves based ultimately upon our early experience, our early, internalized, unconscious associations that give such "higher" aspects their compelling, affective power, their emotional bite as it were. When we "sin," for example, we undergo *separation* from our Lord, Who is unconsciously linked to the caregiver; we experience once more the threat (and the torment) of primal, foundational loss, what Dante calls in the *Inferno* "the eternal isolation of the soul." When we love others as ourselves in response to our Parent-God's directive, we bring to others that primal, foundational love we internalized in response to the timely ministrations of our parental provider. Our "conscience" as we feel it in wrongdoing, and as we express it in our compassionate concern for the welfare of others, is rooted in our deepest affective core, in the part of us that we informally call "the heart," that wordless region from which comes the expression of our basic emotional nature, shaped in the first years of life.

As for the issue of *why* the early period is lost to our explicit recollection, there is no universally accepted, definitive answer because the question (for obvious reasons) does not easily lend itself to empirical, observational investigation. Generally accepted and ubiquitous in the literature, however, is the notion that what we've called the nonverbal, image-based system becomes increasingly unavailable to direct apprehension as it simply gives way to the emergent, brain-based modes of recollection linked to the socially accessible system. As we mature neurologically, the later configuration is the one we are fated to *use* when we employ our will and our capacity to remember. The answer that reigns in the literature, then, is Piagetian: an early "scheme" of cerebral functioning gradually yields to, and is finally absorbed into, a later "scheme." As Johnston expresses the matter, "The inaccessibility of early childhood memories [is] due to a disjunction between the earliest and later modes of processing information. . . . While there is no abrupt neurological watershed corresponding to the offset of infantile amnesia, there is good reason to believe that neurological maturity must be one of the factors that limits early memory."[7] Thus the *way* we remember things changes, leaving the socially accessible system "on top," or "in the light," and the nonverbal, image-based system "below ground," or "in the dark." We have in all this a provocative and relatively straightforward method of talking about a highly disputatious topic in modern (and postmodern) awareness: the unconscious mind, an entity that each person possesses whether or not he's been "repressing" specific and presumably stress-laden aspects of his thought and behavior.[8]

We come now to a major consideration. As the early, nonverbal memorial mode gives way to the later, verbal, socially accessible system, it is "narrative memory" that bears the weight of the past and begins to influence the shape of the future. "Infantile amnesia," states Johnston, "is overcome through the linguistic sharing of memories with others. . . . Various pieces of empirical evidence support the idea of a later onset of narrative memory."[9] By way of illustration, Johnston offers us, among several items, the following representational vignette: "Tessler studied 3 year olds and their mothers on a visit to a natural history museum. She found that none of the children remembered any of the objects that they viewed in the museum if they had not talked about them with their mothers. Mother's talk alone was not facilitative, nor was a child's mention alone effective in leading to subsequent remembering. Creating a narrative together cemented particular objects in memory." And then, summarizing the matter for us neatly, Johnston writes, "Through sharing memories with others language becomes available as a means of reinstating memory." Johnston calls this the "Vygotskian model,"[10] referring to the famous Russian linguist Lev Vygotsky, who flourished seventy years ago and who stressed the social, interactional roots of linguistic behavior. The point is, the two major narratives, or stories, that make up the "world" or the "universe" of the developing person, namely the familial narrative and the religious narrative, are destined to inherit, to contain, to absorb, and to harbor precisely the early, preverbal experience that resides at the core of that person's mind-brain. The affect, the perception, the attachments and longings of the early period as they are steadily internalized during life's first years become the human "stuff" out of which the religious realm is fashioned and toward which religious practice is finally directed. "If the infant's environment provides frequent opportunities for reactivation," notes Johnston, "then theoretically an individual's early experiences could be remembered over a lifetime." Memory turns out to be an "emergent property" of the "cue and the engram,"[11] and it is precisely the "engram" of the first relationship, or what we have called the attractor state as grounded in the basic biological situation, at which religion aims its traditional or sacred "cues," the substance of its doctrinal and ritualistic enactments.

We must ask ourselves, what is *there* in the young person's mind-brain after all to accede with emotion to religion's "story," to the narrative with the loving Parent-God at its center, if not the immediate context of the young person's *life*? Clearly, there is *nothing else*. Equally, as the familial narrative takes shape and the young person increasingly apprehends the inevitable psychic (if not physical) *separation* that looms as its culmination, the religious narrative begins to assume a central, affective position in the psychic economy of the developing individual. While he must eventually relinquish the actual parent, he can retain forever the mysterious Parent-God, the supernatural surrogate whose attractive power emanates unconsciously from that very mnemonic place from which the attachment to the actual parent initially arose. As we become predominantly verbal, narrative creatures as opposed to "primitive," preverbal creatures, lo and behold, there is our religious narrative to greet us, to offer us another loving, protective Parent, another Guide, another Nourisher, another Omnipotent Companion and Ally Whose hand we may clutch as we proceed upon our increasingly separate way. At the affective, perceptual, synaptic level of our existence the religious narrative presents itself as another version of and the direct successor to exactly what we've just experienced interactionally as little ones, and it derives its compelling power, its compelling timeless appeal, from precisely the direction of our implicit recollection: we can't *see* the realistic, empirical link between the two stages, the two systems; all we can do is *feel* the connection inside; the unconscious associations impel us to judge the religious narrative as "true." In other words, the narrative *implic-*

itly confirms what we've just experienced as people; it returns us to our familiar internalized reality at our emergent verbal level of understanding, and this fills us with the irresistible sensation *that we are what we are*, that no break exists in our being, that no separation will snatch us away from our inward emotional reality, or world. In the neurobiological terms that recall the early stages of our discussion, the religious narrative permits us to *map* our early experience onto our ongoing and increasingly separate lives. Reason, needless to say, is not *there* yet to question the assumptions of our supernatural outlook. We simply project our way happily to the spiritual universe that is offered to us by our directional elders. Whereas the arms of the actual biological caregiver held us in the beginning, the arms of the narrative Parent-God hold us now. As the fleshly body of the mother recedes, the spiritual body of the Deity appears mentally to take her place. We will not be alone. With the help of society's institutional promptings, and with the assistance of our transitional (or Winnicottian) capacities to imagine, to play, to create substitutes for the treasured caregiver we must gradually relinquish as we grow, our mind-brain will accord us just what it requires for our peace of mind.

The religious story to which we are introduced as the early, preverbal stage gives way to our narrative style of perception is all-encompassing, all-satisfying, completely reassuring—that is, if we stick to the rules and dutifully propitiate our Parental Provider. We are allied with omnipotence once again; the all-powerful parent returns in the form of the Parent-God. We will live forever, be loved forever, be guided forever, be "housed" forever in the mansions of our benign, supernatural Benefactor, our Shepherd, our Savior and Spiritual Nourisher. All our questions will be answered; all our wonderings about the nature of Nature will be met with some sort of explanation, thus allaying our anxiety over the shape of the unknown. Our religious narrative has, like all good dramatic tales, a beginning, a middle, and an end. We discover our provenance, our duties in mortal life, and our destination upon mortal life's conclusion. We can continue to question and to wonder as much as we like, of course; but we don't *have* to wonder and question; we can rest content in the reassurances of doctrine whenever we wish to do so. All who seek shall find. All who submit shall be comforted. All who kneel to their loving Parent-God shall be uplifted, over and over again, each time they supplicate, forevermore.

Marion Milner observes in one of her characteristically wonderful passages that "the inner structure of the unconscious part of our psyche is essentially animistic. That is, we build up our inner world on the basis of our relationships to people we have loved and hated, we carry these people about with us and what we do, we do for them—or in conflict with them. And it seems that it is through these internalized people that we carry on our earliest relationships, developing and enriching them throughout life; even when these first people no longer exist in the external world, we find external representatives of them both in new people who enter our lives, and in all our interests and the causes that we seek to serve." Milner continues, "And because these internal people contain something of ourselves, they contain, represent, the love and the hate which we first felt for the outside people, so we go on throughout our lives, continually discovering more of ourselves and more of the world, in developing our relationships to them through their substitutes."[12] Our key contextual connection to this material, of course, is that religion comprises for countless millions of people the chief, life-sustaining, life-enhancing "substitute" for the "internalized people" we were obliged to relinquish during the separation stage. Religion, in short, allows us to "people" the world with the idealized, loving, omnipotent image of the Parent-God from Whom the world as "object" emanates. Such "peopling" is indeed religion's chief psychological aim. It urges us at the level of our unconscious, implicit memorial processes to put the parent out there again, to keep the parent at the center of the picture, and thereby to transform the universe around us into a "people place," a place in which we feel at home precisely because a Person resides at the foundation, just as a person (the "object") resides at the foundation of our psyche. To turn the coin over, we are encouraged to make the universe into a person by placing the Parent-God at the center of the universe, and to make the latter a version of the former and the former a version of the latter according to the formula, Parent-Person-God = the Universe, and the Universe = Parent-Person-God. It seems that we have no intention as religious beings of residing in a "non-people place."

Just listen to famous theologian John Polkinghorne as he expounds the truth in his celebrated Yale lectures: "God is not just one entity among the many entities of the world, available to be picked out and examined in isolation. The divine presence is the ground of the world's being, and the Creator is party to every occurrence."[13] Could it be made plainer? The universe becomes essentially a gigantic Person as we map the object of the early time onto the cosmos around us, thus preserving our attachment, our connection to the transformational presence we internalized in the beginning; and we *do* this because our mind-brain itself, at the neurobiological level, has been loaded up with emotive-perceptual associations that affirm the religious view in a way that can only be termed irresistible, particularly as our exposure to religion transpires as we separate increasingly from the original source of our security in the world. We may appreciate more fully from this angle perhaps the psychological implications of C. C. J. Webb's monumental researches undertaken in England half a century ago, which conclude that all religion, at least as we know it ordinarily, is wedded forever to an anthropomorphic perspective on the universe.[14] If a religion is to be a living faith as opposed to a theological exercise, then it is obliged to keep a *human* at the center, for in the recesses of our mind-brain it is a *human* that we *want* at the center. We may also appreciate more fully of course the enormous anxiety that can emerge in individuals and in societies as other narratives, such as science, begin successfully to compete with the religious narrative to which we've been clinging as humans for thousands of years. The proliferation of religious cults, of New Age magic, and of the pseudoscience and quantum gobbledygook that surrounds the surreptitiously religious notions of "intelligent design" and "anthropic cosmology" bears striking current witness to the painful psychological upheaval that may be triggered by what is popularly called "God's death," as anyone can see for himself simply by visiting the New Age bookstore in her neighborhood or by picking up from the newsstand an issue of the *Skeptical Inquirer*.[15] As I will endeavor to demonstrate fully in subsequent chapters, weaning ourselves away from our person-centered universe embodied in our person-centered religious narratives marks a gigantic and problematical step in our evolution as a form of life, for it engages simultaneously two of our most rooted evolutional urges, namely the urge to feel attached and secure (or free of anxiety) as we strive to cope with a difficult and sometimes hostile environment, and the urge to perceive the world around us accurately, to rely upon impersonal analysis, to set aside our soothing fantasies. The time in which we live just happens to be the time when these potentially antithetical evolutional tendencies run directly into one another—producing a clash of titans, if there ever was one.

A ROMANTIC INTERLUDE

Why is the period "richest in experience, the period of early childhood," the one which is "forgotten," asks Ernest Schachtel in his famous, compelling paper, *On Memory and Childhood Amnesia*?[16] While Schachtel lays some weight on the advent of a language-based mnemonic structure and thereby reflects the thrust of our contextual theoretical discussion, his major emphasis rests upon what he describes as "the process of schematization and conventionalization" and "its effect on the raw material of experience, especially childhood experience" (p. 196). Schachtel writes, "By conventionalization of the memory (and experience) schemata I understand those memory processes which are subject to the most conventional schematization and which, therefore, are not capable of reproducing individual experience, but can only reproduce what John Doe is supposed to have experienced according to the Joneses' and everybody else's ideas of what people experience. Every fresh and spontaneous experience transcends the capacity of the conventionalized memory schema and, to some degree, of any schema" (ibid.). Calling infantile amnesia a "normal" process, Schachtel continues,

> One might say that the normal amnesia, that which people usually are unable to recall, is an illuminating index to the quality of any given culture and society. It is that which does not serve the purposes of that society and would interfere with the pattern of the culture, that which would be traumatic to the culture because it would break up or transcend the conventions and mores of that culture. Early childhood

> amnesia is the most striking and dramatic expression merely of a
> dynamism operative throughout the life of the people: the distortion or
> forgetting of transschematic experience, that is, of experience for
> which the culture provides no pattern and no schema. (p. 198)

Thus our memories and our experiences are watered down, trivialized, in
a very real way *destroyed* through the social world's "schematic"
impingement on our lives. We turn into "the Joneses," superficial
automatons, superficial conformists, as we knuckle under perceptually
to the governing demands of "the system" by which we gain our liveli-
hoods and through which we come eventually to exist as suppressed,
truncated, "ordinary" creatures. The richness, the spontaneity, the passion and intensity of the early years have simply vanished for us in our
"fallen," desiccated state, and we end up longing for a mythic "lost paradise," or "Eden," which resonates affectively within us at those levels
that retain some sense of how it used to be. Schachtel contends in a
series of powerful, closing sentences,

> Mankind's belief in a lost paradise is repeated in the belief, held by
> most people, in the individual myth of their happy childhood. Like
> most myths this one contains elements of both truth and illusion, is
> woven out of wishes, hopes, remembrance and sorrow, and hence has
> more than one meaning. One finds this belief even in people who have
> undergone cruel experiences as children and who had, without being
> or remaining aware of it, a childhood with hardly any love and affec-
> tion from their parents. No doubt, one reason for the myth of happy
> childhood is that it bolsters parental authority and maintains a conven-
> tional prop of the authority of the family by asserting that one's parents
> were good and benevolent people. . . . And disappointed and suffering
> people, people without hope, want to believe that at least once there
> was a time in their life when they were happy. (pp. 199–200)

And then, restating forcefully the essence of his position, Schachtel declares,

> But the myth of happy childhood reflects also the truth that, as in the
> myth of paradise lost, there was a time before animalistic innocence
> was lost, before pleasure-seeking nature and pleasure-forbidding cul-

ture clashed in the battle called education, a battle in which the child is always the loser. At no time is life so exclusively and directly governed by the pleasure principle as it is in early infancy; at no other time is man, especially civilized man, capable of abandoning himself so completely to pleasure and satisfaction. The myth of happy childhood takes the place of the lost memory of the actual riches, spontaneity, freshness of childhood experience, an experience which has been forgotten because there is no place for it in the adult memory schemata. (p. 200)

Our nostalgic yearning for our "paradise lost," then, measures the degree to which our social order has succeeded in killing off our primal, essential aliveness.

All of this makes very clear indeed why Schachtel reminds us toward the inception of his essay that for the Greeks Mnemosyne is not only the Goddess of Memory but the mother of the Muses and hence of the arts, by Zeus (p. 189). Cutting through the conventional schemata of the mundane social order, the artist restores us (or can restore us) to the realm of genuine, powerful emotion, to the fresh, lively, spontaneous perception we knew early on, before the world of codified thought and behavior closed around us like a constrictive serpent, removing us from the garden of our early participation in life. Through poetry, fiction, painting, music we are restored to a universe of intense, authentic feeling, authentic engagement, whose roots extend directly into the "lost" early period of our experience. Yet note, what Schachtel has in mind here is *not* the Proustian quest for the remembrance of things past, triggered by a longing to recapture specific events and the affective nuances that accompany those events, but the living, inward awareness that attends the artistic encounter generally as we are swept up in perceptions and emotions that reactivate and enlarge the reservoir of "life" that resides in the early "forgotten" stage of our existence. Schachtel cites in illustration of his meaning German writer Johann Wolfgang von Goethe's magnificent words, penned at the height of the Romantic period: "I do not recognize memory in the sense that you mean it [i.e., the ordinary sense of explicitly recalling discrete events]. Whatever we encounter that is great, beautiful, significant need not be remembered from the outside; need not be hunted up and laid hold of, as it were. Rather, from the beginning, it must be woven into the fabric of our inmost self, must become one with it, create a new and better self in us. . . . There is no past that one is allowed to long for. There is only the eternally new, growing from the enlarged elements of the past" (p. 190). Here is the flowing, verbalized heart of the dichotomy Schachtel strives to create, the dichotomy, or perhaps the conflict, between the realistic requirements of the "adult" social order and the passionate aliveness of the creative realm as it is rooted in the figure of Mnemosyne, the Goddess of Memory, including above all the unconscious memory of the "lost" early time.

Through precisely these materials taken as a whole we may begin to realize the following: it is not only art that emerges as memory's offspring; religion must take its place in that family too, for religion is also rooted in the unconscious recollection of early, foundational, interpersonal events that were subsequently "forgotten" as our mnemonic organization matured synaptically toward verbalization, and toward the practical requirements attendant upon our increasingly separate, self-sustaining condition in the world. I am not referring here, of course, to the stale, codified routines of one's mere religious affiliation, which Schachtel mentions briefly in the one and only nod to organized religion in his paper. I am referring to one's living faith as it is powerfully and joyously expressed in the church, or in the temple, or in the revival tent, or in the mystical interlude, or in the immediate, overwhelming sense of God's presence, or in the spontaneous, implacable moment of conversion, of change, of what we popularly know as "amazing grace," in short, to the kind of religious experience that is, to echo Goethe's words, "woven into the fabric of the inmost self." Let's remember that the notion of one's "paradise lost," of one's "Eden," of one's perfect, blissful beginning in the "sacred garden" is an explicitly *religious* notion, not simply an artistic one; and let's remember too that religion offers us at its core not the powerful, affective reliving of just any arresting "experience," any arresting aspect of "life" or being, but specifically the reliving of a perfect, loving, blissful *union* with a perfect, loving *parental figure* who is no longer "visible" or "discoverable" to explicit memory or indeed to ordinary perception itself but who is projectively and inwardly restored afresh, or mapped onto, or perhaps in Goethe's words enlarged into, the figure of the Parent-God each time the believer activates his religious dimension. And more, this supernatural provider and protector appears in earnest on the creative scene just as the early period begins to fade off into the realm of infantile amnesia and as another kind of conventionalized memory, or conventionalized perceptual "scheme," begins to take its place. Can anyone miss it?

The potent, affective, all-absorbing "life" of religious participation and consciousness to which James refers in his *The Varieties of Religious Experience*,[17] as discussed in chapter 6, enters the human picture through precisely a longing for the parental "presence" who is "lost" to us just as we mature toward those "conventionalized memory schemata" to which Schachtel refers as perceptual testimony to our diminished existence in the constrictive social order. To express the matter from a crucial, related angle, it is not only art that *transforms* us perceptually from dried-up automatons into living creatures, it is also religion that accomplishes the trick, for in our religious participations we refind once more the deep, powerful, inexhaustible affect that resides in the unconscious realm and that reflects implicitly the all-or-nothing emotional intensity that characterized our interaction with the caregiver and that presently characterizes our interaction with the caregiver's successor, the loving, omnipotent Parent-God. And here we are, back once again to the basic biological situation of transforming ministration, or care: over and over again, thousands upon thousands of times, for years, the loving provider transformed our lives, changed our hunger into satiation, our discontentment into satisfaction, our agony into bliss, our emptiness into fullness, and on and on without physiological or psychological end. Over and over again in the beginning we learned and we internalized the dichotomy of staleness and deadness versus freshness and aliveness through our transformational parental engagements, and it is just this "forgotten" or "lost" dichotomy that Schachtel associates with the artistic domain and that we now recognize as a foundational feature of the religious participation that gives millions their "life" and their being within the conventionalized social realm. Where else, after all, could that explosive affect come from when the believer falls on his knees and declares his love for his Parent-God? Most assuredly, then, we must not deny religion its central, rightful place in the home of Mnemosyne's many lively offspring. That the Greeks did not put religion there only attests to a greater difficulty in discovering the unconscious wellsprings of religion than in discovering those of art. The very gods, the anthropomorphic *causes* of things in this world, are themselves the products of the mind. Even the Greeks experienced infantile amnesia.

In the broadest terms, Schachtel's approach to the problem of infantile amnesia reflects an ancient, venerable tradition in Western thinking, namely the clash between nature and culture, between innocence and experience, between the prelapsarian realm and the constrictions attendant upon the "fall from grace." One might even find this cleavage behind the dichotomy of pastoral and urban living, the former attesting to natural, spontaneous existence and the latter to calculation and education in "the way of the world"—meaning of course the world of social exchange. Perhaps the most notable, brilliant, and relatively recent expression of this ideational opposition resides in what we know generally as Romanticism, a social, political, and literary movement of the late eighteenth and early nineteenth centuries, which Schachtel may well have in the forefront of his mind as he writes, not only through the monumental figure of Goethe (1749–1832), whose *Sufferings of Young Werther* is often described as the bible of the Romantic period, but through Schachtel's many allusions to the "poet" and to "imagination" (Romanticism's cardinal mental category) as restorers of our lost affective lives (pp. 191–96). The writings of William Wordsworth (1770–1850) serve as a perfect example.[18] "The world [meaning the social realm] is too much with us," notes this poet in a famous sonnet; "Getting and spending [i.e., keeping up with the Joneses, whom Schachtel picks on] we lay waste our powers [our "life"]; little we see in Nature that is ours [we are cut off from the natural order]; we have given our hearts away [to society, to the "conventional" social forces impinging upon us]." In his great ode, "Intimations of Immortality from Recollections of Early Childhood," Wordsworth observes (as does Schachtel), "there was a time" when the world and everything within it seemed "celestial," glorious, fresh, dreamlike (Wordsworth's terms), and he is thinking, needless to say, upon "childhood," upon the period that precedes the ascension of the social domain, or as he calls it here "the prison-house," whose walls close inexorably on the "growing boy," wresting him away from his intense, feeling interaction with "Nature." Is there not a connection (I mean both literally in the words themselves and figuratively in the ideas) between this and Schachtel's final utterance that *there was a time* [my emphasis] before animalistic innocence was lost, before pleasure-seeking nature and pleasure-forbidding culture clashed in the battle called education, a battle in which the child always is the loser"? Although the connection may be entirely coincidental, there is surely no denying its existence. As for the importance of memory in the forging and enjoyment of art, there can hardly be a better example than Wordsworth's celebrated "I Wandered Lonely as a Cloud" (popularly known as "Daffodils"), in which we find the poet toward the conclusion lying upon his "couch" in "pensive mood" and recalling the "golden" flowers he once beheld as he "wandered" through the countryside. What is especially interesting to us here, however, is Wordsworth's intuitive theoretical link between the child's feeling attachment to the world and his attachment to the *maternal figure* through whom his affective existence emerges in the first instance. Indeed, as we read the following remarkable syllables from *The Prelude* we are reminded of the extent to which the affective attunement between mother and offspring is internalized synaptically to become the foundation of the emerging person's emotional life, including of course his projective, emotional attachment to the Parent-God of the religious sphere (the attractor state):

> blest the Babe
> Nursed in his Mother's arms, who sinks to sleep
> Rocked on his Mother's breast; who with his soul
> Drinks in the feelings of his Mother's eye!
> For him, in one dear Presence, there exists
> A virtue which irradiates and exalts
> Objects through widest intercourse of sense.
> No outcast he, bewildered and depressed;
> Along his infant veins are interfused

The gravitation and the filial bond
Of nature that connect him to the world.
Is there a flower, to which he points his hand
Too weak to gather it, already love
Drawn from love's purest earthly fount for him
Hath beautified that flower, already shades
Of pity cast from inward tenderness
Do fall around him upon aught that bears
Unsightly marks of violence or harm.
Emphatically such a being lives.

(bk. 2, ll. 234–51)

Clearly then, it is the mother's love directed toward the child that attaches him feelingly to his own extension, the world, and in particular to the world of nature and the "flowers" (the daffodils, perhaps?) contained therein.

I am not suggesting, let me make clear, that every subsequent attachment to nature, or to anything else, that the child evinces is a direct reactivation of affective attunement with the maternal figure. But I am suggesting that a person's subsequent attachment to and affective apprehension of the "presence" of the Parent-God consists in exactly such reactivation as it is drawn forth from the realm of one's unconscious memory (infantile amnesia) through priming and cueing (however subtle or subliminal) in the environment. For Wordsworth, not surprisingly, such priming spontaneously transpires smack in the midst of a glorious, natural, religious setting far from the maddening social crowd, a setting, in short, where the "fount" of maternal affection might flow implicitly toward him again. Note this splendid example from the celebrated "Lines Composed a Few Miles above Tintern Abbey": lamenting his divorce from the world of nature and his steady, unremitting absorption into the social domain—what we might call today his "alienation"—Wordsworth observes in a moment of powerful feeling that he is, in spite of everything, still able to experience

A presence that disturbs me with the joy
Of elevated thoughts; a sense sublime
Of something far more deeply interfused
Whose dwelling is the light of setting suns,
And the round ocean, and the living air,
And the blue sky, and in the mind of man:
A motion and a spirit, that impels
All thinking things, all objects of all thought,
And rolls through all things.

(ll. 93–102)

And when he feels this "presence," concludes the poet, he finds himself "still a lover" of "nature," of the "meadows" and the "woods," the "mountains," the "green earth," the "mighty world" (ll. 103–106), which is to say, he finds himself *still attached* to the natural environment, to the "flowers" as it were, to which he was affectively guided in the beginning through the nurturing of his maternal provider, the "dear presence" and the special "filial bond" that, in his words again, "connected him to the world." Nature "never did betray the heart that loved her," writes Wordsworth ("Tintern Abbey," l. 132).

Thus the "lost paradise" for which we long in our "conventionalized" social condition, to echo Schachtel, the "Eden" we affectively crave as we sense its "presence" in our removed, infantile memory, is *peopled.* The loving, parental nurturer resides at its affective core, ready to be projectively and wishfully metamorphosed into the loving Parent-God (or spiritual "presence") when our Edenic days are over and our movement into the social world commences. We must "go it alone," as the old adage has it, but not on the *inside.* There, we may take the caregiver along, as Wordsworth discloses to us poetically, imaginatively, creatively in his wonderful "Tintern Abbey." Within a special psychic "space" the specific contents of which we cannot *see* resides the specific anthropomorphic inspiration of the restorative spiritual sphere to which we cleave as postlapsarian creatures.

I hope the reader will not become impatient with me. Having placed art and religion side by side, I must now sunder them, forever. I mean, although religion and art are clearly connected through their foundational relation to memory, they oppose each other, or differ, in this all-important respect: art makes no truth-claims; it never has, and it never will—not one. Keats's nightingale will never sing; Blake's tiger will never roam the forest. Michelangelo's David will never strike Goliath with a stone; Monet's water lilies, floating beneath a bridge, will never see the close of the soft, spring light. Shortly after Othello kills himself upon the stage, the actor who played him takes off his makeup, changes into his street clothes, and goes home. Art may be symbolically true, of course; it may "hold the mirror to nature," as Shakespeare has it; but it is never literally true, rigorously true, objectively true; it lives entirely and forever in the imaginal land of metaphor. Only a young child or a madman believes in the objective truth of an *objet d'art*.

Religion, by contrast, makes truth-claims; in fact, it makes no other kind. It is totally objectivist in its outlook; it repudiates the attachment of any subjectivity to its central claims, the claims by which and through which it lives as a cultural institution. Let's recall the authoritative words of distinguished theologian John Polkinghorne on the all-encompassing presence of the Deity (see p. 120). One would be very hard-pressed indeed to tease a subjective element out of Polkinghorne's view, which makes the matter as plain as the nose on one's face: God is real, absolutely and finally real, real in every conceivable sense, more real than anything else in the world. Moreover, one may say with complete, unqualified assurance that Polkinghorne's attitude is shared by religious people everywhere; belief in the absolute reality of God is ubiquitous among the faithful. Any disagreement, any dissent, any qualification of this basic tenet indicates one thing and one thing only: disbelief.

Listen with this in mind to Winnicott's famous description of the "intermediate area," and note in particular his closing reference to art and religion:

> The third part of the life of a human being, a part we cannot ignore, is an intermediate area of *experiencing*, to which inner reality and external life both contribute. It is an area that is not challenged, because no claim is made on its behalf except that it shall exist as a resting-place for the individual engaged in the perpetual human task of keeping inner and outer reality separate yet interrelated. . . . I am

here staking a claim for an intermediate state between a baby's inability and his growing ability to recognize and accept reality. I am therefore studying the substance of illusion, that which is allowed to the infant, and which in adult life is inherent in art and religion.

What was that again? "It is an area *that is not challenged* because *no claim is made on its behalf* except that it shall exist as a resting-place" (emphasis added)?[19] Surely this is off the mark, unless Winnicott is referring to the inhabitants of some other planet. As far as earthlings are concerned, although no claims may be made on art's behalf, they certainly are made on religion's behalf. Indeed, people routinely go to war to defend or to assert their religious claims. They sack Jerusalem over their claims; they burn dissenters at the stake, or tear them limb from limb; they drop bombs on each other; they fly airplanes into buildings; they propagandize, they proselytize, they go off on missionary journeys; they would rather die than renounce their religious claims; death itself is preferable to the betrayal of God's word, whatever that word happens to be at some particular moment in some particular place. More claims have been made on behalf of religion than on behalf of anything else in the world; it isn't even close. Some resting place!

Granted, people may feel strongly one way or the other about the work of, say, Henri Matisse, but they don't kill themselves over the matter, that is, unless they are willing to put at risk their reputations in artistic circles. It is equally mistaken, of course, to say that religion as part of the intermediate area is not challenged. Every claim contains a challenge, be it implied or open. That has always been, and is, an integral, inescapable facet of our earthly religious experience: claims and challenges, claims and challenges, for thousands of years, from rival pagan gods to rival monotheistic creeds, from rival interdenominational sects (Protestant-Catholic, Sunni-Shi'ite, Orthodox-Reformed) to rivalrous religious families calling each other names up and down the streets of their towns and cities. I won't repeat the names. Note this brief passage from an article by Leonard George: "In 1950, [Pope] Pius XII pronounced *ex cathedra* that the Virgin Mary emigrated to heaven, body and soul, at the end of her life. (He learned this via 'special divine assistance.') Catholics have no wriggle room here. They must believe this dogma, for as Pius put it, 'if anyone, which God forbid, should dare willfully or call in doubt that which We have defined, let him know that he has fallen away completely from the divine and Catholic faith.'" Or this: "The Cathars' last redoubt was the mountain fortress of Montsegur, which fell to crusaders in 1244. Although the loss of Montsegur was a bitter blow, three other castles in the region— Puilaurens, Fenouillet, and Queribus—endured for some time as Cathar strongholds. The last to go was Queribus, in 1255. Even then Catharism held on in pockets throughout western Europe. Unable to crush this popular heresy either by debate or crusade, the Catholic church invented another strategy: the Holy Inquisition. The rest, sadly, is history."[20] I, or anyone else, could easily cite a thousand similar passages from the history of the world's religions.

Two central points emerge: first, although Winnicott's contributions to our understanding of human behavior are considerable, although his analyses of transitional objects and transitional phenomena assist us greatly in grasping the underlying dynamics of religious conduct, Winnicott was not an esthetician, or an epistemologist, or a historian. He was a brilliant and busy child psychologist. His comments on religion and art were made in passing. He did not explore the implications of those comments. The second and more crucial point is this: because religion, unlike art, makes truth-claims, religion is fated to confront and to deal with the forces of rationality. It must either accommodate or lay to rest the competing philosophic and scientific narratives that people encounter as they move along in the world. Truth-claims, after all, must be defended, demonstrated, set out clearly—in short, justified perceptually in a manner that convinces inquiring minds. Faith may be sufficient for millions, but it is not sufficient for everyone, and as things presently stand, everyone just happens to include a great many shrewd, critical intellects. This is why religion continues to harp on "miracles," of course, and not just faith. The religious realize in their wisdom that doctrine's final support is doctrine witnessed through the natural as opposed to supernatural order. When God suspends the laws of nature, walks on water for example, we know for certain He is God; our faith at such a moment is quite beside the point: we can *see* the truth. Were miracles straightforward and universally beheld, I would not be writing this book. Also, and monumentally, because religion must confront the realm of reason through its truth-claims, it, religion, is not merely vulnerable but mortal: it can die. It can fail to dominate rationality; it can lose out to competing narratives—science, or its cousin, empirical philosophy based on logic. It can contemplate (as it has already contemplated) God's death, to call up Nietzsche's famous pronouncement in *The Gay Science* (1882), or Don Cupitt's similar, more recent remarks in *After God* (1997). Art, as I've indicated, does not carry this burden; it is totally imaginal. It can be trivialized, or debased, or ideologically constrained, or simply ignored, but it can't be killed off. Of the two, art and religion, it is art that is imperishable. Its immortality rests upon the surest foundation of all: no one claims it to be true.

NOTES

1. Richard Restak, *The Infant Mind* (New York: Doubleday, 1986), p. 149.

2. Ibid., p. 169.

3. Emmett Wilson Jr., "The Object in Person," *Psychoanalytic Quarterly* 71 (2002): 382.

4. Joseph Le Doux, *Synaptic Self: How Our Brains Become Who We Are* (New York: Viking, 2002), p. 222.

5. Elizabeth Johnston, *Investigating Minds* (Bronxville, NY: Sarah Lawrence College, 2001), p. 1.

6. Ibid., p. 3.

7. Ibid., pp. 1–2.

8. Freud was among the first psychologists to note the phenomenon of infantile amnesia. He suggested that it might be precipitated both by the repression of infantile sexual experiences and by the onset of changes in the mnemonic systems of the brain, mainly the development of language.

9. Johnston, *Investigating Minds*, pp. 3–4.

10. Ibid., p. 4.

11. Ibid., p. 3.

12. Marion Milner, *The Suppressed Madness of Sane Men* (London: Tavistock, 1987), p. 189.

13. John Polkinghorne, *Belief in God in an Age of Science* (New Haven, CT: Yale University Press, 1998), pp. 116–17.

14. C. C. J. Webb, *God and Personality* (New York: Kraus Reprint, 1971).

15. See, for example, Mark Perakh, "A Presentation without Arguments," *Skeptical Inquirer* 26 (November 2002): 31–34.

16. Ernest Schachtel, "On Memory and Childhood Amnesia," in *Memory Observed: Remembering in Natural Contexts*, ed. Ulric Neisser (1947; New York: W. H. Freeman, 1982), p. 190. Page numbers for the other Schachtel quotes in this section are included in the text.

17. William James, *The Varieties of Religious Experience* (1902; New York: Library of America, 1987), p. 453.

18. All my citations from Wordsworth may be found in *The Norton Anthology of English Literature*, ed. M. H. Abrams, 4th ed., vol. 2 (New York: W. W. Norton, 1979).

19. D. W. Winnicott, *Playing and Reality* (London: Penguin, 1971), pp. 2–3.

20. Both quotations from Leonard George, "To Err is Human, to Forgive Divine," *Georgia Straight* (Vancouver, BC), June 22, 2000, p. 7.

8.

Prayer and Faith

There is no tighter connection in the realm of religious experience than the connection between prayer and faith. They are spiritual symbionts, inextricably intertwined, breathing the same supersensible air, and destined to flourish, or to perish, together. Granting them each a single clause by way of compact definition, I would suggest the following: faith is the willful assertion that God not only exists but is there for one, available to one, involved caringly in one's life and affairs; prayer is faith in action, faith manifested, expressed, the actual calling upon God in the supernatural world. The mutuality, or perhaps the "system," is ironclad: if one has faith, one prays; if one prays, one demonstrates faith; if one fails to pray, faith slumbers; if one ceases to pray permanently, faith dies. And it goes without saying, of course, that faith's demise is also religion's demise. The religious literature supports all this completely; there just isn't any disagreement, anywhere. We may note James's remark that prayer "is the very soul and essence of religion."[1] We may note too this passage from Friedrich Heiler's classic study, *Prayer*,[2] which presents comprehensively the orthodox position and which may be considered axiomatic. As far as this particular topic is concerned, the reader will require nothing further. "Religious people, students of religion, theologians of all creeds and tendencies," writes Heiler, "agree in thinking that prayer is the central phenomenon of religion, the very hearthstone of all piety. Faith is, in Luther's judgment, 'prayer and nothing but prayer. He who does not pray or call upon God in his hour of need, assuredly does not think of Him as God, nor does he give Him the honor that is His due.'" Heiler continues,

> The great evangelistical mystic, Johann Arndt, constantly emphasized the truth that: "without prayer we cannot find God; prayer is the means by which we seek and find Him." Schleiermacher, the restorer of evangelical theology in the nineteenth century, observes in one of his sermons: "to be religious and to pray—that is really the same thing." Novalis, the poet of romanticism, remarks: "Praying is to religion what thinking is to philosophy." The same thought is expressed by the gifted evangelical divine, Richard Rothe, when he says, "the religious impulse is essentially the impulse to pray. It is by prayer, in fact, that the process of individual religious life is governed, the process of the gradual fulfillment of God's indwelling in the individual and his religious life. Therefore, the non-praying man is rightly considered to be religiously dead." (p. xiii)

For our naturalistic, psychological analysis, this is the upshot: to get at the essence of prayer is to get at the essence of faith; to get at the essence of faith is to get at the essence of religion. To turn the coin over, a full-fledged naturalistic understanding of religion requires little more than a full-fledged naturalistic understanding of prayer.

Personal, individual, informal prayer, as opposed to codified, congregational prayer, is my main interest. This opposition, as it turns out, has a complex, disputatious history that is not our business here. It is enough to say that the individualism of prayer is usually traced back to Jeremiah and the psalms of the Old Testament, that Jesus' prayer on the Mount is widely regarded as the model prayer for individual Christians ("Not my will but Thine be done");[3] that Paul views personal, intercessory prayer as a cornerstone of spiritual practice; and that by Luther's day subjective, solitary prayer in which the worshiper gives himself over to a fervent, one-to-One relationship with his God is moving steadily toward the heart of Christianity, first for the Protestant, and then, with rather less momentum perhaps, for the Catholic as well. For both Jews and Muslims,[4] codified, public prayer is the dominant form of worship, although there are noteworthy exceptions—chiefly in the area of mysticism. Accordingly then, what follows will find us exploring from a psychological angle the motivational dynamics of personal prayer in the Judeo-Christian tradition.

This tradition contains at its core (mysticism aside) an essentially anthropomorphic, supernatural Parent-God, or Deity, capable of receiving, understanding, and responding to the personal, private, subjective, spoken and unspoken prayers of individual religious practitioners. He hears and He answers (or chooses not to answer). "All religion," notes Karen Armstrong in *A History of God*, "must begin with some anthropomorphism."[5] I will be dealing in what follows only with such a Deity and only with prayers directed to such a Deity. Conversely, I will not be dealing here with any form of secularized prayer, with prayer as a method of "getting in touch with one's feelings," or "looking inwardly" for one's "true self," with prayer as a "breathless response" to a "magnificent sunset," or a "bird on the wing." Mind you, I have nothing against this sort of thing. I consider myself as spiritual as the next person. I'm just not dealing with it now. God's anthropomorphism, and in particular the way in which that anthropomorphism is treated in the literature of prayer, resides at the very center of my overall presentation. Let the reader prepare himself, then, for what he can think of generally as good old-fashioned prayer emanating from good old-fashioned prayers.

I will rely upon a wide variety of sources, but for much of the discussion I will utilize three pivotal, relatively recent treatments of the subject, namely Heiler's *Prayer*, regarded by Hans Küng as the classical work on the topic and perhaps the most scholarly and comprehensive book on prayer ever to appear in the West; Ole Hallesby's *Prayer*, another classic, translated into several languages, reprinted fifteen times in English alone, and probably the most widely read and influential single discussion composed during the twentieth century; and Romano Guardini's *Prayer in Practice*, a treasured work among Roman Catholics and penned by one of the church's most astute and respected thinkers— undoubtedly another classic treatment. Needless to say, for all three of these authors, prayer and faith are integrally connected: faith depends upon prayer for its existence, and prayer is nothing other than faith's signal manifestation. "We must bear in mind," declares Guardini, "that faith itself depends on prayer. . . . Prayer is the basic act of faith as breathing is the basic act of life."[6] Until we pray, maintains Hallesby, we have no access to God, and God has no access to us. He "cannot gain admittance."[7] To pray is "to believe." Faith is "prayer and nothing but prayer," writes Heiler, echoing Martin Luther, as we've just seen; without prayer, "we cannot find God" (p. xiii). The issue could hardly be plainer. That the Judeo-Christian tradition of individual subjective prayer is ulti- mately petitionary in nature, in other words, that *asking* the Parent-God for help and support resides at its theological essence, is equally plain.

"The heart of all prayer is petition," states Heiler in one place (p. 17); and in another, "The free spontaneous petitionary prayer of the natural man exhibits the prototype of all prayer" (p. 1). "Whether we like it or not," declares C. H. Spurgeon, "asking is the rule of the Kingdom."[8] "Petition is the heart of prayer," writes Patrick Cotter.[9] Prayer is a "reverent petition to God," asserts James Pruitt.[10] The Judeo-Christian tradition of prayer, derived from both the Old and New Testaments, has always been "essentially petitionary," observes Walter A. Elwell in *The Evangelical Dictionary of Biblical Theology*.[11] Prayer is a "palpable thirst to ask," maintains Timothy Jones in *The Art of Prayer*.[12] "Prayer" is a "trustful appeal for aid in our necessity," holds the great sixteenth-century theologian Huldrych Zwingli.[13] "Give us this day our daily bread," requests the Lord's Prayer. One could cite a thousand similar passages.

As for asking and *receiving*, we have the following: "One has only to ask the Father in order to receive what is needed," states Elwell, echoing Scripture.[14] "Whatsoever ye shall ask in prayer, believing, ye shall receive," writes Hallesby, quoting Matthew 21.[15] "Petition" for "divine grace" is "freely bestowed," observes Heiler (p. 243). "God's power" is "capable of giving everything," maintains Guardini.[16] "Asking is our staple diet," asserts Gordon Lindsay; "the spirit suffers when it is not fed the Bread of Life."[17] "Prayer is the spiritual practice of asking God for what you want and accepting that it has been done once you have made the request," suggests Joshua Stone in *Soul Psychology*; "God . . . hears and answers all prayers."[18] "Do you know why the mighty God of the universe chooses to answer prayer?" inquires Richard Foster. "It is because His children ask."[19] "Everything will be given to you," declares Cotter in *How to Pray*; you are merely claiming "what is already yours."[20] Our asking is itself "God's answering," holds Jones.[21] The classical expression on the asking side of the equation has already been cited, of course: "Give us this day our daily bread." On the receiving side we have, from the Twenty-third Psalm, "The Lord is my shepherd; I shall not want" (vv. 1–2). Taken together, these two lines contain the pith of the petitionary mind-set.

My aim here, needless to say, is to establish a clear motivational link between the immediate context of supplicatory ritual and the basic biological situation of asking and receiving as earlier described. With such an aim in view, we must inquire, first, how does one go about this individual subjective praying, this asking the Parent-God for succor and support? Second, do the instructions for prayer as proffered by the authoritative theologians call to mind explicitly the early parent-child interaction, the interaction in which the helpless, dependent little one calls upon the all-powerful provider for nourishment, attention, love, care?

To pray successfully one must adopt a certain attitude, a certain psychological posture, or stance. One does not come to God in just any way but in a very specific way indeed. I'm referring to an attitude of utter dependency, utter helplessness, utter submission, a willful attempt to get rid of one's will entirely. "Helplessness," writes Hallesby, "is unquestionably the first and surest indication of a praying heart. As far as I can see, prayer has been ordained only for the helpless."[22] Hallesby goes on in the personal style that has made his book so influential: "Listen, my friend! Your helplessness is your best prayer. It calls from your heart to the heart of God with greater effect than all your uttered pleas. He hears it from the very moment that you are seized with helplessness, and He becomes actively engaged at once in hearing and answering the prayer of your helplessness." Thus "helplessness is the real secret and impelling power of prayer," the "very essence of prayer," the "decisive factor" that makes us "attached to God" and "more strongly dependent on Him."[23] At the heart of successful prayer, states Heiler, dwells the "expression" of one's "weakness and dependency" (p. 258). One "submits" entirely to "God's will" and strives to make such "submission" a "permanent attitude" (p. 268). In fact, the "feeling of dependence" is the "universal feeling" that "animates" the whole of humanity's relation with the Deity; "nowhere . . . is it revealed so clearly as in prayer" (p. 77). "Man is ever conscious of his want and helplessness," maintains Guardini; "it is only right, therefore, that he should turn to the bountiful and almighty God, who is not only ready to give and to help, but greatly rejoices in it." Unless we "surrender without reservation" to the "Creator," Guardini continues, unless we realize that our very existence depends on God and His grace, our praying will be futile.[24] Whereas our powers are limited, even puny, God's are infinite. He allows us to breathe, to be, and above all to approach Him with "our needs."[25] Identical views may be instantly discovered in a thousand places. Dependence upon and submission to the Almighty reside at the very core of Judaism and of Islam as well.[26] "Thy will be done," writes Cotter in *How to Pray*.[27] The "value of surrender" in prayer is "extraordinary," declares Larry Dossey in *Healing Words*.[28] "God's plan involves daily dependence on Him," asserts Lindsay in *Prayer That Moves Mountains*; "without Him we can do nothing."[29] Nor is it only one's inward attitude, or stance, that determines the emotional, psychological quality of one's praying. One's bodily conduct may also enter integrally into the picture. One can, of course, worship in any manner one chooses, at any time, in any place, in any posture. Yet for countless millions everywhere, inward dependency, helplessness, and submission are outwardly expressed, or mirrored, by prayer's traditional, ritualistic behaviors: suppliants kneel, bow down, close their eyes, fold their hands, even prostrate themselves entirely. Stephen Winward, in *Teach Yourself How to Pray*, cites Psalm 95 as follows: "O come, let us worship and bow down, let us kneel before the Lord." In these "familiar words of the Venite," he observes, "the Psalmist invites us to let our bodies also participate in the worship of God."[30] Let's take a moment now to see how this theme of dependency, of helplessness, of submission is developed in the literature we are employing. Remember, we are looking for open, explicit, indubitable references to the basic biological situation of asking and receiving, in which the helpless little one petitions the caregiver for loving ministration and support.

"If you are a mother," asserts Hallesby, "you will understand very readily this aspect of prayer. Your infant child cannot formulate in words a single petition to you. Yet the little one prays the best way he knows how. All he can do is cry, but you understand very well his pleading cry. All you need to do is to see him in all his helpless dependence upon you, and a prayer touches your mother-heart, a prayer which is stronger than the loudest cry. He who is Father of all that is called mother and all that is called child in heaven and on earth deals with us in the same way."[31] Thus we leave everything "in His hands." We cling in our helplessness to the "spirit of prayer" whenever we pray. We know "the Lord is at our side," and therefore we no longer feel frightened.[32] Indeed, we know He is there constantly, and so we may tell Him "throughout the day," and during the nighttime too, "how dependent we are upon Him." When his own "little boy" comes to him with "round baby eyes" and asks for his assistance, Hallesby writes, he sees at once the manner in which everyone should approach the "heavenly Father."[33] We must "let our holy and almighty God care for us just as an infant surrenders himself to his mother's care."[34]

And by the way, Hallesby is perfectly aware of the psychological dimension of the discussion; he is not using the theme of dependency in some metaphorical fashion: "Psychologically," he states, "helplessness is the sustaining and impelling power of prayer."[35] Heiler agrees (p. 32) and also turns to childhood in illustration. The feeling of "dependence and impotence" is the key to successful praying, for we have no genuine power of our own: we are like "children who can do nothing" (p. 36). It is precisely this childlike mind-set, this childlike "trust and surrender," holds Heiler (pp. 130–31), that marks all the "eminent men" with a "genius for prayer," all the "great men of religion" (p. 253). We turn to God "in prayer," writes Guardini, "as the child in distress turns to his mother." Jesus taught us, Guardini goes on, "that we should turn to the Father and ask Him" for our "daily bread," for the "necessities" of our "daily life."[36] This is because the Almighty knows best what is "needful" for us. He knows how to love us truly, how to look after us in every respect—in a word how to "care" for us in our "helplessness" and "want."[37] "God will be found" in supplication, claims Buttrick, "not by our seeking" but "by a response . . . to One of whom we are dimly aware—as a child, half waking, responds to the mother who bends over him."[38] When we pray, maintains Jones, "we take hold of His willingness to listen and move; we exercise our right as children to influence a loving parent."[39] Cries Horatius Bonar in *The New Book of Christian Prayers*: "Lead me by Thine own hand, choose out the path for me."[40] Once again, a thousand similar quotations may be instantly found in the literature of prayer. The dependent child relying on the loving Parent-God is probably the Western world's most common depiction of the supplicatory relationship. Thus a culminating question arises: why does successful prayer hinge so decisively upon the assumption of an infantile, childlike state, a state of helplessness, dependence, and submission that is persistently rendered in terms that recall the early parent-child interaction?

The ritual is designed to trigger the attractor state, to "prime" the worshiper for the reawakening and projection of the core relationship with the biological caregiver. One's praying becomes the "cue" for the emergence of implicit, state-dependent memory, for the inward perception and feeling that one is still united with the parental object, now transmuted through religious narrative into the invisible, compassionate Deity of the putative supernatural realm. This is why the worshiper "turns to God as a child in distress turns to his mother"; why he "lets God care for him as an infant surrenders himself to his mother's care"; why he adopts an attitude of "childlike trust," of utter "dependency" and "helplessness," frequently upon his knees (preambulation). In the performance of this remarkable enactment or "play," the heart of religion and faith, the worshiper seeks unconsciously to undo the past, to reverse the flow of time, to restore the enormous advantages he possessed as a symbiotic partner or "organ" of an omnipotent, loving protector and provider. The rite of prayer attests on the one hand to the preciousness and power of the first relationship, to the severity of our early needs, to the depth of our conditioning as little ones when asking and receiving were the order of the day, to the persistence of our longing for unconditional love and care—in a word, to the urgency of our unconscious requirements as they arise from the foundational years. On the other hand, and just as significantly, the rite of supplication reflects the anxieties and the exigencies of the moment, the problematical now of the pray-er's existence, his present concerns, his present wishes (including those for the future), his present need for reassurance and support. Writes Walter Burkert, "Rituals are complicated, ambivalent, and not seldom opaque even to those who practice them. . . . It makes more sense to see them as cultural attempts to make the 'facts of life' manageable and predictable; to perform an act of artificial social creation, as if to veil biology."[41] We don't have to puzzle very long to espy the biology that is veiled by supplication: separation from the matrix; the loss of infantile omnipotence; dealing with a dangerous, unpredictable world; the inescapable facts of accident, illness, aging, and death. The point is, when Freud suggests that religion is based upon an "infantile model" he has in mind the projective image of the mighty father looking out for the vulnerable child: "Over each one of us there watches a benevolent providence which is only seemingly stern and which will not suffer us to become a plaything of the pitiless forces of nature."[42] As we may now appreciate, however, the wishful imposition is considerably more decisive, considerably more radical than that: the very asking and receiving in which the infantile situation is rooted turn up though implicit memory at the heart of religious ritual. Religion is not merely based imagistically on an infantile model; it actually recreates one in prayer. Suppliants, spurred on by their synaptic structure, by the very neurological makeup of their mind-brains, act out their infantile wish. The biological foundation of infantile life is ritualistically transformed into the cornerstone of religious practice.

The procedure resembles what James Frazer terms in *The Golden Bough* "homeopathic magic" or "imitative magic," in which the practitioner, applying his crude, erroneous idea of "cause and effect," seeks to accomplish his purpose through sheer mimicry (I can destroy my foe by stabbing his effigy).[43] However, the practice of individual, subjective prayer goes well beyond mere homeopathy: the imitative, magical element, namely the recreation of the basic biological situation in which the little one calls upon the big one for succor and support, is undergirded by the monumental fact that the original experience is actually *there*, at the synaptic, neurological level. The Parent-God is fashioned through a psychological projection that is firmly based on the *reality* of a corresponding inward, biological content. What makes the whole arrangement so difficult to fathom, so "mysterious," so problematical, so contentious, is that the inward content that drives the rite dwells entirely in the realm of infantile amnesia and thus can't be directly discerned by anyone, neither theologian, nor worshiper, nor psychological sleuth. The magic runs deep. One might figuratively express the matter this way: as prayer goes forward and the worshiper turns to his Parent-God, his implicit memory whispers to his wish and his wish whispers back to his implicit memory. Accordingly, the "slate" on which one's culture inscribes its religious narrative is loaded with the record of one's infantile experience; the faith on which practitioners rely is impelled by the force of a dynamic, appetitive unconscious, as manifested magnificently in the ritual of prayer.

We continually hear from the religious experts themselves that prayer is rooted in the unconscious, reaches into the unconscious, arises from the unconscious, engages the unconscious regions, and so forth, but we are never offered anything specific on this score, never told how the process works, never made aware of the connections. "Religious emotions in the pious man," states Heiler, "force their way unconsciously and unexpectedly, from evident and inner necessity, to expression in prayer. Prayer wells up from the subconscious life of the soul" (p. 233). And again, "Men take over faith in God from the community in which they were born; but how it first arose cannot here be discussed; doubtless it flowed from a whole series of psychological forces" (p. 3). Prayer, asserts Dossey, is grounded in "the power of the unconscious instead of the conscious mind;" it "need not always be 'thought.' . . . 'Unconscious prayer' is possible."[44] When we pray successfully, holds James, "subconscious forces take the lead."[45] One's "whole subconscious life," one's "impulses, . . . faiths, . . . needs, . . . divinations," has "prepared the premises of which [one's] consciousness now feels the weight of the result."[46] As for those premises themselves, as for the "divine personages" that determine the attitudes and practices of the believer, including his supplication, they are "exerted by the instrumentality of pure ideas, of which nothing in the individual's past experience directly serves as a model."[47] We may now appreciate, however, that something *is* there in the "individual's past experience" that *does* "directly serve as a model." I am referring, of course, to the basic biological situation, internalized deeply into the worshipper's mind-brain and explicitly extended in theological handbooks as the chief imitative prerequisite to successful supplication. No one invented prayer. It arose from the unconscious strata through the irresistible interaction of neurological structure and wishful affect. It was and still is dedicated to the evolutionarily valuable proposition that we are not separate, and alone, and impotent, and mortal, in an enigmatic, indifferent universe. Surely from this perspective we may now grasp why the doctors of prayer inform us that we *receive* simply by *asking*, indeed, that our asking *is* our receiving. It goes like this: when we *ask* we restore the early period; we trigger in the unconscious the symbiotic union we enjoyed in the beginning; we jog through our prayerful *state* the state-dependent memory of our attachment to the loving provider. Merely to pray, then, is to gain what we're seeking.

SUPPLICATION AT WORK

The appetite for symbiotic merger, the longing to undo the past, to dissolve ego boundaries and reunite with a succoring, all-powerful provider appears with striking, unmistakable clarity everywhere in the literature of supplication. How could it not? The passion for symbiotic union is but a variation on prayer's central figure, namely that of the helpless child crying out to the mighty Parent-God. As Guardini says, "The longing for union" is "to some degree present in every prayer which deserves the name."[48] In this way, the most primitive, elemental asking and receiving that one enacts in prayer (which is faith's counterpart, remember) stems from the most primitive, elemental experience one undergoes early on, namely that of existing as an "organ" of the parent, that of being oneself and the caregiver too, that of possessing, as Christopher Bollas puts it, an "other self."[49] The "yearning for union," maintains Guardini, is the "first motive of prayer." Our "soul longs for union with God." "We cannot be without Him." When we pray, "our prayer becomes love, for love means seeking to be completely at one with another autonomous being."[50] Yet, Guardini goes on, "only God can create that nearness that fulfils our yearning." Because desire for the Almighty is "inborn in human nature," we "cry" for Him "again and again." Guardini sums everything up with the assertion that "the yearning for God, for union, *is also prayer*" (emphasis added).[51] Let's look further.

Prayer's "deepest motive," observes Heiler, "is the burning desire of the heart which finds rest in blissful union with God" (p. 104). The "yearning for blessed union," Heiler continues, is capable of "over-bearing" all the other "themes" which often find their way to supplication, namely "guilt, grace, and sin" (p. 127). In fully successful prayer, states Heiler, "God and the soul are bound together in indissoluble unity" (p. 142). The "contrast of subject and object which rules the soul's normal life is dissolved" (p. 141). One "fuses with Him in deepest unity" (p. 142). One encounters Him "face to face" (p. 160). "God is in me and I am in Him," cries Elsa of Neustadt (cited in Heiler, p. 142). "I sink myself in Thee; I in thee, Thou in me," exclaims Tersteegen (cited in ibid., p. 190). "Thou alone art my food and drink," pronounces Thomas à Kempis (cited in ibid., p. 209). "If I am not united with Thee I shall be forever unhappy," insists Gertrude of Hefta (cited in ibid., ibid.). "I am Thou and Thou art I," declare ecstatic, mystical pray-ers worldwide (see ibid., p. 190). Famous historian Arnold Toynbee expresses it this way: "When prayer—the communion between human person and divine person—has been raised to its highest degree of spiritual intensity, it is transmuted into another kind of experience. At this higher spiritual level, personality is transcended, and, with it, the separateness that is personality's limitation. At this supra-personal spiritual height, the experience is unitive. At this height, God and man do not commune with each other because, at this height, they are identical."[52]

Avows one of James's subjects as he describes his sensations during heartfelt supplication, "I was immersed in the infinite ocean of God."[53] Rabbi Irving Greenberg renders it similarly: in "prayer," he announces, one has "an oceanic feeling of connectedness."[54] Proclaims New Age guru Larry Dossey: "We have for so long defined ourselves as separate personalities that we have fallen into the hypnotic spell of believing that separation, not unity, is the underlying reality." However, adds Dossey, if we pray sincerely, if we allow ourselves to become "God-realized," we soon learn that love is a "living tissue of reality, a bond that unites us all," not merely to one another but to "a loving God" as well.[55]

The powerful sense of merger with God achieved through supplication is often associated of course with mystical moments; yet we must not be distracted by this from prayer's common, basic, integral connection with union. "Mystical prayer," affirms Heiler, is merely "the sublimest kind of prayer" (p. 225). Indeed, for the great saint and bishop of Geneva Francis of Sales (ca. 1600), "prayer and mystical theology are one and the same thing" (cited in Heiler, p. 194). As Guardini reminded us, the "yearning for union" is prayer's "first motive."[56] We must also note here the intimate relationship between mystical prayer, with its dissolution of ego boundaries, and what James calls the "faith-state." James writes, "Faith, says Tolstoy, is that by which men live. And *faith-state and mystic state are practically convertible terms*" (emphasis added).[57] Earlier we described faith as the accompanying inward assent to the practice of supplication, as the unconscious longing for symbiotic union with an idealized version of the caregiver. Accordingly, the psychology of faith is quintessentially expressed in the experience of mystical prayer. To feel merged with the Almighty, to have the sensation of ego boundaries dissolving, to emotionally become, or be, the divine Other, to achieve a perfect, mirroring, face-to-face union with an all-powerful provider is the psychological core of what we know generally as religious faith. When the infantile model—prayer—triggers its coincident infantile affect—faith—one enjoys in the present what one lost in the past: symbiotic fusion with a loving, succoring parental presence. Such is the power of prayer to accomplish its central goal, the reversal of time: maturity to infancy, death to birth—world without end.

Of special fascination is the extent to which the urge for prayerful union with God reflects, or better, picks up, the phenomenology of the early parent-child interaction. To adopt the infantile model is to reexperience psychologically key relational features of the intimate, primal bond. "As a true mother dedicates her life to the care of her children," writes Hallesby, "so the eternal God in His infinite mercy has dedicated Himself externally to the care of His frail and erring children."[58] Specific, clinical details on the biological side of this simile actually present themselves as wondrous, "spiritual" attributes on the religious, supplicatory side. Needless to say, if prayer re-creates through implicit memory the asking and receiving of life's initial stages, as it surely does, then the appearance of those clinical traces in supplication is exactly what we should expect. We noted in the work of Bollas, for example, the manner in which the caregiver transforms the infant's world. "It is undeniable," Bollas declares, "that as the infant's other self, the mother transforms the baby's internal and external environment." If the infant is "distressed," Bollas continues, the "resolution of discomfort is achieved by the apparition-like presence of the mother" who arrives in a timely manner to remove the distress.[59] Bollas calls this a "primary transformation": emptiness, agony, and anger become fullness and contentment.

Over and over again during life's opening stages—thousands upon thousands of times—the parent and the child are joined in such ministering, transformational encounters. When we discover the Lord through our supplications, Heiler informs us, "a wonderful metamorphosis takes place" (p. 259). No longer do we feel uncertain about things; no longer do we have sensations of doubt or dread. Rather, we undergo "the blissful consciousness of *being cared for*" by a "protecting higher Power" (p. 260, emphasis added). "Confidence, peace, hope, and trust" suffuse us, "often quite suddenly" (as in the descent of grace), and always, Heiler notes, involuntarily and unconsciously (p. 259). Surely the reader will recognize at once what is going on here. The adoption of the supplicatory infantile model (as a response to some sort of crisis or stress) triggers the old transformational feelings that reside at the core of maternal ministration, maternal care. We undergo again the elemental transformational experience that we underwent thousands of times during the early period, when our call to the succoring figure brought about a change in our internal and external environment. To pray is to reactivate both wishfully and adaptively a basic, primitive, biological conditioning that simply went too deep ever to be forgotten or relinquished. What served us well at the start will, through supplication, continue to serve us well along the way. We will ask, receive, and feel transformed—which is to say, better—by the time the process concludes.

Everywhere in the literature of prayer we come upon this theme. "God was present, though invisible," declares one of James' praying subjects; "he fell under no one of my senses, yet my consciousness perceived him." And then, "It was . . . as if my personality had been transformed by the presence of a *spiritual spirit*."[60] We might recall here Bollas's point that the mother's appearance in response to the infant's summons has an "apparition-like" quality. "Prayer has true transformative power," states Terry Taylor in *The Alchemy of Prayer*.[61] Not only is God always there but just by connecting to Him through supplication we are altered alchemically, our leaden existence turning suddenly to gold. To pray, observes Guardini, is to shed our old being and enter into a nascent state of spiritual communion, at the heart of which resides "the seed of a new life." This seed, this new life, says Guardini—and here is the early biological arrangement itself—"is given to us to tend as the new born child is given to the mother."[62] "Change me into Thyself," cries David of Augsburg (cited in Heiler, p. 183). "Take me up and transform me," cries Peter of Acantara (cited in ibid.). Clearly then, to supplicate, to indulge the infantile model of asking and receiving, is to engage in what Bollas calls "the wide-ranging collective search for an object that is identified with the metamorphosis of the self." The suppliant "sustains the terms of the earliest object tie within a mythic structure" (i.e., the overall religious creed). The object is sought for its "function as a signifier of transformation." The quest is "to surrender to it as a medium that alters the self."[63] In many instances, of course, a specific crisis sparks the longing for the transformational presence, as was exactly the case early on. Yet a basic, underlying motivation of prayer as a whole is to experience the hit of transformation over and over again, in one's daily existence, just as one experienced it regularly during the addictive, crisis-ridden phase of the initial parent-child interaction. As I mentioned earlier and as we may now see distinctly, the attainment of grace in its myriad, endless shapes and forms, which arise chiefly from prayer, marks the sharp reinfusion of the infantile transformational process into the life of the changed or saved individual. There is nothing miraculous or mysterious at work here. Grace is readily explained in purely naturalistic, psychological terms.

The early dyadic intercourse is loaded with periods of what Daniel Stern described for us in chapter 5 as affect attunement. Mother and infant interact on the same bodily and emotional wavelength; they share a common energy, a common telepathic understanding of each other's dispositions and requirements. Mother often knows baby's needs *before* baby makes them fully known through his squalling or squirming. Writes the Psalmist, specifically in the context of supplication, of course, "Before a word is on my tongue, you know it completely, O Lord" (139:4). Writes Isaiah, also in the context of prayer and reflecting God's voice itself, "Before they call, I will answer: and while they yet are speaking, I will hear" (15:24). Writes Matthew in the New Testament, echoing the words of Christ, and still again in the context of asking and receiving, "Your Father knows before you ask Him" (6:8). According to Jones, "God may influence and speak without our knowing it." Moreover, even if our clumsy efforts to "address" Him are "akin to the child's first efforts to address his parent," God "hears them" through his "caring involvement."[64] God hears "all your uttered pleas," states Hallesby, "from the very moment that you are seized with helplessness." He "becomes actively engaged at once in hearing and answering your prayers." Indeed, He knows what your supplication involves "before it has been formulated in words" because He knows exactly what "is present in the soul."[65]

Are we to regard it as merely coincidental that the Parent-God, whom we approach as helpless, dependent children, possesses as one of His cardinal attributes the telepathic ability to read our requirements before we have pronounced them, exactly as the caregiver was able to do early on? Think about it. At only one stage of our lives, during only one period of our actual experience, was an astonishing telepathic arrangement like this one not only the case but the norm. On a daily, hourly, even moment-to-moment basis, over and over again, thousands of times, for years, the empathetic caregiver intuited or read our requirements and responded to them in a timely, synchronous way.[66] Our smallest bodily sign begot her attention. Before we even asked, she was there, caring for us. Later, when we pray as men and women, the very trait that defines the good object, the very telepathic ability that distinguishes her, turns out to be a central, defining feature of the Parent-God to whom we turn for ministration, for care. He too knows all about our needs before we make them known to Him as His children. We are instructed by theologians to adopt an attitude of childlike dependency, to call upon the Almighty "as a child in distress turns to his mother,"[67] and when we do so we find that He possesses the very telepathic powers that our original caregiver possessed and exercised again and again on our behalf. Of course we don't have a coincidence here. We have the direct transference of an early, specific, interactional, biological trait from the natural caregiver to the supernatural parental presence who resides at the foundation of our infantile, supplicatory model. Just as we can readily understand grace in naturalistic terms as the reinfusion of the infantile transformational process into the life of the "changed" individual, so we can understand naturalistically and psychologically God's miraculous telepathic powers as the suppliant's unconscious attribution of the good object's primary quality to the succoring, empathetic Creator who assumes her life-sustaining function. In the beginning was a caregiver who could intuitively fathom, and meet, our needs. Our wishful, religious inclinations will not allow such a one to slip away.

Kant remarked in a famous *mot* that prayer was "strictly a soliloquy" (cited in Heiler, p. 100), and when he did so he was both right and wrong. Prayer is indeed a soliloquy in that it involves no one and nothing outside of the individual who prays. At the same time, prayer evinces the trace of a relationship, a relationship that is acted out as the suppliant goes about his business. I am referring of course to the infantile model, which resides at the foundation of the practice itself. There are two at the unconscious ground of prayer because there were two at the psychological place of prayer's origins. By the time the suppliant indulges his grown-up asking and receiving these two—the vulnerable, needful infant and the ministering parental figure—have blended through the process of psychological internalization into one—one helpless, dependent suppliant beseeching his Parent-God for His assistance and care. The spiritual wheel comes full circle, back to its biological origins as those origins now reside in the mnemonic structure of the one who asks and receives, the one who still perceives the world as problematical and dangerous, and the one who copes with his anxiety by fashioning through prayer a version of the one who soothed him early on.

NOTES

1. William James, *The Varieties of Religious Experience* (1902; New York: Library of America, 1987), p. 417.

2. Friedrich Heiler, *Prayer: A Study in the History and Psychology of Religion* (1932; Oxford: Oxford University Press, 1997). Page numbers for the individual Heiler quotes in this chapter are included in the text.

3. See Heiler, *Prayer*, p. 123.

4. For Jews, see Louis Jacobs, *The Jewish Religion: A Companion* (New York: Oxford University Press, 1995), p. 380; for Muslims, see Heiler, *Prayer*, p. 304.

5. Karen Armstrong, *A History of God* (New York: Ballantine Books, 1993), p. 48.

6. Romano Guardini, *Prayer in Practice*, trans. L. Loewenstein-Wertheim (London: Burns and Oates, 1957), p. 209.

7. Ole Hallesby, *Prayer*, trans. C. Carlsen (1948; Leicester, UK: Intervarsity Press, 1979), p. 24.

8. C. H. Spurgeon, quoted in Richard S. Foster, *Prayer: Finding the Heart's True Home* (New York: HarperCollins, 1992), p. 179.

9. Patrick Cotter, *How to Pray: A Guide to Deeper Spiritual Fulfillment* (Boca Raton, FL: Globe Communications, 1999), p. 13.

10. James Pruitt, *Healed By Prayer* (New York: Avon Books, 2000), p. 1.

11. Walter A. Elwell, ed., *The* Evangelical Dictionary of Biblical Theology (Grand Rapids, MI: Baker Books, 1996), p. 622.

12. Timothy Jones, *The Art of Prayer: A Simple Guide* (New York: Ballantine Books, 1997), p. 108.

13. Huldrych Zwingli, quoted in Heiler, *Prayer*, p. 271.

14. Elwell, *Evangelical Dictionary*, p. 622.

15. Hallesby, *Prayer*, p. 22.

16. Guardini, *Prayer in Practice*, p. 63.

17. Gordon Lindsay, *Prayer That Moves Mountains* (Dallas: Christ for the Nations, 1996), p. 37.

18. Joshua Stone, *Soul Psychology: How to Clear Negative Emotions and Spiritualize Your Life* (New York: Ballantine Books, 1999), p. 168.

19. Foster, *Prayer*, p. 179.

20. Cotter, *How to Pray*, p. 14.

21. Jones, *The Art of Prayer*, p. 110.

22. Hallesby, *Prayer*, p. 13.

23. Ibid., pp. 14, 17, 16, 21.

24. Guardini, *Prayer in Practice*, pp. 78, 64.

25. Ibid., p. 134.

26. For Judaism, see Keith Crim, ed., *The Perennial Dictionary of World Religions* (New York: Harper and Row, 1989), p. 385; for Islam, see John R. Hinnells Jr., ed., *The Penguin Dictionary of Religions* (London: Penguin Books, 1991), p. 152.

27. Cotter, *How to Pray*, p. 28.

28. Larry Dossey, *Healing Words: The Power of Prayer and the Practice of Medicine* (San Francisco: HarperSanFrancisco, 1993), pp. 100–101.

29. Lindsay, *Prayer That Moves Mountains*, p. 37.

30. Stephen Winward, *Teach Yourself How to Pray* (London: English Universities Press, 1961), p. 46.

31. Hallesby, *Prayer*, p. 14.

32. Ibid., pp. 105, 102, 119.

33. Ibid., p. 121.

34. Ibid., p. 20.

35. Ibid., p. 25.

36. Guardini, *Prayer in Practice*, p. 77.

37. Ibid., p. 78.

38. George A. Buttrick, *So We Believe, So We Pray* (New York: Abingdon-Cokesbury, 1994), p. 30.

39. Jones, *The Art of Prayer*, p. 107.

40. See Tony Castle, ed., *The New Book of Christian Prayers* (New York: Crossroad, 1986), p. 61.

41. Walter Burkert, *Creation of the Sacred: Tracks of Biology in Early Religion* (Cambridge, MA: Harvard University Press, 1996), p. 75.

42. Sigmund Freud, *The Future of an Illusion*, trans. J. Strachey (1927; New York: W. W. Norton, 1964), p. 26.

43. James Frazer, *The Golden Bough* (1900; New York: Mentor Books, 1959), p. 40.

44. Dossey, *Healing Words*, p. 18.

45. James, *The Varieties of Religious Experience*, p. 195.

46. Ibid., p. 73.

47. Ibid., p. 55.

48. Guardini, *Prayer in Practice*, p. 59.

49. Christopher Bollas, *The Shadow of the Object: Psychoanalysis of the Unthought-Known* (London: Free Association Books, 1987), p. 13.

50. Guardini, *Prayer in Practice*, pp. 55, 57, 55, 58.

51. Ibid., pp. 58, 56, 58, 56.

52. Arnold Toynbee, quoted in Leonard R. Frank, ed., *Quotationary* (New York: Random House, 1998), p. 636.

53. Quoted in James, *The Varieties of Religious Experience*, p. 359.

54. Irving Greenberg, *The Jewish Way* (New York: Simon and Schuster, 1993), p. 142.

55. Dossey, *Healing Words*, pp. 114, 115–16.

56. Guardini, *Prayer in Practice*, p. 55.

57. James, *The Varieties of Religious Experience*, p. 382.

58. Hallesby, *Prayer*, p. 15.

59. Bollas, *The Shadow of the Object*, pp. 13, 33.

60. Quoted in James, *The Varieties of Religious Experience*, p. 69.

61. Terry Lynn Taylor, *The Alchemy of Prayer: Rekindling Our Inner Life* (Tiburon, CA: H. J. Kramer, 1996), p. 15.

62. Guardini, *Prayer in Practice*, pp. 7, 8.

63. Bollas, *The Shadow of the Object*, pp. 14–15.

64. Jones, *The Art of Prayer*, pp. 139, 67.

65. Hallesby, *Prayer*, pp. 14, 13.

66. See Daniel Stern, *The Interpersonal World of the Infant* (New York: Basic Books, 1985), p. 124.

67. Guardini, *Prayer in Practice*, p. 77.

9.
Angelic Encounters

Angelic beings have fascinated human beings for thousands of years. During several historical periods the fascination has developed into something of an obsession. One thinks of the Middle Ages, or more specifically of the thirteenth and fourteenth centuries, which saw a steady stream of artistic renderings, philosophical debates, and theological analyses, most notably perhaps the fourteen angelic books of Saint Thomas Aquinas's monumental *Summa Theologica*. The Black Death brought this golden age of angelology to an end—an end that was sealed officially, for Protestants at least, by Martin Luther's thundering condemnation of all the angelic tribes in the early sixteenth century. The mid-Victorian period also witnessed a growing absorption with angelic beings, who began to show up profusely in statuary, painting, and literature (we'll eventually have a look at one of Robert Browning's angelic poems). Freshly minted artistic depictions of angels adorned not only chapels and graveyards but also the drawing rooms of middle- and upper-class citizens with a robust appetite for these divine, winged creatures. By the inception of the twentieth century, angels had become both familiar and fashionable across the Continent, and in North America as well. The most recent period of absorption is of course our own.

"Over the last ten years," writes Sylvia Browne, "angels have penetrated the deepest consciousness of humankind."[1] We are witnessing, in

155

the words of Rupert Sheldrake and Matthew Fox, "the return of the angels."[2] In *Angels, A to Z*, James Lewis and Evelyn Oliver put it this way: "Not since the Middle Ages, when angels were thought to oversee all things material, have these winged beings loomed so large in the popular imagination. Angel books, angel jewelry, angel newsletters, specialized angel stores, and even an angel cover story in *Time* magazine (December 1993)—clearly we are in the midst of a national phenomenon, a steadily rising interest in celestial beings that is not just confined to the New Age movement. As a statistical indication of increasing interest, a 1992 Gallup Youth poll found that 76% of American teenagers believed in angels—up from 64% in 1978." These authors offer a general psychological and sociological explanation of this "national phenomenon" when they note, "In an age of uncertainty and upheaval, it is extremely comforting to believe in the existence of spiritual beings whose principal employment is the protection and encouragement of human beings."[3] Certainly one important source of the current angel craze are the sermons and writings of Billy Graham, particularly his best-selling volume *Angels: God's Secret Agents* (1954), which refuses to disappear from the bookstores and which guides many thousands of individuals yearly to the putative angelic realms. We might also observe, taking the hint from Lewis and Oliver, that angels have come to be bound up inextricably with the vastly influential New Age movement and its absorption in shamanic guides; channeled advisors; benign, loving goddesses; and even space aliens, who, says Keith Thompson in *Angels and Aliens*, may be in actuality our latest version of angelic companions arriving from the beyond to enlarge our minds and enhance the quality of our lives.[4] These days, one has only to turn on the television during prime time to find some angelic melodrama fashioning its profundities and mysteries for our consumption.

But the history of angels is not my concern here. If the reader craves knowledge of this vast, complex subject, she can walk over to the library and get started. It is enough to say, in passing, that angels appear to have originated in ancient Persia as Zoroastrianism with its two chief theological figures of Good and Evil hastened the dispersal of numerous, older, traditional spirits and demons, who eventually found their way, metamorphosed, into postexilic Judaism and the Old Testament (e.g., Jacob's angelic encounter in Psalm 91); into Christianity through the Old Testament, the Apocrypha (the books of Tobit and Enoch), and the angelology of Dionysius the Areopagite; and finally into Islam (the angel Gabriel dictates the Qur'an to Muhammad). The angelic presence in Christianity has been highly disputatious from nearly the beginning, by which I mean the Patristic period, with angels accepted by one official Council only to be rejected by another. For some Christians (such as Graham), angels glorify the Almighty and enhance His influence; for others (Luther), they distract Christians dangerously from the centrality of God, Who reigns in Christian hearts when devotion is directed toward Him and only Him. What angels are doing in this book should be obvious enough: I turn to them in an effort to develop my contextual contentions about the nature of religious belief—where it comes from and what it means.

ASKING AND RECEIVING IN DISTRESS

Our angelic protectors and companions discover their way to us through a variety of channels, one of which is prayer. Here are a few examples.

Diane has just enjoyed the midnight service at her country church. It is a snowy Christmas Eve, a very cold night in fact, yet she decides to trudge her way home through the mounting drifts and plunging temperatures. Before long, she finds herself exhausted, lost, and in considerable danger. Sensing the panic surging up within her frame, Diane cries out to the wintry sky, "Oh, God, I'm so afraid. Help me to get home!" Immediately upon concluding her supplication, she hears "beautiful music" and feels herself "floating on top of the snow," as if "she were in a dream." A moment later, she is standing in front of her house, safe and sound. Although "she has no memory of moving" since uttering her prayer, she is convinced an angel, "commanded by God," carried her lovingly to her "front door." She declares herself "exultant."[5]

Leaving her two small children at home in her husband's care, Peggy sets out in the Lincoln for the early-morning shift at a nearby hospital. It is a cold, wet, snowy day, and the roads are treacherous. As she "hits a curve" near a bridge several miles from her destination, Peggy suddenly loses control of her car, which begins to swerve dangerously, wildly, above the "frozen marsh some thirty or forty feet below." The vehicle is "obviously going to plunge through the guardrail." Wondering in sickly terror what will "become" of her children, Peggy cries out, "Oh God, help me!" An instant later, "a warm glow" begins to illuminate "the spinning car's interior." As she beholds this "glow," Peggy is "filled with an indescribable reassurance." The light "warms" her, "bathes" her in "contentment." It is, well, "heavenly." Peggy knows, "without exactly knowing how she knows," there is "no reason to be afraid." And sure enough, the car comes safely to a stop at the edge of the perilous slope. Amazed and profoundly grateful, Peggy "still likes to tell people about the day an angel met her on a bridge and gave her a glimpse of heaven."[6]

A similar "miracle" occurs when Alex loses control of his vehicle "on an icy road." Sliding toward the shoulder in fear, Alex calls to the "Archangel Michael" for assistance. "His car immediately move(s) back into the middle of the road—as if it ha(s) been pushed by a hand." There are no words to describe Alex's gratitude toward his angel for watching over him with such love and compassion.[7]

Scaling the face of a lofty cliff with her boyfriend, Chantal gradually recognizes the danger they've created for themselves. It is as treacherous to go up as to go down; the material at their hands and feet is crumbling, and only the tiniest of ledges supports their combined weight. Suddenly, without warning, Dale plunges to his death below. Horrified, yet mindful of her own precarious position, Chantal cries out, "Oh, God! Please don't let me die that way!" Immediately upon uttering this supplication, Chantal feels "as though the gateway between heaven and earth" has "opened." She sees "angels all around" her, like a "wall of protection," "buoying" her up, "holding" her, "closing in" to "keep her from falling." The "next thing" Chantal remembers is "looking up and seeing the cliff high above" her. "Somehow" she has "managed" safely to descend "more than three hundred feet of slippery wet shale." When she describes her ordeal to the sheriff an hour later, he is truly amazed. He can't understand how anyone could have made it down that cliff. Having encountered the angels, maintains Chantal, she appreciates not only that

God "exists" as a "loving, caring Being" but that His angels will also "always be with" her, to "follow" her, and to "assist" her "throughout life." "I don't think I saw [the angels] as much with my eyes as with my spirit," Chantal concludes.[8] Her "vision," in other words, did not amount to a full-blown hallucination.

Wayne, Paul, Heather, and Kelly have been "decreeing" (making prayerful contacts) with their angels for several weeks when they all pile into a car together and set off for church. A few moments later the unfortunate teens become involved in a terrible accident. An "18-wheeler" runs a red light and plows into their vehicle. Trapped in the wreckage but still alive, the youngsters are being steadily crushed by the weight of the metallic debris that presses down on them. They are in imminent danger of death. "Do your calls" [to the archangel Michael], breathes Heather to Kelly, who has become a veritable genius at "decreeing." Silently asking Michael for assistance, Kelly (who can't speak) "swears the truck instantly lift(s) a few inches," giving her and her companions time to twist free of the wreckage. At last they can "breathe." As help arrives and workers spend "hours" removing the teens from the horrid, tangled mess, they remain "perfectly calm, comforted by the presence of Michael," who has "saved them all."[9] From the angel literature that surrounds us today, I could cite hundreds of similar accounts. Indeed, thirty minutes in a well-stocked religious or New Age bookstore will provide the seeker with as much as he can handle.

We recognize at once in these vignettes a striking variation on the basic biological situation, as we've described it from the outset and particularly in the chapter on prayer just concluded. An individual is in distress, in need of succor and support; the individual cries out. Then what happens? A powerful, loving caregiver arrives to transform the situation. Pain and fear are changed to comfort and security. The crisis passes. Over and over again during the course of the early period this is exactly what the infant experiences, and not only experiences but internalizes deeply into his mind-brain as a central affective, synaptic strategy for dealing with the world that lies before him developmentally. As the previous chapter makes plain, religious narrative and practice—prayer above all—are overwhelmingly devoted to underscoring and strengthening this behavioral configuration in the human creature, who copes on his own with the environment he inhabits. Indeed, the official theological instructions for individual, subjective prayer actually require the practitioner to enact an *imitation* of the basic biological situation itself. We must turn to God in supplication "as an infant in distress turns to his mother," declares Guardini.[10] "All we can do is cry" to God, asserts Hallesby. We must "let our holy and almighty God care for us just as an infant surrenders himself to his mother's care."[11] We must adopt an attitude of helplessness, of dependency, of submission. We can do nothing for ourselves. We can only trust in God. And if we mind our teachers and supplicate successfully, if, in short, we succeed in "priming" ourselves so as to jog our state-dependent memory and thus *map* our previous experience onto our present situation, we make contact, we feel God's presence; He comes to us in love and compassion; He assists us; He cares for us; we are with Him; He is *there*. With the angelic encounters we've just sampled, by contrast, *there is no reason to imitate anything*. The actual situation creates both the attitudes the pray-er is encouraged to adopt, and the results the pray-er is encouraged to await. The individual who prays is *already* in "distress" (Guardini), *already* helpless, *already* needy, dependent, vulnerable, and submissive. In a word, the individual in these vignettes is thoroughly *primed* for the emergence of the attractor state and the reactivation of the early pattern that marked the core of his interaction with the loving provider—the basic biological situation. The prayer that summons the angelic helper is *forced* out of the pray-er by the circumstances in which he discovers himself. Here, we see prayer returning to its origin as biological "cry" (Hallesby), biological call for assistance, the *sound* the baby makes as he summons his precious provider. Accordingly, prayer *verbalizes* the instinctual, primitive communication uttered by the little one in the exigency of his needs, from nourishment and protection to succor and love. Elizabeth Clare Prophet offers us the ideal prayer for "summoning" angelic assistance in her practical handbook, *How to Work with Angels*. It goes as follows: "Help me! Help me! Help me!"[12] For the user of words, this is about as close as it gets to simply bellowing out one's gut-level "distress." We've all heard the cliché that there are no atheists in foxholes. Each of the situations in which the individual finds himself in our foregoing angelic encounters is a "foxhole," that is, a crisis capable of jogging implicit memory and reactivating the oldest and most engrained defensive pattern in the human range of hallucinatory, protective responses.

As for the magical quality of such primal enactment, we note Roheim's observation that "magic must be rooted in the child-mother situation because in the beginning the environment simply means the mother. Therefore, wishing or manifesting the wish is the proper way to deal with the environment." And again, "Magic originates from the child's crying when he is abandoned and angry; it is not merely the expression of what actually takes place in the dual-unity situation, but is also a withdrawal of attachment from the object to the means by which the object is wooed, that is, from the mother to the word and back again to the mother."[13] Here is the origin of not merely prayer's magic but the magic inherent in a wide range of human activities that impinge upon the supernatural realm, such as casting spells, channeling guides, and commanding invisible spirits: from the mother to the word and back again to the mother. As we have seen, the first relationship harbors, in addition to the joys of symbiosis, the sensations of omnipotence and narcissistic entitlement. When Erich Neumann reminds us in his celebrated book, *The Great Mother*, that "the original magical intention to move and influence the upper powers is preserved in almost all prayer,"[14] he draws our attention to the *willful* component in Prophet's instructional supplication, "Help me! Help me! Help me!" The baby may be weak and dependent, but he still has to summon the caregiver, just as the pray-er has finally to utter his prayer. Referring to the "ours and theirs" mentality the "religious" sometimes display toward the "heathenish" practices of "primitives" and "savages," Mary Douglas writes in *Natural Symbols*, "Sacraments are one thing, magic another; taboos are one thing, sin another. The first thing is to break through the spiky verbal hedges that arbitrarily insulate one set of human experiences (ours) from another set (theirs)."[15] She continues,

Sacramental efficacy works internally; magical efficacy works externally. But this difference, even at the theological level, is less great than it seems. For if the theologian remembers to take account of the doctrine of the Incarnation, magical enough in itself, and the even more magical doctrine of the Resurrection and of how its power is channeled through the sacraments, he cannot make such a tidy distinction between sacramental and magical efficacy. Then there is the popular magicality in Christianity. A candle lit to St. Antony for finding a lost object is magical, as is also a St. Christopher medal used to prevent accidents. . . . Both sacramental and magical behavior are expressions of ritualism. . . . I see no advantage . . . in making any distinction between magical and sacramental.[16]

Douglas renders the matter even more succinctly in *Purity and Danger*: "The division between religion and magic" is "ill-considered."[17] Whether we like it or not, then, we will find it ultimately untenable to make rigid, hard-and-fast distinctions between the realm of religion and the realm of magic in respect to both the human intentions that stand behind them and the perceptual features that accompany their expression. Permit me to apologize for the complexities—or better perhaps, the contradictions—that often lurk in human behavior.

A POTPOURRI OF ANGELIC ENCOUNTERS

Note this rich, compelling expression of the psychological pattern we discovered earlier, in our initial angelic vignettes. (I will highlight the major theoretical links.) "As a child," writes Karen, "I remember feeling the ecstatic presence of angelic beings—of joy and love all around me. I was not alone."[18] (The quotation reflects Winnicott's transitional realm, the "transitional objects" that move the child both toward the caregiver and away from the caregiver as separation proceeds. Karen's "objects" are of course psychical.) The most important "angelic presence" in Karen's life, however, turns out to be a real person, namely her father, to whom she is deeply attached: "He became my dearest angel. . . . I loved his big hands, the smell of his pillow in the morning. I loved his peacefulness and humor and his depth in quiet times. . . . My father was an angel" (pp. 28–29). Underscoring for us the omnipotence and primary

narcissism that reside in the parental bond and that often turn up in religion and magic as the practitioner identifies with an all-powerful God
and luxuriates in his position as one of God's special, beloved children,
Karen states that under her father's influence she felt like "Lois Lane"
interacting with her "Superman." She had only to touch "Daddy's little
finger" and she "could fly" (p. 29). Karen's adored and adoring father—
a Harvard-trained psychoanalyst as it happens—died suddenly of a
heart attack when Karen was barely thirteen and on the verge of adolescence, with its separation issues. The news "hit" her, she declares, "with
the force of an atom bomb." "The walls fell down, the floor dropped out,
the roof blew off, the sky caved in and I exploded." And then, in three
simple words that capture the central psychological dilemma of those
who turn to angelic and other religious beings in the first place, from
childhood onwards, "I was alone." What of Karen's mother? Absorbed in
her own grief and her own problems, the woman is unable to give her
daughter the solace she now requires. Nor do other people such as relatives and friends step in to fill the gap. "No one even held me," the
bereaved girl sadly notes (ibid.). Thus commences what Karen calls her
"disease" (p. 30), her ever-present "loneliness," her sense of "meaning-
lessness" and futility, her powerful "feelings of abandonment." The disease proves unrelenting.

For ten years Karen "drifts" through the world, a depressed, "lost,"
self-destructive "soul" (ibid.). She turns to alcohol, to drugs, to promis-
cuous sexual relations in an effort to numb the pain. Attending this high
school and that college, living in this small town and that big city, she
finally winds up in a tiny apartment near Manhattan's Central Park. One
summer evening she joins the crowd and attends a Simon and Garfunkel
concert in the park. As she takes in the music, she finds herself
"uplifted" and "inspired" by the "love and vulnerability" in the voices
of the youthful singers (p. 32). When she gets home, she wanders aim-
lessly over to her typewriter and taps out the sentence, "Simon and Garfunkel are angels." That "one sentence," states Karen, "changed my life
forever." She writes, "The word 'angel' suddenly lit up in Broadway neon
in a flash of light inside me. It was as if I had never seen it before. A door
opened in my heart and I heard music. I felt as if a spiritual bomb went

off in my psyche and filled my head with fairy dust." She continues, "Angels. It was like remembering a tremendous secret, one I never should have forgotten. There was something gigantic in that word, something timeless, almost taboo in its purity, something utterly mysterious yet inherently important to my life. Angels were a key to something enormous. They were a piece of a sacred door to a forgotten part of my own soul" (ibid.). (Several major items emerge here, and they are all inextricably related. First, the music of Simon and Garfunkel primes Karen for a resurgence of the loving attachment she knew during the early, symbiotic [preverbal] period and the later, transitional stage marked by the advent of language. Secondly, although Karen's mother appears to fail her child during the time in which the father disappeared, the mother was presumably "good-enough" [to use Winnicott's famous expression] to nurture and to raise a normal offspring who was capable of creating benign transitional entities [angels] and of transferring her affections to the male parent, as girls frequently do. We might also note how the specific *word, angel*, holds the key to the restoration of the vital, life-giving attachment. As Roheim renders the matter in discussing the origins of magic, the essential move is "from the caregiver to the word and back again to the caregiver."[19] There could hardly be a more vivid illustrative "case" than the one we have here.)

Once Karen *has* her word, her "angel lit up in neon," she simply will not let it go. "I instantly became captivated, infatuated. I started writing angel sentences, angel thoughts. They came to me out of thin air. For weeks, I wrote about angels in taxicabs and elevators, in subways, coffee shops, and walking down the street. . . . I laughed and cried. They were magical words. They came from a different place than I was familiar with. They came from Heaven" (pp. 32–33). And then, "I experienced something stainless, deathless, and immediate in the thought of an angel that I'd never known anywhere else. My angel thoughts were a thread of light for me to follow" (p. 33). (The "thread of light" Karen follows in her "angel thoughts" functions as a kind of psychic umbilicus that leads her toward the inward, idealized, "heavenly" attachment upon which her well-being depends. Her mind is now striving to *map* the early, symbiotic period onto the "disease" of separation and loss, something she was incapable of doing throughout the period of her self-destructive grief. She is being pulled toward what we have contextually termed the attractor state. Although Karen "hears music" [Simon and Garfunkel?] as her "heavenly" transformation occurs, she does not experience full-blown hallucinations, yet.)

The return of Karen's transitional companions holds her steady for a couple of years. She is writing about angels, she is beginning to prophesy, and she is trying to publish her work. Then disaster strikes again in the form of a lost relationship, this time with a treasured lover upon whom she relied for companionship. "Heartbroken," feeling that she has "hit bottom" for a second time, Karen decides to attend "chapel" on a regular basis and to "request guidance" from her angelic friends (ibid.). In short, she begins to *pray*. (The transitional pattern of inward attachment is no longer adequate for Karen. She must go deeper, must follow the "thread" all the way to the foundational levels that reflect and fully restore the basic biological situation, the symbiotic attachment to the caregiver and the omnipotence and narcissism that characterize the primal bond.) The defensive, restorative strategy works, which is to say, the "asking and receiving" trigger the synaptic connections, the unconscious, state-dependent memories, Karen seeks in the midst of her latest, painful separation. No longer does she simply *think about* and *dwell upon* angels as symbols, as *words*; she experiences their *actual presence* (as James's subjects experienced the presence of God), hears their voices, talks with them, knows indubitably they are *there*, just as her own *body*, her own *sensorium*, are *there*. Let's note the material that captures the aftermath of her passionate, successful supplication: "To my blissful amazement, I asked questions and heard real answers, eloquent sentences, whole paragraphs, life-altering speeches, flowing just for me" (ibid.). (Karen is beginning to channel supernatural entities; the transformational object is talking; religion [as we usually conceive of it] is fading off into magic [as we usually conceive of it].) "As I became more receptive, I found these loving . . . angels right inside me, sitting next to my every thought. . . . I laughed and cried with them, letting go of my hardened pain. . . . Soon I felt continuously surrounded by angels and deeply loved. I knew my needs were finally, fully appreciated, and I felt . . . befriended for the first time since my father's death" (pp. 33–34). (Narcissism or perhaps "self-esteem" is restored through loving contact with the primary internalization; Karen's "high" is the flip side of her anger at being "low.") "My worries ceased, . . . my insecurities ended. . . . Now I have a sense of safety and protection that extends beyond the boundaries of my activities and the activities of the world" (p. 34). (Here is the original symbiotic union, providing an all-encompassing sense of security, of being *held* by an all-powerful parental provider; the "boundaries" established in separation are removed.) Karen is changed, transformed, "graced" (p. 36): "Little by little the angels have brought me back out into the sunlight and surrounded my heart with the fresh air of living. My heart is alive now because it knows it has angels" (p. 35). (The search for the transformational object within the mythic structure of religious, angelic lore is reaching its benign, defensive conclusion.) Most of all, Karen now believes, now *feels*, that she will never be *alone* again; she is attaining through her hallucinatory experience the central goal of all religious and much magical behavior: "Angels don't die, you see [as Father died]. . . . You can't lose them as you lose people. The deep answer to my dilemma was simple. Angels are eternal. . . . Angels will always take care of us [note Karen's ineluctable dependency]. They will never go away" (ibid.). (The primal trauma of Mahlerian separation, painfully reawakened by the father's sudden demise, is expunged through prayerful restoration of the basic biological situation (now the attractor state) fetched from the land of infantile amnesia and projected into the supernatural, angelic sphere. Here is Erikson's "hallucinatory sense of unity with a maternal matrix,"[20] religion's underlying, unconscious obsession in the widest, most general sense.) Karen sums up this phase of her angelic adventures by observing that "out of necessity" she began to "pray" and that "out of love" the angels began "to speak to me." And then, "angels: the word has become the seat of my existence" (p. 36). Once again we appreciate the accuracy of Roheim's formulation: from the caregiver to the word and back again to the caregiver. The preverbal mind-brain (or the unconscious) wishfully maps the basic biological situation onto the current problem or crisis that confronts the individual. Religion is largely an institutional framework designed to facilitate precisely such mapping.

It isn't long before Karen manages to make contact not with mere angels but with the Almighty Himself. It is one thing to "believe in God," she notes; it is another to have direct, personalized access to His divine, "omnipotent ear" (p. 37). (Karen seeks unconsciously to complete her defensive return to the early period by reactivating her participation in the omnipotence of the original parent-child bond and of course in the narcissistic gratification that accompanies dual unity.) Pouring out her heart, praying with great intensity, Karen asks for a "sign" (ibid.). Is He there? An instant later Karen hears a kind of tapping sound coming from the direction of her typewriter, the one on which she wrote the sentence that brought down the angels. But how can this be? She is alone in the room. Is God signaling to her? Sure enough, almost simultaneously with her question, she receives her answer: more tapping emanates from the typewriter. "God," Karen concludes from this extraordinary incident, has given her, Karen, her own "private miracle" (ibid.). She is now in ear-to-Ear contact with an omnipotent Being Who is singularly devoted to *her* wants, *her* needs. (Thus does Karen magically restore the egocentric position of primary narcissism and omnipotent merger. Her earlier sensation of angelic presence, along with the experience of inwardly hearing her angelic messengers, blossoms directly into external, aural hallucination within a prophetic context—the typewriter as the source of Karen's special, inspired knowledge of the angelic sphere.)

Shortly after God makes His presence known to Karen (who speaks to us prophetically now as an expert on angelic beings), Karen makes contact with the dead, specifically her precious "daddy" (p. 38). The denial of death is at hand. It goes like this: praying earnestly in "chapel," Karen suddenly *sees* her dead parent in her mind as a "vision." She writes, "It was not my imagination, because it was so real. I saw him just outside the building on the little footbridge in the sun, leaning over the rail looking at me and the swans. In my mind, I went to him, and with his arm around me, we gazed at the swans together, just like in the old days. . . . I had a long, long conversation with him that day. It soothed my soul no end" (pp. 38–39). Nor do the "visions" cease: "About a week later, sitting at my desk, I felt that my father was with me again. . . . He was communicating how much he loved me, telling me he had received all my love as well. It was important for me to know not to grieve for him. He explained that he was surrounded by very loving beings, that his spiritual progress was continuing in a marvelous, rewarding way, and that we would always, always know each other. He . . . let me know I was being carefully watched over. It was a most transforming encounter" (p. 39). (The unconscious "program" is now revealed to us in its entirety: from the father's sudden demise and the traumatic separation that succeeded it to the plangent music which primes Karen for the reawakening of her transitional companions in "neon," to the obsession with the word *angel*, to the growing hallucinatory tendencies that through prayer and the consequent triggering of the attractor state ultimately restore the lost parent who now abides *here*, with Karen, forever more.) Without exception, the psychological features and items that inform this emotional, affective odyssey derive from a synaptically configured, deeply internalized relationship with real human beings, and from nowhere else. What Karen offers us in this candid, autobiographical account of her "angelic" transformation is a veritable lesson in the naturalistic, bodily origins of the putative supernatural domain.

Although prayer constitutes the official, theological method for engaging one's guardian angel, or angels,[21] a great many angelic encounters transpire without the presence of overt, explicit supplication. Here are a few representative examples from the literature, similar in content to hundreds of others currently sitting on the shelves of the bookshops and libraries. A child of twelve named Margaret finds herself racing home one summer afternoon in the midst of a terrible thunderstorm. Her father has advised her to wait the storm out at a friend's house, but Margaret has ignored her father's words. "What if Daddy was right?" she asks herself. "What if a bolt of lightning really did hit?"[22] A few moments later, standing "exposed and vulnerable" near a neighbor's swimming pool, the girl begins to panic: "A thunderclap that shook my teeth broke over me and lightning seemed to reach nearer the ground. . . . I was positive that the next lightning flash would spear me like a fish." At precisely this point Margaret sees her guardian angel: "She was standing just a few feet from me, the most exquisite, holy, beautiful being I have ever seen. To this day, the image has remained vivid in my mind. She was surrounded with a blue-white light, brighter than the lightning, that glistened and shimmered in spite of the storm. She had a beautiful complexion, and her thick hair was long, and golden, and wavy, and her eyes were a vivid blue. Around her head was a golden circlet like a headband."[23] Margaret goes on, "I remember that the wonderful white light obscured the lower half of her body so that I couldn't see her legs or feet. I just remember the upper part of her body. She was very tall. The sight of my angel cut into my fears as a hot knife cuts into butter. Her face was so peaceful, so quiet and confident, and I felt some of that peacefulness come into me." And finally, this time with indication of both seizure and an aural hallucinatory component: "Time seemed to stand still while I stood there; at first I was a little taken aback and stunned, even apart from my fear of the storm; and then she spoke to me. I don't remember the exact words anymore, but I know she told me not to be afraid, to be calm, that I wasn't paralyzed anymore—I could walk away from the pool. . . . I found that my legs worked once more, and I wasn't trembling in fear. Suddenly I felt very peaceful and safe. It's a feeling you never forget. . . . All of my fears of being struck down by lightning went away, and I began to run toward my home."[24] The absence of explicit supplication here suggests that "prayer," under certain conditions, may well occur entirely within the unconscious regions of the mind-brain. The crisis we behold—the terrified child in the midst of the thunderstorm—is such that the internalized caregiver in the narrational, hallucinatory guise of "angel" simply arises from the unconscious level to bring relief to the distressed individual. The "guardian" comes through. The "prayer" involved in this instance is not forced out verbally from the mouth of the believer, as it was in our opening vignettes; rather, it implodes into consciousness in the form of the "creature" itself: the angel *is* the asking symbolified, and the angel *is* the receiving imagistically rendered. The "cry," in short, emerges *implicitly* from Margaret's "paralyzed" condition as a kind of frozen, visual, hallucinatory scream, one that fetches immediately the benign, succoring, maternal apparition. Let's recall for a moment Bollas's pivotal description of the early period during the course of which the mother, "as the infant's other self," actually "transforms the baby's internal and external environment," over and over again, thousands of times, on a daily, hourly, moment-to-moment basis, changing pain into pleasure and distress into security. "The resolution of discomfort," writes Bollas, "is achieved"—and here are the decisive words—"by the apparition-like presence of the mother," who arrives in timely fashion to address the child's needs, to make things "right."[25] The apparitional angel we witness in Margaret's harrowing adventure is a direct, visual, unconscious reactivation of the "angel" we internalize into our synaptic structure during the first weeks and months of our existence on the planet.

Alone at home one day in the seventh month of her initial, difficult pregnancy, Jana, who is thirty, finds herself experiencing short, sharp pains in her abdomen. At first she does not worry very much about her discomfort, assuming such pains are "normal" for a woman her age.[26] However, when the pains not only persist but dramatically increase in their intensity, Jana realizes that something may be terribly wrong: "The agony took my breath away. I thought for certain I would pass out. . . . I feared for my baby's life." Staggering toward the couch to rest a moment before calling the doctor, Jana suddenly "feels" a "heavenly presence, an angelic presence in the room." In words that bear significantly on the hallucinatory component of religious experience, she declares, "It was as though it [the angelic presence] came through the ceiling of the den, although I didn't see it actually come through the ceiling. In fact, although I saw it clearly, I didn't really see it at all. I can't begin to describe what I experienced, because it wasn't from this world."[27] Helping us to apprehend the way in which the supernatural entity drifts in from the realm of implicit memory to interfuse itself with current perceptual events, thus creating an awesome, "spiritual" moment for the one who cannot perceive the naturalistic origins of the occurrence, Jana continues: "The presence I felt was bigger than I was, or maybe it was a light, an essence, a being, a totality. All of those words are partly true, but none of them is really accurate. I saw, but not with my eyes. I heard, but not with my ears. It was all beyond my senses, so much so, in fact, that they were obsolete, almost a hindrance. . . . But it was real, much more real than I am, much more concrete than any of my senses. In comparison with that spiritual presence, I was the one who felt light, of little substance. It was the angel that was real."[28] And again, this time with language that recalls the basic biological situation, the original, symbiotic interaction with the *transformational object* at the center: "As I watched, this being, this presence came down, as soft as a feather, and settled over me and around me, beneath me and within me, filling me with its presence and its love and healing. At once, all of the pain that was racking my body simply dissolved into the being's energy and was transformed." Observe how Jana underscores the role of *love* in all this: "I feel that the angel just saturated me with love, not like any love I've ever known or that we know fully on earth. The love was indescribable, but I knew it was love, love of everything, unconditional, unquestioning, all-inclusive."[29] The mysterious, unearthly, "unknown" quality of this pervasive angelic "love" is linked directly to the "forgotten" primary years, the years that are no longer accessible to explicit recollection and that comprise the core of our affective nature as it emanates from the unconscious sphere. As Tomkins reminded us in previous chapters, the early period is essentially and foundationally *affective*.[30] It is *feeling* that resides at its developmental center. It is *feeling* that reinforces the instinct of attachment, bonding the child with the life-sustaining parent. Let's also note, finally, how Jana's vivid portrayal captures the inevitable, traumatic *separation* from the initial symbiotic interaction as it is implicitly reawakened here: "But when the angel began to separate its presence from me, lifting up, so to speak, from me, I felt the separation keenly. I wanted to go with it; the longing was sharp and urgent. In that moment, I didn't care about anything on earth any longer. . . . I said, 'please don't go!' . . . I still cry when I think of it."[31] So perceptually authentic is Jana's angelic encounter, so reflective is it of the mind-brain's primal, synaptic internalizations and of the powerful, interactional conditioning that marks the early time, that the departure of Jana's angelic caregiver actually triggers the old program, the anxiety and sadness of the child's developmental move away from the symbiotic orbit, as we traced that move contextually through Mahler's clinical depictions.

The most decisive, unqualified separation we experience as grown-ups is of course our demise, our biological, affective disappearance from the world forever. It will come as no surprise that this traumatic hour is frequented by angelic figures. If we crave supernatural magic to ease our way in the world, we also crave it to ease our way out.

1. Dying of peritonitis in a hospital bed, young Joey, age eleven, exclaims, "Look, Mother, there are angels all around us, and one is more beautiful than the rest." When Joey's mother declares her inability to detect the angels, Joey insists, "See, they're right here, so close I could touch them." Anderson writes, "Joseph's grieving mother was struck by her son's attitude of profound joy and peace. It became a consolation to the entire family."[32] The angels soothe both the dying and their grief-stricken survivors, who also undergo the trauma of separation.

2. Visiting a friend on her deathbed, one of Anderson's subjects reports having spied a group of angels in the hospital room, an entire "company" of them, in fact: "Oh! There are angels here."[33] Just to approximate the terrifying specter of cessation may be enough to trigger the attractor state, to awaken the defensive, angelic program buried deep within the mind-brain of the believer.

3. On the point of expiration, Andy suddenly senses the presence of his "angel." He writes, "I felt my angel reach out to me and wrap his (or maybe her or its) arms around me in a gesture that was so protective and loving and caring and understanding I have no words to describe it. And whether or not I actually heard words [i.e., was on the brink of hallucination], my angel communicated to me that I was going to be all right. I felt such reassurance and peace, and I understood that I was in the care of a loving God who had sent the angel as a sign of that love [the religious, orthodox aspect of angelic narrative]. The immense strength of that angel flowed through me, healing me, restoring me to life. I can't possibly convey what it was like to share in the life energy, the personal strength of the angel [the attunement and omnipotence of the primal symbiosis]. And then the experience softly dissolved, and my spirit was reunited with my body." Andy concludes, "In whatever time or timelessness it took for that angel to wrap its arms around me, something deep in my heart changed for the better and forever. When my consciousness was restored I was different, and I knew I was different. . . . Not

only did I see the need for a complete change in my life, I felt empowered to make those changes, because the strength of my angel was with me, too."[34] Here, the "near-death experience," as such moments are dubbed today, underscores for us theoretically not only the loving symbiosis of the primal bond but also the deeply internalized transformational nature of the early parent-child interaction. Omnipotence, attunement, and transformational affect are integrally conjoined in the defensive reactivation Andy captures for us with this angelic vignette.

Not only do angelic encounters transpire in the absence of overt, explicit supplication; they also transpire in the absence of overt, explicit crisis. Granted that crisis and prayer are the usual accompaniments of these supernatural events (babies are always demanding or requiring something), our angelic friends often appear spontaneously in neutral or even benign motivational contexts. Here are four brief, representative examples. As we go, note in particular the emphasis on security, love, energy, and transformation.

1. Caroline is experiencing the blahs; her life seems flat, boring, humdrum, meaningless as she goes about her business. "Is that all there is?" she asks herself.[35] After communing with a close friend one day, Caroline becomes convinced that she has "not been feeding" her "spirit." She decides to take up meditation and also to start walking in the country. Several weeks later, upon returning home from an outing, she feels as though she can "see and hear beyond what [she] would see and hear in a normal sense of awareness" (the incipient move toward a hallucinatory episode). A few days after this, alone in her office at work, Caroline begins to detect a "presence" in the room, a "presence" that shortly turns into an outright "vision." Here is the account: "I looked up, and it seemed to me as though the entire end of the room had opened up, and a light was growing in its place. The back wall, the floor, the ceiling—all faded away, to be replaced by the most incredibly beautiful light I have ever seen. I had the impression that the light had far more substance than the room, and had overlaid its reality onto that of the room, replacing it, for the moment, or that the room had become a tunnel, with one end

completely open to the light. . . . And standing there in the midst of the light appeared a very quivering, vibrating, pulsating being of light with outstretched wings that curved down a bit at the tips, as though they were reaching out to embrace me, and a face that was very loving." Caroline goes on: "The angel was . . . tall. The room was about eight feet from floor to ceiling, and I had the impression the angel was taller; perhaps the body was about ten feet tall. Keep in mind that the end of the room had totally faded out. . . . I felt such love reaching out toward me and all around me as I had never experienced before. I had the sensation of knowing I was never alone, that this being was always with me in some way to comfort me [the primal symbiosis restored; separation denied]. The face was full of compassion, loving, soft, and gentle. There was a tremendous love energy in the room.[36] As the "vision" begins to "fade," Caroline knows that her life has been "transformed" forever. "Bathed" in angelic "energy," she decides to leave her old job as a clinical, homeopathic assistant and move into the field of "relaxation therapy" on her own. The blahs are gone for good. Caroline now possesses the "answer" for which she has always been "searching."[37]

2. "Angels have been a positive and visible presence in my life as long as I can remember," writes Fran. "I am unafraid and secure when they are around. I have learned to distinguish their presence by a certain feeling. It is not euphoria or elation or wild heart-pounding. It's security, serenity." One day, Fran is invited to attend the mass in which her young son's class is participating. As the service commences, Fran begins to see "lights" coming into the sanctuary "from all directions." So bright are these holy presences, these "angels," that Fran has to "close her eyes." When she opens them a moment later, the angelic presences are gone. Fran is not sure why angels entered the church at that particular moment, but she is confident an explanation will eventually be granted to her by the Almighty.[38]

3. Ralph and Marion are enjoying a walk through the woods one crisp spring morning. "We frequently took walks in the country," notes Ralph, "and we especially loved the spring after a hard New England winter." In the midst of their "happy, peaceful" stroll, they suddenly hear "voices in the distance." "We have company in the woods this

morning," Ralph remarks to Marion. But when they "turn to look," they see "nothing." A moment later, they perceive that the "sounds" are not only "behind" them but "above" them as well.[39] Ralph writes, "How can I describe what we felt? Is it possible to tell of the surge of exaltation that ran through us? . . . For about ten feet above us and slightly to our left was a floating group of glorious beautiful creatures that glowed with spiritual beauty. We stopped and stared as they passed above us. There were six of them, young beautiful women dressed in flowing white garments and engaged in earnest conversation. If they were aware of our existence they gave no indication of it. Their faces were perfectly clear to us, and one woman, slightly older than the rest, was especially beautiful. Her dark hair was pulled back into what today we would call a ponytail. . . . She was talking intently to a younger spirit whose back was toward us. . . . Neither Marion nor I could understand their words although their voices were clearly heard. The sound was somewhat like hearing but being unable to understand a group of people talking outside a house with all the windows and doors shut."[40] A moment after this angelic group has "floated past" them, Ralph turns to Marion and asks, "What did you see? Tell me exactly, in precise detail. And tell me what you heard." He then declares to the reader, "She knew my intent—to test my own eyes and ears to see if I had been the victim of hallucination or imagination. And her reply was identical in every way to what my own senses had reported to me." Ralph comments on the remarkable, extraordinary episode this way: "Perhaps I can claim no more for it than that it has had a deep effect on our own lives. . . . Since Marion and I began to be aware of the host of heaven all about us, our lives have been filled with a wonderful hope. Phillip Brooks, the great Episcopal bishop, expressed the cause of this hope more beautifully than I can do: 'this is what you are to hold fast to yourself—the sympathy and companionship of unseen worlds.'" From that fateful moment on, both Ralph and Marion have experienced "a feeling of assurance about the future."[41]

4. Amber has just arrived home for the Christmas holidays and is feeling good about it. The only discordant note is her recent separation from her husband, who won't be there to enjoy the season with

her. As she walks about the familiar countryside one quiet, peaceful morning, "appreciating how beautiful" everything is, she suddenly spies an angel standing right in front of her: "At first, when I saw her I didn't even know what I was seeing. It was a formless shape, a bright light. . . . Then I saw the most beautiful thing I ever saw in my life. The white was so white and her wings looked like the stomach on a duck—fine and soft and white. It was the most incredible thing I ever saw! It's not like you could have reached out and touched her. It was like a vision with your eyes open. Like she was somewhere else, but I saw her." Not long after this Amber notices the disappearance of a painful "cyst" from which she has been suffering for years. "Since I saw the angel," she writes, "it's completely gone. No more pain!" Moreover, "My husband and I are back together." Amber now sees "miracles happening around [her] all the time." She will never again be the "selfish girl" she was before she spied her "beautiful angel."[42]

The path to theory is somewhat different here from that of our previous vignettes, where the pray-er reactivates through his ritualistic behavior the basic biological situation of asking and receiving, and where crisis triggers the attractor state through the subject's sharp, unconscious longing for the protection and care of the early symbiotic interaction. The underlying psychodynamics of the encounters we've just examined are rather more diffuse and not as easily teased out. We can of course speculate: Caroline may be struggling with a mild depression that is about to run its course. Her pivotal conversation with a friend in which she is encouraged to "feed" her spiritual life may well have served to prime her for the emergence of her "angel," much as the music of Simon and Garfunkel primed Karen for the emergence of her transitional companions. Fran is obviously a "religious type," that is to say, an individual given to experiencing supernatural presences through deep-seated hallucinatory tendencies in her own personality working in combination with her lifelong religious training. She is prone to crave continuous, symbiotic contact with her unconscious inducers of "security and serenity." Amber may be experiencing a forceful combination of "priming" or precipitating factors: her separation from her husband, her return to the familiar setting of "home," and the advent of the Christmas season, a time of warmth, closeness, belonging. The combination may have triggered the emergence of symbiotic and transitional longings as we witness them symbolized in the figure of her "beautiful angel," the supernatural agent of her physical and emotional transformation (the cyst, the end of "selfishness"). Ralph and Marion may offer us an example of how supernatural or spiritual occurrences can be transferred psychologically from one individual to another through a process of unconscious suggestion, or contagion. The voices the two of them ostensibly heard may well have been those of real people present in the woods; however, when no real people were discovered during the brief interval of their investigation, they embarked upon their uncanny, angelic adventure. Needless to say, their religious background, fully disclosed to us by the end of the account, contributed something to their amazing visions. But we can't be sure—not only in reference to Ralph and Marion, but also in reference to Fran and Amber and Caroline. Just as prayer and crisis do not always result in angelic encounters, so angels may emerge (as I earlier stated) in the absence of crisis and prayer. Like all supernatural creatures, they are licensed by the mind-brain to come and go against an endlessly variegated background of unconscious, affective longings, or needs. What we can underscore confidently here, in keeping with our overall contextual approach, is the following: *the attractor state tends to attract.* The unconscious wish for the early time, for the security and love of the first relationship, is always alive and humming with seductive psychological energy beneath the surface events of our existence. Through innumerable precipitating or "priming" factors in innumerable particular motivational contexts, an endless variety of human beings are drawn to their idealized, Edenic beginnings as those beginnings emerge disguisedly from the mnemonic mists of spiritual experience, including the hallucinatory experience of angels.

Note this compelling angelic narration that takes us straight to the psychological border between what we usually think of as magic and what we usually regard as religion. "From my earliest childhood recollections," writes Kim, "I can vividly remember the presence of special, unseen companions who talked with me, and protected me. As a child, I fully accepted and believed in the reality of their existence." Kim continues, "One day I became suddenly curious about why such special companions would choose to play with ordinary little me. My companions explained they were my guardian Angels who were sent from heaven to guide and watch over me."[43] And then, with another suggestion of a hallucinatory component and reminding us of the commonality of hallucination among preschoolers, Kim explains, "Although I couldn't see them, I could always hear their voices whispering inside my head, and I began to develop a method of communication with them that allowed us to privately talk back and forth, as if we were communicating over a telepathic telephone. Even as a small child, I would practice communicating with my Angels by thinking about a question, and moments later, they would reply with an answer that I could readily understand. It was so effortless and so much fun to practice, I discovered it didn't take any time at all for me to fully develop this communication with my Angels, and soon we became the best of friends" (pp. 3–4). Here we recall Winnicott's depictions of the transitional realm, the psychological space of benign illusions in which the child manages to move toward the caregiver and away from the caregiver all in the same psychological moment. Kim's angelic experiences come to an abrupt halt when she turns eleven; however, they are by no means gone for good.

In her early thirties Kim discovers herself in crisis, a major goad of angelic encounters, as we have seen. Her business is bankrupt; her marriage is on the rocks; she is eating everything in sight; and she finds herself unable to sleep. She declares, "I was an emotional wreck, . . . killing myself with stress. . . . I was at the lowest point of my life. . . . I felt like a total failure" (pp. 6–7). At precisely this juncture, "suddenly," and "without any warning," the angels rush back into Kim's existence: "The intuitive messages began again from my Angels" (p. 6). The "intuitive information" began "exploding inside of me." "I was 'picking up' psychic energy from everyone and anyone who came near me. The intuitive information from my Angels came into my head loud and clear, just as it had when I was a child." Confused at first, Kim comes gradually to realize that her life is being altered by her angelic friends. She begins to offer to those around her not only advice but psychic messages and interpretations that she's receiving from the beyond (the commencement of hallucinatory channeling, common among both religious prophets and magicians). She tells a doorman to call his sister in Florida, and it is a good thing that he does (p. 7)! She reassures a coworker who has just undergone medical testing that her tests will come back negative. She smilingly remarks to an acquaintance that marriage is in the cards, and soon! And when she learns that her predictions and instructions turn out one and all to be "right" (p. 12), she finally understands that she has of a sudden been gifted with supernatural powers, presented with a higher calling. It is a "heavy responsibility," but she has "no other choice" (p. 8). She must give in and go along with her transcendent destiny (the restoration of omnipotence and primary narcissism through hallucinatory regression to the early period). Accordingly, Kim sets up shop and before long becomes an influential spiritual counselor who receives with gratitude and grace the monies her "clients" pay her for her spiritual guidance, or as she puts it toward the close of her account, "for my time" (p. 180).

Surely the reader spies the underlying psychodynamics at work here. We have an individual in crisis, desperate, with self-esteem destroyed, emotionally and physically sick, facing marital separation, and given to angelic, supernatural encounters. Although Kim does not cry out for her "angels," as do our pray-ers, her severe distress primes her unequivocally for the psychic, hallucinatory return to her former companions, the transitional substitutes of the early years who lead back to the "object," the ultimate, naturalistic source of religiomagical activities. With the arrival of her "angels" Kim's life is transformed. Just as the actual caregiver arrives upon thousands of occasions to rescue and reassure the baby, to transform the baby's distress into satisfaction, so do Kim's supernaturals arrive to facilitate her transformational requirements in the midst of her crisis. From an impotent, sick, demoralized "failure," Kim, phoenixlike, is changed into the special, gifted receiver of angelic messages and the remarkable, telepathic guide of the mere mortals who surround her. Most of all, perhaps, she no longer finds herself alone. Not only does she have her admiring customers; she also has her angelic guardians, and she has them forever. As she expresses the matter prophetically, "We have the great privilege of being wrapped in an invisible cocoon of Angelic support, encouragement, love, and protection throughout our lives" (p. 13). It would be hard to find a metaphor for the symbiotic interactions of the early years more vivid than this "invisible cocoon" of love and protection.

THE HALLUCINATORY NATURE
OF RELIGIOUS EXPERIENCE

The conspicuous presence of hallucination in our potpourri of angelic encounters serves to underscore the thesis of our discussion as a whole: all religious experience is ultimately hallucinatory in nature. Note the word "experience." I do not have in mind here religious discussion, or theological argument, or intellectual affirmation of belief in the Parent-God. I have in mind only religious experience, which I will extend along a continuum of hallucinatory features or strength. At one end of the continuum (the weak end) the believer experiences a sense of God's presence, a feeling that the Almighty is somehow "there," not simply as a concept, an "idea," but as an actual, inward, affective accompaniment of his mental and bodily being. Prototypical expression of this basic religious experience may be discovered of course in a thousand places (some of which we've already examined) and is neatly captured for us in James's classic, *The Varieties of Religious Experience*, in which one of James's subjects declares, "God was present, though invisible; he fell under no one of my senses, yet my consciousness perceived him. It was . . . as if my personality was transformed by a *spiritual spirit*."[44] In other, later passages James strives to explain such a sense of God's presence through reliance on the general notion of "energy" working in tandem with the practice of prayer: "Energy which but for prayer would be bound," he states, "is by prayer set-free and operates in some part, be it objective or subjective, in the world of facts." And again (this time with a more noticeable religious flavor), in prayer "energy from on high flows in to meet demand and becomes operative; . . . spiritual energy, which otherwise would slumber, does become active."[45] To move along the continuum (toward the strong end) is to discover an increase in the hallucinatory component, as in for example our angelic encounters where subjects, in some instances, "see" things "but not with their eyes" and "hear" things "but not with their ears" (see Jana's account above); in other, stronger instances, subjects hear "actual" angelic "voices" and "stare" at "actual" angelic "faces," insisting all the while that their experience is not "hallucinatory" or "imaginary" (see Ralph's account above). As Emanuel Swedenborg, the famous eighteenth-century beholder of angels, expressed it in response to the charge that he was imagining things, "I have seen, I have heard, I have felt."[46] We are now in a position to understand naturalistically and psychologically how this seeing, hearing, and feeling come about, all the way from the mere sensation of God's presence to the full-blown sensorial witnessing of an angelic visitor. To put it somewhat differently, we are in a position to set aside permanently any and all reliance on the "transmundane" sphere (to use James's term), on "energies" emanating from "on high" to "meet" the "demand" (supplication) of the believer who feels, or otherwise sensorially perceives, the "actual" presence of the Parent-God or one of His manifestations.

Let's recall Erikson's pivotal assertion, cited above, that religion's aim is to create in the believer "a hallucinatory sense of unity with a maternal matrix." The process through which this "sense" comes about, or is actualized, has been the focus of this book to this juncture. I won't try to write the book again here but will merely state the following: during the course of the early period the basic biological situation of asking and receiving between caregiver and offspring is internalized synaptically into the mind-brain of the developing child to become a rooted perceptual-neurological response to subsequent events (an attractor state). Over and over again, thousands of times, for years, the needful child asks and receives through the ministering interventions of the all-powerful parental provider. Mnemonic development among humans is such that virtually all of this precious, foundational interaction is fated to go "underground," to pass into the unconscious realm through the advent of what neurobiology terms infantile amnesia. Accordingly, and in reference to religious experience, one remembers the early period *implicitly* when one is *primed* to do so by a wide variety of inward or external cues, including most notably (1) supplication, the theological instructions for which draw directly upon the asking and receiving of the basic biological situation, and (2) crisis, in many forms such as physical danger and personal setback (loss), which awaken implicit mnemonic longings for intervention by the succoring caregiver who is now projectively present as the benign Parent-God of religious narrative.

The perceptual-affective bridge from infancy and early childhood to the realm of the religious supernatural resides in what Winnicott terms the transitional stage of illusion (ages two to six, and frequently evincing hallucinatory features),[47] wherein the developing youngster discovers through play methods of arousing implicit memories of symbiotic interaction and thus moving both toward and away from the caregiver in the same psychological moment (i.e., separation anxiety is contained). Later, when religious practice (prayer) or religious narrative ("the omnipotent Parent-God loves you and protects you") jogs implicit memory by creating *states* that match the early time and thus restores the basic biological situation of asking and receiving, the believer not only returns unconsciously to his initial, primal symbiosis with the loving provider, he harbors the strong, conscious sensation that the objects of his religious devotion are present, are "there" in "reality," because he has inwardly fused those supernatural, projective entities with the *real people* upon whom his development (his "creation") depended "in the beginning." It is the "naturals" who engender the "supernaturals" within the unseen, "mysterious," unconscious realm. The inward experience of divine, spiritual presence or the hallucinatory experience of divine, spiritual manifestation can be awakened through an endless variety of association cues many of which cannot be directly discerned by either investigator or experiencer because of their subliminal or otherwise elusive quality.[48] Religious experience, then, is a kind of affective and perceptual *confusion* (taken in the etymological sense, from the earlier "fused"). The believer, with very good reason and entirely within the normal, nondissociative range of his perceptual and affective growth, erroneously takes the religious object to be externally existent. The religious narrative to which he accedes not only promises protection and care; it arouses at the synaptic level of his very mind-brain the unconscious, internalized materials that engender his confirmational experience of the Parent-God and His loving angels.

Although hallucinations are commonly associated with, and present in, mental disorders such as schizophrenia and psychosis, their mere occurrence in individual cases does not indicate psychological disturbance anymore than a crazy dream establishes the craziness of the dreamer.[49] Indeed, odd as it may appear at first glance, hallucinations are an ordinary, everyday occurrence within the full range of human behavior and can be precipitated by such mundane factors as fatigue, hunger, solitude, a bump on the head, or, as we may now appreciate, a heartfelt religious supplication. As a child, many years ago, I once spent a summer on a farm. Mice, as it turned out, were everywhere, and when I crawled into my bed at night I often had the distinct, horrid sensation that several of the furry little critters were running up and down my legs. Throwing the covers back and switching on the light—all in one swift, frantic motion—I immediately discovered to my amazement and relief that nothing whatsoever was there—other than my legs, I mean. That hallucinations are common among very young children in the midst of what Winnicott calls the transitional stage of illusion is of course well known. "People may experience hallucinations as part of their normal developmental stages," writes Derek Wood, "especially during the preschool years, in the 2–5 year old range." Wood continues, "Common causes of hallucination in people without a psychiatric diagnosis are exhaustion, sleep deprivation, social isolation and rejection, severe reactive depression, amputation of a limb (phantom limb syndrome), a reaction to medication, a reaction to hallucinogens such as LSD, a reaction to other drugs such as heroin and cocaine."[50] Terry Lynn Taylor offers us the following on this score: "When I asked children to draw pictures of angels, they usually put wings on them and depicted them watching over children doing things. . . . If you ask children who draw angels whether everyone sees the angels who are watching over them, they will usually say no and yes. They know that some people do see them, and that others do not."[51] Discussing a wide range of perceptual phenomena, Frank Bruno defines hallucinations straightforwardly as follows: "Hallucinations are false perceptions. The individual may see something or hear something that cannot be detected by others. Invisible companions, bugs crawling under the skin, the presence of dead friends or relatives, or the smell of nonexistent onions frying are all examples of hallucination."[52] Neil Bockian says simply that hallucination consists in "perceiving things that are not really there, such as hearing voices no one else hears."[53] Thus the inextricable tie between hallucination and religious experience in no way attests to the insanity, or abnormality, or instability of such experience within the world of human perceptual behavior. The presence of God in the experience of an ardent supplicator, for example, is neither more nor less than a "false perception" called up through unconscious associations emergent in the psychodynamics of prayer.

It is supremely important to our purposes here that hallucination commonly occurs when individuals find themselves *alone* and *in danger*, in other words, when circumstances unconsciously kindle the attractor state and restore the individual to the internalized program for union and intervention that is the synaptic, experiential heart of the basic biological situation taken deeply into the structure of the mind-brain during the early period. F. S. Smythe, for example, writes of a mysterious "friendly presence" in a vivid account of his attempt to climb Mount Everest in 1933: "A strange feeling possessed me that I was accompanied by another. *In its company I could not feel lonely nor could I come to any harm.* It was there to *sustain me* on my *solitary* climb up the snow-covered slabs. When I halted and extracted some mint cake from my pocket, it was *so near and so strong* that instinctively I divided the mint into two halves and turned round with one half in my hand to offer it to my companion" (emphasis added).[54] Elizabeth Clare Prophet's experience of angelic presences occurs during her eighteenth year, precisely as she is towed into the open sea on water skis for the first time: there it is, straight ahead, the deep, vast ocean; and lo and behold, angelic guardians suddenly arrive upon the scene. "I was headed out toward the ocean," Prophet states. "Suddenly I realized that I had entered another dimension. I could see not thousands but millions of angels. I could see that they were my friends, brothers and sisters, spiritual companions. . . . And I knew *I would never be alone* because the angels would always be with me" (emphasis added).[55] Supplication is explicitly, theologically, practically designed to arouse the attractor state through the pray-er's rigorous, orthodox imitation of the early parent-child interaction. We turn to God, maintains Guardini, "as the child in distress turns to his mother" (cited above). Through crises, and in particular crises of separation and danger, we experience not the ritualistic activation but the spontaneous activation of the attractor state and the hallucinatory, defensive appearance of "friendly" religious or nonreligious entities who extinguish our fears and erase our aloneness. The point is, the human animal, or "man" as we used to say, is often described by twentieth-century thinkers as a "theological being,"[56] that is, as a "being" whose chief inclination is to fashion a "reality" in which supernatural powers both accompany his journey through the world (denying separation) and offer him a chance at immortality through sacrifice as that journey comes to its conclusion (the final separation denied). What our contextual discussions reveal is the extent to which this "theological being" relies on hallucination to accomplish his astonishing purpose: the denial of separation and death. For it is "man's" hallucinatory capacity, his unconscious potential to resuscitate through implicit, state-dependent memory the *human* "immortals" of the early time, that engenders the supreme religious "mystery," namely the "mystery" of the "supernaturals" who are experientially "there" to annul separation and expunge the terrors of death. Theological man, in a word, emerges from hallucinatory man.

PHENOMENOLOGY OF ANGELS

Let's take a few pages, now, to explore the way in which angels are conceived, projected, and presented in the recent and current literature that strives to render their divine, supernatural essence. Some of this we've already determined, of course, through our potpourri of angelic encounters; but we can deepen and sharpen the overall picture by disclosing with some detailed precision the kind of affective longings that power the attractor state and provoke the "false perceptions" of religious (and in this case angelic) experience. What lies partially concealed at the theoretical level in our numerous angelic adventures we can bring fully into the light for the reader's careful inspection and evaluation. It may well be that the materials to follow, psychologically striking in themselves, are revealing not only of our relationships with angels but of our fundamental humanity as well.

Angels mitigate the pain of separation, obscuring the inescapable fact of our aloneness and separateness in the world. In the most general psychological sense, they serve a transitional purpose, one that reflects the purpose to which the child puts "the object" as he copes with the separation crises of his development. As we saw in our earlier theoretical sections and in the work of Mahler particularly, the process of separation never ends; it becomes a continuous lifelong issue, ever-pressing for some, intermittent for others, but always there at the level of our affective experience. The angels, more intimate, more personal, more approachable for many people than the Almighty seated upon His throne in heaven, emerge in the literature as vivid extensions of the stage when the developing youngster attempts through his transitional creations to retain his symbiotic contact with the caregiver at the same time that he moves away from the symbiotic orbit into the wider world. To express the matter metaphorically through figures we've only just set aside, the angels allow the believer to remain anchored in the security of the parental union as he ventures out into the sea of his own private, personal, existential voyage. We may recall Elizabeth Clare Prophet's realization, cited above, as she discovered her angels while being towed on water skis into the open ocean: "I knew I would never be alone." Here are a few arresting examples of this ubiquitous theme. "Since we were conceived," writes Eileen E. Freeman, "there has never been a time when our angels have left us or ceased to concentrate their attention on us, not even for a moment. . . . Our special angel is joined to us as long as we are on earth in an indissoluble partnership more intimate—and less well known or understood—than marriage. There is nothing anyone can ever do to rid themselves of their guardian angel. Even death itself is not a divorce."[57] Your "angels," are "always with you," declares Sylvia Browne; no matter who you are, or where you are, or what you are, you can be certain they are "there."[58] You have "one special angel that's with you all of the time," states Joan Webster Anderson in an interview; "you have other angels who come around you when you need some extra help." It is a "wonderful thing to believe," notes Anderson, who goes on, reflecting the hallucinatory component of specific transitional behaviors, "you can talk to your angel your whole life and he or she will always be there for you." In this way, concludes Anderson, those who are able to "communicate" with their angel will never resemble "children who have no one to nurture them," will never have to feel "alone" or "abandoned."[59] The "primary message" of the angels, writes Goldman, is this: "We are not alone."[60] It could hardly be more emphatic than that.

But our angels are not simply "there," to be "with" us, to blot out feelings of separateness and aloneness. On the contrary, they are busy doing things, acting on our behalf, concerning themselves with the requirements of our lives here on Earth, as all "good objects" should be doing. The pure transitional function is only the beginning for these projective "false perceptions." The first thing the angels do—and one might describe it as the first and foremost thing—is love us. That is, they fulfill the need for an affective accompaniment to the instinct of attachment to the primary caregiver on which our survival as dependent primates entirely rests, as we saw earlier in the work of Tomkins. Our angels are fairly dripping with their love for us; it is infinite, powerful, unconditional, and as pure as an infant's brow. The expression here is truly memorable: "No entity, other than God," writes Browne, "can ever provide us with the unhesitating magnitude of unconditional love than an angel can."[61] Our angels, says renowned angelologist Sophy Burnham in an interview, are always "loving us beyond our wildest imaginings that it is possible to be loved." Accordingly, "You don't see an angel with your mind. You see an angel with your heart."[62] Here is the accent on experience, on the inextricable unconscious tie between the projective religious entity and the internalizations of the early time, which reside, as it were, below the surface of our ordinary perception, thus opening the way for cued, confirmational affect to well up "mysteriously" from the realm of infantile amnesia. Our angels, states Goldman, not only tell us we are part of an "eternal family" and thus "never alone"; they tell us also that we are "unconditionally loved." In fact, she declares, our angels have "no other purpose" than "to love" us. Loving us is their only "function," their only "need"; they have no "personal desire."[63] What an idea! They have "only unlimited love," and it is for "us" and us alone. Our angels, holds Freeman, do not merely want to "communicate" their "love" for us; they "need" to. With this in mind, we can finally understand why they are there: "to love us." That is their "nature." And if for some reason we find ourselves struggling to love them back, they'll "empower" us to do so, to "love" them "face-to-face."[64] Even death can't stop the loving, maintains Freeman in another place, for death only leads to the "loving embrace of the angels," whom "we never have to leave again."[65] Here is the primal infantile wish in all its affective glory (tied, once again, to the biological instinct for attachment): endless, unconditional love from an infinite, eternal, perfectly loving source that has no other business in the universe but loving you. The ideal "object" of one's conscious and unconscious longings stands, or perhaps floats, naked before us announcing our foundational, infantile need: to be totally loved forever. This is what we are, love sponges; and this is what drives an attractor state powerful enough to rear up the supernatural, religious world as a whole: the fear of separation, including the separation of death; the thirst for attachment; and an inexhaustible appetite for loving attention. *Ecce homo.* Moreover, we may also understand at this juncture precisely what it is that possesses the power actually to bend our mind-brains such that they perceive falsely, hallucinate, or manufacture as supernatural presence or vision beings that are not "really there." It is not merely "the world" in some general sense that love makes "go 'round." It is the world of our human perceptions that love has the ability to distort or "confuse" as we seek high and low in the supernatural sphere for something, some god or some angel, capable of replacing the "object" we've lost and of assuaging our anxieties and love-hungers as we go about our separate lives on the planet.

When we combine the angelic promise always to be "there" with the angelic inclination to love us dearly and forever, we spy the affective undercurrent that produces the angel as ideal "companion," as a projective version of the "evoked companion" depicted earlier by Daniel Stern as the available trace of the "object" who has been internalized into the synaptic core of the child's mind-brain during the early period. And it is of course the capacity to evoke companionship, to call up the "object" through the developing mind-brain, that carries the youngster into the transitional stage, where he discovers through play the imaginary companions who hold him steady as he negotiates his emotive way through the anxieties of separation from the primary caregiver, a separation that both psychic growth and social surroundings require. As Stern writes, our evoked companions "never disappear."[66] They "lie dormant" throughout our lives to be repeatedly aroused by a wide variety of affective cues, including of course the notion of the loving angel that the individual encounters through religious narrative, to make use of as he wishes along the way.

"We are your companions," announces the "Archangel Uriel" to Prophet as she channels his messages from the divine to the earthly sphere for our benefit.[67] "Angels want to be our friends," writes Freeman, striving to illuminate their nature. "They are companions on the journey of life on this planet." Their aim, she continues, is to "share" that journey with us, to "guide" us and "support" us as we go. Unlike other putative "companions" whom we may find "in the realm of pure quackery," our angels are the real thing, our "authentic friends" upon whose "touch" we can always depend for "enrichment" and "growth."[68] In Sophy Burnham's view, "everyone is attended" by an "angel," in fact, "by more than one." Burnham goes on, "When we're spirits on the other side and decide to be born—we have already chosen the companions that will be with us for our entire lifetimes. . . . And when we die, which is to say when we go back to living, we will be with those spirits again and they are our friends." She concludes, "Any angel that you call on can bring you thousands more."[69] From our psychodynamic perspective, Burnham's "other side" is of course the implicit, amnesiac realm, the realm of unconscious memory, the source of our religiomagical projections, the wellspring of our heartfelt conviction, especially pressing perhaps in our anomic, urbanized, technological era, that we are "companioned" through life by "dozens" or "thousands" of unseen, loving, supernatural "friends." Loneliness is a powerful trigger of what we've been calling the attractor state, as is the notion of death, which Burnham seeks to erase simply by dubbing it "living."

The traditional angelic role with which we're all familiar is of course that of angel as "guardian." To explore this facet of angelic projections will move us toward the zone where religion and magic unite and also toward the psychological place where matters of loving companionship join up with considerations of power. As we've seen, angels are not simply "there"; they are busy loving us and keeping us company. But as vulnerable mortals on an imperfect and dangerous planet we require more than symbiotic affection: we require protection, security, strength—and to get that we require angelic companions who reflect the all-powerful, omnipotent quality of the original care-giving figures. In short, we require angels who are able to "watch over" us, to make sure we're "all right" and will remain "all right" as we confront a continuous stream of earthly trials. We need "angels" to "protect us" so that we may "get through our difficulties," states Anderson in an interview. Referring to the title of her book *An Angel to Watch Over Me*, Anderson stresses that we must "ask" our angels for "their protection" and their "help" to ensure that "everything is going to be okay" in our lives.[70] When we are united with our angelic companions, says Goldman, we know with certainty that "someone" is "watching over" us, someone who is "always near," a "guardian angel" who can "offer assistance" when assistance is required. We must be able, concludes Goldman, to call upon our angels "in bad times as well as good." "Don't wait for disaster," she lessons; "attract them now."[71] We are under "divine surveillance," declares Billy Graham; the angels are "watching" us and "ministering to us personally"; they are "concerned" with our safety and well-being. Indeed, holds Graham, "in times of danger" and of "crisis" when we are "miraculously preserved," we can be sure that our angels, our "wonderful friends," were there, through God's grace, to "protect us."[72]

As I've just suggested and now wish to underscore, this accent upon angelic power, guardianship, protection primes the believer for an implicit, unconscious return to the omnipotent dual unity of the early period wherein the child experiences, as "nearly a fact," to cite Winnicott's words,[73] the parent's all-powerful quality as an aspect of his own being. With ego boundaries as yet unestablished, parental omnipotence takes up its magical place within the little one's internalizing mind-brain to remain potentially arousable forever after, as witnessed in an endless variety of expressions, from the Superman comic to the arcane spell of the New Age wizard or witch. The current gravitation to angels, then, is inextricably tied to the omnipotence that is associated traditionally with their presence and existence. It is not simply love but power as well that triggers the attractor state we've been describing all along. The way this goes in the literature is unforgettable. Note the following from Billy Graham, who is very taken with the theme of angelic might: "Think of it!" he cries out. "Multitudes of angels, indescribably mighty, performing the commands of heaven!"[74] And they are there for us, to work on our behalf, to do our bidding as we direct our supplications toward the spiritual region. *We* get the power: "If you are a believer," asserts Graham, "expect powerful angels to accompany you in your life experiences. . . . Take courage, your angels are nearer than you think. . . . After all," Graham continues, citing Scripture, "God has 'given His angels charge of you in all your ways. On their hands they will bear you up, lest you dash your foot against a stone' (Psalm 91)."[75] So great, so "mighty" are our angelic "friends," holds Graham, that they possess the capacity to vanquish death itself: "You may be filled with dread at the thought of death. Just remember that at one moment you may be suffering, but in another moment, you will be instantly transformed into the glorious likeness of our Savior. The wonders . . . and grandeur of heaven will be yours. You will be surrounded by these heavenly messengers sent by God to bring you home."[76] And it is of course "home" in the deepest psychological sense that serves as the underlying allure of the angelic literature as a whole, the "home" of the original, loving "guardians," the original omnipotent caregivers and providers to whom we were indissolubly and magically attached during the inception of our mortal days and from whom we had eventually to separate as we commenced our solitary journeys, small though we were.

Note how Prophet deals with the theme of power, of omnipotence, and note in especial the magical flavor of her ideas. (We've already had a taste of this through her notion that our prayer, "Help me! Help me! Help me!" can *summon* an angel to our side.) The angels, she maintains, are waiting for us to "give them assignments." If we ask them to assist us, they will do so, but we have to "ask" (the basic priming of supplication). She then writes, "Not only can you ask them to help you personally but you can also direct them—*even command them*—to perform larger tasks" (emphasis added).[77] You can "get" the angels "to work for you," states Prophet, sounding for all the world like a confident magician about to send her spirits off to do some job. We naturally wonder, as we confront all this, what Prophet's angelic spirits are "like," that is, what form they take, what appearance they assume. Well, says Prophet, they are "gigantic beings," with "wings as big as jumbo jets." So "large and powerful" are they, in fact, "that they can simply dissolve seemingly insurmountable problems, even on a global scale." These, precisely these, are the entities we may "command." And when one performs this commanding correctly, when one gets the magic right through specific, decisive directions, it is not merely one or two or three spiritual giants that "go to work for you" but "millions."[78] Moreover, these supernatural, angelic "jumbos" do not merely serve you with their omnipotence; they see to it that you get "strength" as well, strength of both body and mind. The angels, holds Prophet, can make us so "intelligent" that we have the capacity to "pass" any "test," to understand virtually anything within our state of "illumination." We can even expect "flashes of insight" on the level of "Einstein" with his "theory of relativity." And there is more. Our omnipotent angels can actually "put us in touch with the mind of God," from Whom we may directly receive a host of "life-changing revelations."[79] Our psychological studies reveal that primary narcissism generally emerges with the sensation of omnipotence during the early period. The dependent little one feels very, very special in the arms of his all-powerful provider. For some, this narcissistic attitude never relinquishes its hold upon the developing mind. Accordingly, and with the words of Prophet ringing in our ears, we must not exclude *self-love* from the constellation of unconscious affect that pulls the necromantic believer toward the realm of the mighty angels. The ability to "command" these "gigantic beings" sets one gloriously apart from the rest of ordinary humanity.

As we've noted on several occasions, the basic biological situation contains at its core a transformational parental object, a caregiver who, in Bollas's words (cited above), actually "transforms the baby's internal and external environment," over and over again, for years, changing discomfort into contentment and distress into happy relief. It can hardly come as a surprise that, as adults susceptible to religious narrative and given to religious experience by virtue of our hallucinatory capacities, we should jump at supernatural beings who promise us regular, ceaseless transformation throughout the course of our lives. Are we down? Are we blue? Are we somehow dissatisfied with the way things are going? Well, with the angels around we surely know what to do about it. And if actual transformation, actual specific, material change fails to occur, we always have the inward transformation that obtains merely from fantasizing the possibility of miraculous alteration. If it did not come this time, it may come the next, and "knowing" that, in and of itself, assists us in our distress. The attractor state is significantly driven by our unconscious recollection of the endless transformation that marks the very essence of the early time. Pray to your "angels of love," instructs Prophet, and they will "transform you." If you're lacking love, you'll get it; if you're fighting with your boss, the fighting will stop; if the kids aren't getting along, they will; if you can't find "the relationship you want," you'll find it. As the Archangel Chamuel has revealed to Prophet, the "forces of anti-love" will "be gone" when you start contacting your angelic guides.[80] The "angels in our midst," holds Freeman, have the capacity to "transform" not merely our personal lives but the "world" in which we reside as well. In her section titled "Transformations," Freeman contends that at this very moment the "whole earth is hovering on the edge of a transformation so glorious that we have no idea how to describe it."[81] We'll have grown so "loving," we'll have "changed" so totally, that we'll "hardly need help to see and walk with our angels." Referring to the transformational experiences that occurred during the course of her own development, Freeman observes, "I learned that when I was touched by my angel Ennis at the age of five, it was with such transformation in mind, to free me of the fears that would have paralyzed my life [the well-known pattern of fear triggering the hallucinatory presence of supernaturals, as we've seen]. And as I've grown over the years, I've come to know God intends for all of us to live lives filled with love." We can all experience God's "grace," which is freely "bestowed" (grace as the sharp, unconscious infusion of the infantile transformational process into the life of the adult, associated here with angelic beings).[82] There is an old "saying" about the "angels," notes Anderson in her volume *Where Angels Walk*, and it goes like this: "How many angels are there? One—who transforms your life—is plenty."[83]

Note these wonderful lines (ll. 23–38) from Browning's poem "The Guardian Angel" (1848), inspired by a picture at Fano, Italy, in the midst of the nineteenth century:

> Dear and great Angel, wouldst thou only leave
> That child, when thou hast done with him, for me!
> . . . .
> If this was ever granted, I would rest
> My head beneath thine, while thy healing hands
> Close-covered both my eyes beside thy breast,
> Pressing the brain, which too much thought expands,
> Back to its proper size again, and smoothing
> Distortion down till every nerve had soothing,
> And all lay quiet, happy and suppressed.
>
> How soon all worldly wrong would be repaired!
> I think how I should view the earth and skies
> And sea, when once again my brow was bared
> After thy healing, with such different eyes,
> O world! As God has made it! All is beauty;
> And knowing this, is love, and love is duty.
> What further may be sought for or declared?[84]

Here is the transformational object in its pure, classic form, leaving the "child" and moving to the grown-up, who longs poetically to lay his head upon the maternal "breast," to feel the guardian's "healing" hand suspend his distorted, worldly sight, thus changing him back into the soothed, "quiet, happy and suppressed" infant of the early period. And were this to occur, were the poet to find his way somehow back to the primal time, to the perfection of the beginning, he would suddenly behold an Edenic earth and sky, a "world" as "God has made it," a place where everything is beautiful and love abounds—indeed, where our "duty," our very responsibility as humans, is "love"—as it is for the parent. What attracts individuals to the angels today is significantly bound up with precisely what attracted Browning to his "guardian angel" at Fano a century and a half ago. The attractor state is unconsciously rooted in the longing for the transformational object. Our angelic soothers will provide us with a world that contains nothing but "beauty" and "love." We will have the "breast" we were forced to relinquish during the course of the separation stage. As Prophet informed us earlier in this section through the revelations of the Archangel Chamuel, "the forces of anti-love" will "be gone."

Through supplication, through asking and receiving, through turning to God "as an infant in distress turns to his mother" (in Guardini's words, cited above), the worshiper *primes* himself unconsciously for a return to the original symbiotic union with the caregiving object. The *state* of prayer triggers *state-dependent memories* that reside at the core of the *attractor state* and that declare that the Almighty is *there*, experientially, sensationally *there*. Much the same thing occurs when believers seek to attune themselves with their angels through carefully constructed trance states. As we have seen, affect attunement during the early period serves as the emotional, perceptual foundation of the newcomer's emerging selfhood. Like the asking and receiving of the basic biological situation, such attunement is synaptically internalized into the structure of the neonate's developing mind-brain. When the parent is "able to read" the infant's "feeling state" from the infant's "overt behavior" and performs "some behavior" that "corresponds in some way" to the infant's, writes Stern, and when the infant is "able to read" this "parental response" as "having to do with his own original feeling," we encounter the kind of intersubjective relatedness from which the individual's "core self" is constructed.[85] Stern dubs this empathetic responsiveness between caregiver and child "affect attunement," observing that it comprises what is meant when clinicians speak of parental "mirroring" (see chap. 5). In this way, attuning with one's angels, like praying to one's angels, constitutes an unconsciously cunning means to remove ego boundaries, to restore the original, affective merger of the early time, to reestablish the primal attachment through which the little one discovered his foundational bliss and from which he was forced to separate as his growth proceeded in its postparadisal direction. Let's bear in mind, the trance state induced by attuning with one's angels is not some technique for releasing stress or achieving a *state* of relaxation. The attuning individual is working to establish a tight, affective connection with supernatural figures who are entirely and lovingly devoted to his welfare, and to that alone.

"When angels touch our lives," writes Freeman, "they do so by coming down to our level, by changing their angelic 'wavelength' to match ours so we can apprehend them."[86] How they do this is a "mystery," states Freeman, but we can follow certain procedures to initiate our own personal, private contact. We can choose a "quiet room" or "outdoor location," take a "few minutes" to get used to where we are, begin to "sit still," and then "seek" to "become more angelically attuned." As we "grow in this commitment," concludes Freeman, "our own wavelength will more closely match that of our angels, who live for love."[87] To reach our angelic guides, maintains Paul Roland in his volume *Angels*, we work "to have a sense of their presence on a daily basis" and to bring that "sense" with us when we go about our "meditation." Relaxed yet focused, unwilling to become overly eager, we "still our mind" and "listen." "Don't try," instructs Roland; "let go and let your angels draw near." As you proceed to "close your eyes" and "focus on your breath," you also "visualize" a number of glorious angels from the world of Scripture: Gabriel, Uriel, Michael, Raphael.[88] Such "visualization" not only brings you "harmony and balance," states Roland; it helps you to "imagine" a "circle of white light around you, below your feet, and above your head," to "protect you" and to "create a sacred space" wherein your "angelic guides" may dwell. When you've "completed your contact with the angels," Roland advises, you can slowly "become aware of your body sitting in the seat, and when you are ready," you can "open your eyes."[89]

In another instructional passage, titled "Making Contact," Roland asks the reader to "relax," to request his "guardian angel" to "draw near," and to "visualize" himself being "wrapped" in "its wings of multi-colored auric light." "Repeat the exercise as many times as you feel necessary," lessons Roland; "focus on your breathing" and "when you are ready return to waking consciousness." All such "exercises," Roland concludes, will assist you in drawing your angel toward "your own energy field," where it can become your "constant celestial companion" and "source of inspiration."[90] When she meditates upon her angels, claims Joan Borysenko, she begins by fantasizing "light" washing over her, pouring through her, until her "heart" becomes "lighter and lighter" and she feels herself "encased" in "an egg of light." The "bulk" of her meditation, she goes on, consists in simply "sitting" in that divine, "angelic presence throughout the day." The vibrations she experiences during this extended period call to her mind the illusory "space" between "atoms" in "quantum mechanics" and the theories of "Einstein." All such "space" is in fact "just made of light." Nothing could be more erroneous than the "idea that we are separate form one another." At the "energetic level" of vibrations, says Borysenko, "everything is related to everything else."[91] Let's note how Sheldrake and Fox characterize the way in which, and the extent to which, a guardian angel is familiar with the "person" over whom he has charge: "[He] would have a unified and wide-ranging knowledge of the person's being through a direct cognition of the fields underlying the person's thoughts, actions, intentions, and relationships," the person's "innermost being and becoming." Yet "it's not just a matter of receiving vibration, but also of responding to it as well," these authors observe in a subsequent passage.[92] There could hardly be a more vivid projective description of the caregiver's preternatural sensitivity to the child's behavioral world or of the two-way vibrations that constitute the core of what we've described as affect attunement. It is the real, human interaction between the real mother and baby that provides the experiential foundation, or the "energy," of the transcendent, mystical "space" in which the angel seekers sit and attune with their putative supernatural companions. Their goal is the jogging of state-dependent memory and, through that, the reawakening of the early, delicious attunement that said at the affective level, my existence is inextricably interfused with the caregiver's; we revolve around each other in an orbit of empathy and love; this is the universe.

A FINAL ANGELIC WORD

Angels have assumed a wide variety of forms across the centuries. The reader with an appetite for the iconography might begin by turning to Lewis and Oliver's *Angels, A to Z*, which is an especially handy and readable compendium, loaded with illustrations. What we must stress here, however, is the ever-present anthropomorphism of angelic depictions, the humanness of our angelic friends, and guests, and guardians. "It is the power of angelic generosity to take on bodily form to assist us, to help us, to communicate with us, and to be recognized by us," write Sheldrake and Fox, who go on to suggest, correctly I believe, that "incarnation seems to be a necessary means by which human beings learn anything, including even the divine."[93] From the psychodynamic perspective that governs our discussion, such anthropomorphism immediately calls to mind Milner's observation, already cited in chapter 7, that "the inner structure of the unconscious part of our psyche is essentially animistic. That is, we build up our inner world on the basis of our relationships to people we have loved and hated; we carry these people about with us and what we do, we do for them or in conflict with them." Milner goes on, "And it seems that it is through these internalized people that we carry on our earliest relationships, developing them and enriching them throughout our life; even when these first loved people no longer exist in the external world, we find external representatives of them both in new people who enter our lives, and in all our interests and the causes that we seek to serve." Milner's words help us to grasp the deep, unconscious purpose behind much of the angelic belief and testimonial we see around us today.

Threatened by not only the personal dangers and separations that are an inescapable aspect of one's life experience, the current angel seekers and worshipers find themselves confronting scientific views that suggest that the universe is anything but a "people place," anything but a secure, comforting home for our vulnerable, perishable organisms and our fragile, pregnable psyches. We look out upon a cosmos that is utterly indifferent to our existence on our little planet as it floats in the immensity of "our" galaxy, not to mention many billions of other galaxies. Evolution holds that we exist by way of sheer materialistic happenstance (natural selection). And modern psychology, especially psychoanalysis, suggests that much of the time we don't even know what we're doing. The point is, just as physical danger and interpersonal crisis can trigger the attractor state and prompt through implicit, state-dependent memory an affective, perceptual, hallucinatory return to the loving symbiosis of the early period, so can the basic, existential dread that may arise from the materialistic, scientific outlook we continuously, diurnally confront. It may well be, of course, that our macrocosmic anxieties stem from both the implications of scientific materialism and our tendency to project into that harsh view the personal, private anxieties we inherit from our familial interactions within and without the home, as Milner suggests. Accordingly, a significant portion of the current angel literature is devoted to "angeling" the cosmos, to "peopling" or anthropomorphizing the universe in such a way as to transform it (recall here the transformational object) into a living, even a maternal entity that is disposed to love us, hold us, protect us, nurture us, and provide us with a permanent home, canceling out in the process any and all suggestions of separation, insecurity, danger, and the old, familiar bugbear of mortality. Moreover, the angelic literature that strives to accomplish all this is wont to dress itself up as "science," as "physics," as "objective analysis"; in short, it is bent upon supplanting the enemy with pseudoscientific claims, the chief one of which is that "light" or "energy," being "immaterial" or "bodiless," is some sort of "spiritual" stuff and thus an emanation of the divine. As the expression (from *Hamlet*) has it, the foe will be "hoisted with his own petard." Let's look now at a representative example of this wishful, angelic thinking, an example that turns out to be the very text of Sheldrake and Fox, to which we resorted a moment ago when striving to capture humanity's tendency to "incarnate" its angelic inventions.

According to Sheldrake and Fox, the angels are "returning" to the earth at this time because a "living" as opposed to a "dead" cosmology is also "returning." We are witnessing the revival of the "ancient, traditional teaching" that "when you live in a universe and not just in a man-made machine, there is room for angels." Sheldrake and Fox then ask, "What do they do," these angelic beings? At this point in our discussion we don't have to puzzle very long over that question: "Angels make human beings happy," according to these authors; they "guard" us, "defend" us, "heal" us, "understand" us, and of course "love" us.[94] We get the whole dimension of the early period, from omnipotence to protection, to ministration, to empathy, to unconditional love. "Angels are not abstract intellectuals," we are informed (p. 3); "they are loving, understanding beings. Loving invades their understanding. Their knowledge is heart knowledge." Above all, however, the angels are here to tell us that "the whole cosmos" is "alive" (p. 6), that the "mechanistic worldview" is "now being superseded" by "a new vision of a living world." Nature is being "rebirthed" as a "developing organism"; no longer is it merely a "thing" (p. 8). The "fields and energy" that inform the vast universe, hold Sheldrake and Fox, attest ultimately to a vast creative process" that includes not only our "Mother Earth" but all the "galaxies" that surround it: "Galaxies are alive and not just microbes, plants, and animals," they write (p. 11). We "are talking about superhuman consciousness." A specific illustration goes like this: "If people are prepared to admit that our consciousness is associated with . . . complex electromagnetic patterns, then why shouldn't the sun have a consciousness? The sun may think. Its mental activity may be associated with complex and measurable electromagnetic events both on its surface and deeper within" (p. 19). How did Milner put it a couple of paragraphs ago? "The inner structure of the unconscious part of our psyche is essentially animistic." Who would doubt it here? The upshot of Sheldrake and Fox's animistic ruminations is of course in keeping with the passionate transitional aims of angelic and religious thinking as a whole: "The universe is a friendly place" (p. 13). It is "benign" (p. 12). We can "trust" it. It "smiles" upon us (ibid.). We "can relax" (p. 13); all of which is to say, the universe is an unconscious, animated version of the maternal breast upon which we long to rest our anxious heads as we cope with our separateness and smallness in the world. We don't have to be threatened any longer by "science"; we don't have to look out upon a vast, indifferent cosmos and feel the powerful anxieties and dreads that perforce accompany our materialistic vision. If the galaxies attest to unfathomable mysteries, unfathomable distances, unfathomable vortices of time and space, and if such attestations make us tremble in our boots, well, we can simply erase all that by postulating angelic presences everywhere and *transforming* the unfathomable cosmos and its mysterious "quanta" into a version of the maternal provider. Presto change-o!

The length to which Sheldrake and Fox carry these infantile projections is truly amazing. Here are a few more examples that should serve to crystallize the essence of their presentation: (1) "The universe is our home, and everything we're talking about is our home" (p. 20). (The essence of the notion of home is the notion of mother.) (2) "Photons are immortal"; the "quantized" movement of the angels "is just like Einstein's description of the movement of a photon of light" (p. 21). (We are all essentially "quanta" at the Einsteinian level of vibrations, and therefore we are all "immortal." There is no death in our "living universe.") (3) "Everything mirrors God" (p. 38). (The universe of Sheldrake and Fox is an unconscious version of the mother's face.) (4) "The whole is more than the sum of its parts" (p. 38); "everything we're talking about is encapsulated in our soul field," which is also an "angel field," which is in turn a living "electromagnetic field" (p. 40). As the "human field awakens," it discovers a complete absence of "disconnection" or "isolation" in the cosmos (p. 41). (There is no separation.) (5) "Angels are connectors" (p. 40); they speak for "interconnectivity" (p. 41). Every angel that ever existed is still among us in some part of the "living universe." Even the angels who watched over the dinosaurs are still here (p. 118). True, they may be somehow "recycled," "retrained," and "relocated" to be of better, more up-to-date "service," but they are here, of that we can be sure. (Again, there is no separation, ever, for anything that was, is, or will be. The fear of separation in humans is such that it can transport them to any absurdity that might possibly be thought up. Dinosaur angels, indeed!) The psychodynamic meaning of the angelic revival we witness around us today is captured fully and perhaps unforgettably in the work of Sheldrake and Fox. Everything comes together through the heads they put together.

The old question arises, is it not possible that Sheldrake and Fox are *ultimately* right? That is, even if our religious beliefs, including our belief in angels, are triggered by an unconscious return to the early time and to the powerful hallucinatory sensations of certainty or "thereness" that accompany such a return, could not the Almighty be *using* these unconscious perceptions and affects to bring us into His divine presence? Would that not be a natural, logical way for Him to find us, and for us to find Him? Is He not, after all, our Parent-God? My reply to this question is always the same, as the reader by this time doubtless knows: I haven't a clue. What produced the originative stuff of the universe, or what is now occurring in the supernatural sphere, is entirely beyond my capacity to determine. I am making a psychological argument that is intended to offer explanations that are firmly rooted in naturalistic as opposed to supernaturalistic assumptions. If the reader wants an answer to this fascinating ultimate question, I suggest he approach a theologian, an individual who is qualified to tell him in no uncertain terms where the universe ultimately came from and what everything ultimately means.

NOTES

1. Sylvia Browne, *Sylvia Browne's Book of Angels* (Carlsbad, CA: Hay House, 2003), p. 28.

2. Rupert Sheldrake and Matthew Fox, *The Physics of Angels: Exploring the Realm Where Science and Spirit Meet* (San Francisco: HarperSanFrancisco, 1996), p. 1.

3. James R. Lewis and Evelyn D. Oliver, *Angels, A to Z* (New York: Gale Research, 1996), p. xiii.

4. Keith Thompson, *Angels and Aliens: UFOs and the Mythic Imagination* (New York: Addison-Wesley, 1991).

5. Joan W. Anderson, *Where Angels Walk* (New York: Ballantine Books, 1993), pp. 81, 82.

6. Ibid., pp. 106, 107.

7. Elizabeth Clare Prophet, *How to Work with Angels* (Corwin Springs, MT: Summit University Press, 1998), p. 7.

8. Quoted in Eileen E. Freeman, *Touched by Angels* (New York: Warner Books, 1994), pp. 138, 139–40.

9. Prophet, *How to Work with Angels*, pp. 43, 44.

10. Romano Guardini, *Prayer in Practice*, trans. L. Loewenstein-Wertheim (London: Burns and Oates, 1957), p. 77.

11. Ole Hallesby, *Prayer*, trans. C. Carlsen (Leicester, UK: Intervarsity Press, [1948] 1979), pp. 14, 20.

12. Prophet, *How to Work with Angels*, p. 14.

13. Geza Roheim, *Magic and Schizophrenia* (Bloomington: University of Indiana Press, 1955), pp. 11–12.

14. Erich Neumann, *The Great Mother*, trans. R. Manheim (Princeton, NJ: Princeton University Press, 1970), p. 115.

15. Mary Douglas, *Natural Symbols: Explorations of Cosmology* (London: Routledge, 1996), p. 7.

16. Ibid., p. 9.

17. Mary Douglas, *Purity and Danger: An Analysis of the Concepts of Pollution and Taboo* (New York: Ark Paperbacks, 1984), p. 28.

18. Karen Goldman, *Angel Encounters: True Stories of Divine Intervention* (New York: Simon and Schuster, 1995), p. 28. Page numbers for the other Goldman quotes in this section are included in the text. Even though Goldman is the author of her own book, unlike the previous case studies in this chapter, she will be referred to by her first name in the text for consistency.

19. Roheim, *Magic and Schizophrenia*, p. 12.

20. Erik H. Erikson, *Young Man Luther* (New York: W. W. Norton, 1958), p. 264.

21. See Anderson, *Where Angels Walk*, p. 10.

22. Quoted in Eileen E. Freeman, *Touched by Angels* (New York: Warner Books, 1994), p. 121.

23. Quoted in ibid., p. 122.

24. Quoted in ibid., p. 123.

25. Christopher Bollas, *The Shadow of the Object: Psychoanalysis of the Unthought-Known* (London: Free Association Books, 1987), p. 33.

26. Quoted in Freeman, *Touched by Angels*, p. 115.

27. Quoted in ibid., p. 117.

28. Quoted in ibid., pp. 117–18.

29. Quoted in ibid., p. 118.

30. Silvan S. Tomkins, *Affect, Imagery, Consciousness*, vol. 1 (New York: Springer, 1962).

31. Quoted in Freeman, *Touched by Angels*, p. 120.

32. Quoted in Anderson, *Where Angels Walk*, p. 17.

33. Quoted in ibid., p. 16.

34. Quoted in Freeman, *Touched by Angels*, pp. 126–27.

35. Quoted in ibid., p. 81

36. Quoted in ibid., pp. 85–86.

37. Quoted in ibid., p. 87.

38. Quoted in Anderson, *Where Angels Walk*, pp. 179–80.

39. Quoted in ibid., pp. 228, 229.

40. Quoted in ibid., pp. 229–30.

41. Quoted in ibid., pp. 230, 231.

42. Quoted in Goldman, *Angel Encounters*, pp. 229, 230.

43. Kim O'Neill, *How to Talk with Your Angels* (New York: Avon Books, 1995), p. 3. Page numbers for the other O'Neill quotes in this section are included in the text. Like Karen Goldman, O'Neill is the author of her own case study and will be referred to in the text as Kim for consistency.

44. William James, *The Varieties of Religious Experience* (1902; New York: Library of America, 1987), p. 69.

45. Ibid., pp. 417, 428.

46. Emanuel Swedenborg, quoted in O'Neill, *How to Talk with Your Angels*, p. 13.

47. D. W. Winnicott, *Playing and Reality* (London: Penguin, 1971).

48. See David G. Myers, *Intuition: Its Powers and Perils* (New Haven, CT: Yale University Press, 2002).

49. See Fred Alan Wolf, *The Dreaming Universe* (New York: Simon and Schuster, 1994), p. 128.

50. Derek Wood, "What Is a Hallucination?" *A Mood Journal*, May 2003, p. 1.

51. Terry Lynn Taylor, *The Angel Experience* (San Raphael, CA: Amber-Allen, 1998), p. 51.

52. Frank Bruno, *Psychological Symptoms* (New York: John Wiley and Sons, 1993), p. 47.

53. Neil Bockian, *New Hope for People with Borderline Personality Disorders* (New York: Prima Publishers, 2002), p. 212.

54. F. S. Smythe, quoted in Anderson, *Where Angels Walk*, p. 17.

55. Prophet, *How to Work with Angels*, p. 1.

56. Ernest Becker, *The Denial of Death* (New York: Free Press, 1973), p. 175.

57. Freeman, *Touched by Angels*, p. 147.

58. Browne, *Book of Angels*, p. 118.

59. Joan Webster Anderson, quoted in Rex Hauck, *Angels: The Mysterious Messengers* (New York: Ballantine Books, 1994), p. 22.

60. Goldman, *Angel Encounters*, p. 129.

61. Browne, *Book of Angels*, p. 45.

62. Sophy Burnham, quoted in Hauck, *Angels*, pp. 79, 81.

63. Goldman, *Angel Encounters*, pp. 209, 94.

64. Freeman, *Touched by Angels*, p. 145.

65. Ibid., p. 121.

66. Daniel Stern, *The Interpersonal World of the Infant* (New York: Basic Books, 1985), p. 116.

67. Prophet, *How to Work with Angels*, p. 80.

68. Freeman, *Touched by Angels*, pp. xi, xii.

69. Burnham, quoted in Hauck, *Angels*, p. 83.

70. Anderson, quoted in Hauck, *Angels*, pp. 27, 29.

71. Goldman, *Angel Encounters*, pp. 96, 97.

72. Billy Graham, *Angels: God's Secret Agents* (New York: Doubleday, 1954), pp. 72, 93.

73. Winnicott, *Playing and Reality*, p. 13.

74. Graham, *Angels*, p. 20.

75. Ibid., pp. 24, 25.

76. Ibid., pp. 154–55.

77. Prophet, *How to Work with Angels*, p. 9.

78. Ibid., pp. 81–82.

79. Ibid., p. 49.

80. Ibid., pp. 56–57.

81. Freeman, *Touched by Angels*, p. 68.

82. Ibid., p. 70.

83. Anderson, *Where Angels Walk*, p. 126.

84. Robert Browning, "The Guardian Angel," in *The Complete Works of Robert Browning*, ed. H. Scudder (Cambridge, MA: Houghton Mifflin, 1895), p. 194.

85. Stern, *The Interpersonal World of the Infant*, p. 139.

86. Freeman, *Touched by Angels*, p. 152.

87. Ibid., pp. 162, 163.

88. Paul Roland, *Angels* (London: Judy Piatkus, 1999), pp. 3, 6, 8, 9.

89. Ibid., p. 11.

90. Ibid., pp. 73, 104.

91. Joan Borysenko, quoted in Hauck, *Angels*, pp. 68, 69.

92. Sheldrake and Fox, *Physics of Angels*, pp. 13, 143.

93. Ibid., p. 89.

94. Ibid., pp. 2–5. Page numbers for the other Sheldrake and Fox quotes in this section are included in the text.

10.

Conclusion: Are We "Wired for God"?

T he widespread notion that we are "wired for God" or "genetically endowed" with a "need" for "faith"[1] emerges from our
psychodynamic context as a misperception of human behavior—an
understandable, wishful, natural misperception to be sure, but inac-
curate nonetheless. Are the many millions of people throughout the
world who do not believe in God the products of faulty wiring? Has their
elemental, primal nature been somehow distorted or suppressed? I
don't think so. At the foundational, genetic level we are wired for the
struggle to survive, to continue existing as biological organisms on the
planet, to secure nourishment (energy), to excrete waste, to sleep, and
to grow. One might suggest that we are genetically inclined to move
toward that which gives us pleasure and away from that which gives us
discomfort or pain; yet even here, in the area of something as basic as
pleasure and pain, environmental factors intrude upon the scene. Pain
may emerge as a preliminary to pleasure, or pleasure as the harbinger
of pain, thus defeating categorical explanations. As the biological program continues to unfold, we find ourselves walking upright, talking to
one another, and expressing an inaugural interest in sexual matters. By
this time, however, environmental factors have become so pervasive, so
mixed up with whatever genetic directions we possess, that it proves
impossible to make rigorous distinctions between the realms of nature

and nurture. Even a tendency as basic as attachment cannot stand up in isolation from the environment. Virginia Demos writes, "Bowlby's alternative to Freud's psychic energy model, namely a specifically committed, preorganized attachment system built into the brain, is . . . not supported by neuroscience. The brain is composed of several fundamental modular, functional systems, which initially operate in a more general, abstract manner, systems including the perceptual, cognitive, affective, motoric, and homeostatic. These systems do not have preset or preorganized specific goals such as attachment. It is far more likely that in humans attachment patterns gradually emerge and become organized as the result of lived experiences."[2] We will be turning to precisely such "lived experiences" in relation to precisely the "goal" of "attachment" very shortly. The whole issue is summed up neatly for us in Robert Plomin's *Development, Genetics, and Psychology*: "Genetic influence is embedded in the complexity of interactions among genes, physiology, and environment. It is probabilistic, not deterministic; it puts no constraint on what could be."[3] Surely our cursory, rudimentary overview of this vast, complex field makes abundantly clear the untenability of the proposition that we are "wired for God" or "genetically endowed" with a "need" for "faith." The only truth we can wrest from such a view is that some people are gratified to think of God as built into us by nature. The names that fit in here span the centuries, from Saint Augustine to Saint Thomas Aquinas, to John Calvin, to Friedrich von Schelling, to Carl Jung, to choose but a few.

As we experience the world developmentally, affective, interactional patterns take shape to become engrained synaptically at the foundation of our perceptual lives through the process of psychophysical internalization. Because our mind-brains are moldable, flexible instruments, these internalized interactional patterns turn out to be transferable across experiential space. "Even the adult brain is 'plastic,'" observes Sharon Begley, "able to forge connections among its neurons and thus rewire itself. Sensory input can change the brain, and the brain remodels itself in response to behavioral demands. Regions that get the most use literally expand. In terms of which neural circuits endure and enlarge, you can call it survival of the busiest."[4] Thus we may mourn the loss of one caregiver as we transfer our developing affections and needs to another caregiver, expanding the base of a "busy" interactional pattern at the neuronal level. We may negotiate the traumas of the separation stage and the anxieties of our dawning independence in the world by transferring our experiential, symbiotic longings to a substitute parental figure in the form of a Parent-God offered through religious narrative at the societal level to ensure our homeostasis, and thus our productivity, as emerging members of a cohesive group. As interactional, affective patterns become established at the synaptic level, they begin to look like "instincts," like automatic, genetic, programmed responses. For the vast majority of earthlings involved in the basic biological situation, an initial pattern of attachment develops experientially between caregiver and child as the process of biological survival moves ahead. The baby clamors or otherwise communicates his wishes, and the mothering figure responds. This asking and receiving serves eventually to forge an affective, perceptual bond that powerfully and permanently impinges on our lives, all the way to the end. We've been describing this bond as an "attractor state," a neurally based perceptual and emotional configuration that strives to locate and draw unto itself a wide range of subsequent experience that "echoes" or unconsciously restores the original symbiotic union, the alliance of caregiver and child through which our successful struggle to survive transpired early on. Present at the start if we're normal, healthy humans in normal, healthy settings, our "intelligence" for life, for security, for "energy," to put it in the most elemental terms, never sleeps. What we wanted and needed in the beginning we will discover and employ again as we go. Indeed, we'll send our flexible mind-brains in hallucinatory directions if necessary, but we'll have what we emotively, internally require.

NEUROBIOLOGICAL ANGLES

Let's take a moment to note how this contextual perspective harmonizes with current neurobiological thinking on the nature of our perceptual apparatus, our "mind-brain," as I've been calling it. In their volume

The Origin of Minds, Peggy La Cerra and Roger Bigelow maintain that as people develop toward maturity, their developing neural interconnections reflect their individual, cumulative experiences in the world. Steadily coalescing into what they term an "adaptive representational network," these interconnections guide the individual toward behavior that is conducive to his survival and well-being. In regard specifically to how all this occurs, La Cerra and Bigelow describe the adaptive representational network as "a network of neurons that memorializes a brief scene in the ongoing movie of your life, linking together your physical and emotional state, the environment you are in, the behavior or thought you generate, and the problem solving outcome."[5] What we have here, of course, is what is called in the literature an autocatalytic or self-generating feedback loop, characterized thus by Michael Shermer: "New experiences stimulate neurons to grow new synaptic connections. Those new connections are distinctive to every individual mind, which then responds to the environment in an idiosyncratic way, producing a behavioral repertoire of responses. This network evolved as an adaptation to help organisms survive in an ever-changing environment."[6] Surely at this juncture we need not struggle to determine the foundational "scene" that is "memorialized" into the ongoing "movie" of one's life, the "scene" that "links together" one's physiology, emotion, thought, environment, and behavior, the "scene" that becomes the inspirational "star" of the religious domain.

It is the "scene" of the basic biological situation, the scene of "asking and receiving" (prayer) at the hands of the loving provider, the "scene" that is repeated thousands of times, to be internalized into the "adaptive representational network" of the child's flexible mind-brain through his robust "memorial" capacities. This is what gets "wired" into us, to govern or to direct the manner in which we respond to the "experiences" we're obliged to encounter as we develop toward maturity. When we confront our separation from the caregiver during the transitional period we fashion "new" substitutive attachments through the illusory objects we discover and create.[7] When independence or autonomy looms and our transitional companions fade away, we find through religious narrative the figure of the Parent-God, Who adopts the caregiver's role, Who watches over us, protects us, guides us, succors us, and loves us, either directly or through His ministering angels. Moreover, those in charge of religious doctrine urge us, even instruct us, not merely to *do* what we did in the beginning as little ones (ask a big one for assistance) but inwardly to *become* what we *were* in the beginning. We are told to become "little children" again, to turn to our Parent-God in prayer as infants in distress turn to their mothers.[8] We must "let our holy and almighty God care for us just as an infant surrenders himself to his mother's care."[9] The primal interactions that were foundationally "memorialized" and that now exist chiefly in the realm of infantile amnesia, or at the level of unconscious process, will be awakened through state-dependent memory to exert their compelling influence upon us as we enact religion's chief rite, supplication. The result is assured, at least for millions of adherents: we will *feel* the presence of the indwelling Parent-God as we go about our religious business; our "busy" infantile, neurological pattern will be further expanded, enlarged. We will *know* God exists because we will find Him "there" as we unconsciously associate our original symbiosis with the "mysterious" union that divinely transpires. We will accept the "false perception," the hallucinatory "presence," because we wish to, and also because we have no way of seeing or understanding what is actually occurring in our mind-brains. Our "experience" will tell us, neurally, this is so, and for most of us that will be enough. We will have achieved what James calls the "faith-state" by which men "live" (cited in chap. 3). It is indeed exactly that; it springs directly from the biological heart of the early period, from the "scene" of the basic biological situation, from the *asking and receiving* that ensured our biological survival in the world to become, through the workings of unconscious association, the "mysterious" center, the "mysterious" essence and soul, of religious, supernatural enactments. Need it be added that our successful accomplishment of all this, our successful rediscovery of our original source of survival and well-being, should have grand adaptational consequence, that we should proceed more calmly, more securely, more effectively, more productively in our lives through our regular indulgence in our foundational, joyous, life-sustaining "scene," thus emerging as more useful members of the group that depends upon us and upon which we in turn depend? The ultimate significance of Herbert Benson's notion that we are "wired for God" now appears: the notion itself instantiates the neural pattern upon which we are focused. The notion itself confirms the presence of the unconscious, memorial forces operating deep within us. They have done their work: they have fashioned the "false perception" that the Almighty is innately existent at the root of our lives.

ORIGINS

I believe we gain insight here into the origins of religion as they are presented in the anthropological literature. The variety and scope of explanation is of course enormous, but the essential thought belongs to Edward Tylor, offered during the late nineteenth century and skillfully presented to us by Marvin Harris: "It is not the quality of belief that distinguishes religion from science. Rather, as Edward Tylor was the first to propose, the basis of all that is distinctly religious in human thought is animism, the belief that humans share the world with a population of extraordinary, extracorporeal, and mostly invisible beings, ranging form souls and ghosts to saints and fairies, angels, and cherubim, demons, jinni, devils, and gods." Harris continues,

> Wherever people believe in the existence of one or more of these beings, that is where religion exists. Tylor claimed that animistic beliefs were to be found in every society, and a century of ethnological research has yet to turn up a single exception. The most problematic case is that of Buddhism, which Tylor's critics portrayed as a world religion that lacked belief in gods or souls. But ordinary believers outside of Buddhist monasteries never accepted the atheistic implications of Guatama's teachings. Mainstream Buddhism, even in the monasteries, quickly envisioned the Buddha as a supreme deity who had been successively reincarnated and who held sway over a pantheon of lesser gods and demons. And it was as fully animistic creeds that the several varieties of Buddhism spread from India to Tibet, Southeast Asia, China, and Japan.

Harris asks, finally, "Why is animism universal? Tylor pondered the question at length. He reasoned that if a belief recurred again and again in virtually all times and places, it could not be a product of mere fantasy. Rather, it must have grounding in evidence and in experience that were equally recurrent and universal. What were these experiences? Tylor pointed to dreams, trances, visions, shadows, reflections, and death."[10] Following this pivotal lead, we now understand that religion's informing animism is more integrally rooted in our neurological makeup than Tylor could have imagined more than a century ago. Again in Milner's words, "The inner structure of the unconscious part of our psyche is essentially animistic" (cited in chap. 7). We take people in, and we set them up neurologically at the foundation of the "feedback loop" through which we process information and experience as we go.

Accordingly, we unconsciously project into our version of the world "out there" the people we've internalized into the world "in here," and chief among these of course the parental figure upon whom our survival, our very existence depends during the early period, when our unconscious, animistic "loop" commences its flexible growth. Through a variety of complex, metamorphic developments arising from the peculiar environment we inhabit (our "culture"), the "internalized object" births the Parent-God of religious narrative, the One Who "takes over" or "takes charge of us" as the original internalized parental presence gradually recedes into the existential background. The universe remains animistic, with a humanlike figure at its center, because we want the universe to remain "like us." Only if it remains so can we approach it with true intimacy and feel secure, special, and loved within its confines. To be "home" we must continue to "incarnate." Am I suggesting in all this that other items have no importance when it comes to the catalysts of religious conviction? Certainly not. No question that dreams, visions, and recollections of the dead, and the very nature of language itself where "disembodied" words and symbols assume "reality," play a contributory role in creating the sensation of God's presence. But at the ground of the entire animistic edifice is the unconscious structure of the psyche, the unconscious structure of the human mind-brain, into which the monumental people in our lives were internalized—as Scripture has it—"in the beginning" (Genesis 1:1). As for "God's Word," it comes long, long after our animistic inclinations are underway, and it "lives" because those very animistic inclinations magically, religiously grant it "life." In a nutshell, "God's Word" is coextensive with the animistic Deity it sacredly contains. Just ask any man of God.

FROM CULTURE TO CULTURE: THE FACE OF DIVINITY

As I hinted a moment ago, the way such religious, animistic arrangements of the world "look" from one culture to another is anything but uniform. The variations, in fact, are staggering. We get a very good sense of them in Robert Coles's volume *The Spiritual Life of Children*, where we have a chance to witness dozens of animistic configurations in their early stages of development. Allow me to summarize the essence of Coles's findings in a few brief sentences. For the Jewish child, God is the traditional guide, linked integrally with the ancestors, the "tribe." Being a good Jew is largely an ethical matter, one of being good to other people, of striving to make the world a decent place in which to live. Intensely attached to the family's religious and spiritual life, the Jewish child discovers in his Deity the "rock" of his existence, the source of his hope and his strength.[11] For the Muslim child, the accent is upon surrender and obedience. Allah is mercifully inclined to be there for the believer, yet one must be careful not to displease Him through recalcitrance and neglect. If one surrenders through supplication, and does so on a regular basis, Allah will strengthen and protect him in both this life and the next.[12] For the Christian child, Jesus is companion and friend, always glad to see and to be with His children. He came to earth to make Himself known to all, and by doing so, He experienced firsthand what it is like to be human. One discovers Him through prayer, during the course of which He becomes an intimate, personal guide to one's conduct in this world and to one's salvation in eternity.[13] Looking over his work as a whole, Coles entertains the following "interesting possibility": "that at least one small part of the unconscious is not Freud's 'seething cauldron' after all, but rather, as Isaiah would have it, an alert 'watchman,' asking and being asked, 'what of the night?'"[14] What this suggests in our particular psychodynamic context of interpretation is apparent: the unconscious is working to locate for us sources of attachment and security as we undertake our separate, dangerous journeys through the world. Such "location" is inextricably bound up with our animistic tendency to people the environment with projective versions of the parental, care-giving figure.

Of major importance to us in exactly this regard is Coles's finding that 90 percent of nearly three hundred youngsters between the ages of five and ten draw a simple human face when asked to render their personal conception of God.[15] They do not draw a body; they do not draw a giant; they do not draw a delineated creature of any kind. They draw, once again, a simple human face. Surely we understand whence this face comes: it is the product of the empathetic parent-child interaction, which resides at the foundation of religious experience as a whole. It begins to take shape as the caregiver's empathetic visage appears above the edge of the crib or the playpen. It begins to take shape as the child opens his mouth in his high chair to receive another spoonful of plums from his empathetic nourisher, his adored and adoring parental presence. Over and over again, thousands upon thousands of times during the early period, the little one looks into the empathetic face of the big one, and the big one looks back. Over and over again the child internalizes into his "feedback loop" this empathetic visage, this face, as the bedrock of his own emerging identity, his trust in life, his very selfhood.

Permit me to recall a few remarks from a previous chapter. The genesis and the formation of the self derive form the initial mirroring experience with the mother. For the past few decades, this unique, remarkable aspect of our origins has been studied intensively by a wide variety of observers and has come to be regarded generally as a central structural occurrence of our normal development. An inborn tendency on the part of the infant prompts him to seek out his mother's gaze and to do so regularly and for extended periods. The mother sets about exploiting this mutual, face-gazing activity. As eye-to-eye contact becomes frequent, and easily observed by the investigator, the mother's continual inclination to change her facial expression, as well as the quality of her vocalizing, emerges with striking clarity. Usually she smiles, and nods, and coos; sometimes in response to an infant frown, she frowns. In virtually every instance, the mother's facial and vocal behavior is an imitation of the baby's.

Accordingly, as the mother descends to the infant's level, she provides him with a particular kind of human mirror. She does not simply give the baby back his own self; she reinforces a portion of the baby's behavior in comparison with another portion. She gives the baby back not merely a part of what he is doing, but, in addition, something of her own. As Winnicott expresses the matter, "In individual . . . development *the precursor of the mirror is the mother's face*" (cited in chap. 5; emphasis added). Of particular interest in this connection is Winnicott's answer to his own question, "What does the baby see when he or she looks at the mother's face?" He writes, "I am suggesting that ordinarily, what the baby sees is himself or herself. In other words, the mother is looking at the baby and *what she looks like is related to what she sees there*" (emphasis added). Thus the process that engenders one's selfhood appears to go as follows, once again in Winnicott's aphoristic style: "When I look I am also seen, so I exist."[16] Precisely in that "seen," precisely there, resides the jewel of parental empathy. Have we a variation upon the cogito in this? I was seen, therefore I am? Is it possible that Descartes missed, in his notorious monadic formulation, the empathetic, relational origin of his and everyone else's existence?

The point is, when we discover God in the social realm, we discover Him as an extension of the empathetic object, as a version of the internalized caregiver we have seen and loved during the course of our early experience. This is the personal, individual, subjective core of religion, and as the core, it can never be sundered from the theology, no matter how sophisticated and mature the theology may get. Religious belief can't be broken up, let alone gutted of its emotional foundation. God is there for those who believe in Him because the empathetic object is there. The very basis of religious feeling, the very root itself, is both infantile and naturalistic. Moreover, because the empathetic object is connected inextricably to the advent of one's selfhood, one's identity as a person, to find God in supplication, to detect His presence in prayer, feels exactly like finding or detecting the self, or better like refinding or redetecting the self's origination in the face of the loving provider. The most important theological use of the term *face*, we learn from *The New Interpreter's Dictionary of the Bible*, is to indicate "the presence of God."[17] "Cause thy face to shine," cries the Psalmist (87:7). "Lead me on, Dear God! To see Thy face," cries nineteenth-century Anglican preacher Frederick Faber.[18] Within the Judeo-Christian tradition of personal, subjective prayer, one meets his Parent-God "face-to-face." Indeed, unless such "face-to-face" contact occurs, unless one reaches the level of one's mind-body internalizations—the object in short— one's supplication fails to attain its spiritual goal. The reader may be thinking, Is not the putative infantile model you offer but a metaphorical or symbolic representation, an imaginative depiction of God's 'face' designed merely to guide the believer to an appropriate interaction with his Creator? Why must you insist on both its origination in infancy and its direct, causal connection to religious faith? I insist because religion, like everything else, goes all the way down to the developmental roots of our internalizing mind-brains, to the unconscious strata where our neurological feedback loops begin to process the foundational "scenes" of our experience in the world. As I stated earlier, we don't "invent" religion and its cardinal expression, prayer; we act out our passionate, unconscious concerns as they emanate from our elemental, psychophysical interactions with other people. From the soil of what psychology calls "object relations" spring the psychodynamics of what religion calls "spiritual relations."

BRAIN WAVES

Just as Benson's remark that we are "wired for God" is misleading, so is it also misleading, or perhaps I should say superficial, to suggest that religious experience is neither more nor less than a certain kind of "brain wave" or an instance of "low activity" in the "orientation association area." I am referring on the one hand to the work of Michael Persinger of Laurentian University in Canada, who has attracted to himself a fair bit of notoriety by wiring his students up and then subjecting their temporal lobes to various magnetic patterns. When his students report "experiencing God" (along with a good many other things), Persinger cries bingo—God has been disclosed for the natural, electrical, material, inducible entity that He ultimately is.[19] On the other hand, I have in mind the work of Eugene D'Aquili, Andrew Newberg, and Vince Rause (mentioned in the preface), which finds that mystical, out-of-the-body experiences transpire on a regular basis when monks and nuns, through meditation or prayer, put the orientation association area (OAA) in a dormitive mode, which results in a neuronal confusion of the boundaries that demarcate a feeling of being in one's body and a feeling of being out of it.[20] Accordingly, the sensation of being at one with the universe, or with its divine Creator, is the result of behaviorally provoked cerebral departures from the mind-brain's normal mode of functioning. Surely the trouble with all this is perfectly obvious. To find "God" or "oneness with God" in the brain is no different than finding anything else there: everything we experience is mediated by the brain. What we require is the understanding of how these putative supernatural experiences came to be "in the brain" in the first place, psychologically, developmentally, naturalistically. *Why* does feeling "out of one's body" signify a union with the universe? Where did *that* idea come from: to be merged with the cosmos? How did people get to be monks and nuns? Why does stimulation of the temporal lobes turn up an image or a sensation of divinity? Why should such a thing as "divinity" be there at all? Might it have something to do with our *experience* in the world?

To behold an end result of our experiential development across time and in culture by electronically stimulating our brains or examining the cerebral apparatus may be entertaining or even useful in some way, but it hardly tells us who and what we are in any meaningful, human way. True, the developmental, psychological theories offered here might well be off the mark, might well be oblivious of decisive, behavioral, experiential factors that have simply eluded our imperfect investigations. But at least the theoretical cupboard we are opening to the reader is not bare; at least she will find *some* sort of developmental, human account that works to suggest how the supernatural domain may have arisen—I don't mean *ultimately* of course. From *that* perspective, it is God's "brain" that may have made ours. *He* may reside behind the experiments we run, the switches we pull, the currents we enkindle in our labs. I mean an account based upon our passionate, affective interactions, the biological, earthly dimension, which it is religion's goal to supersede and ours to put at the center of all mature, psychological inquiry.

EARTHLY AND CELESTIAL HARMONIES

I want to get at this further by turning for a final time to the relevant "spiritual" literature. If the reader has gained something already from his exposure to the classics of prayer, as well as from our selection of angelic encounters, he may well gain more from the following discussion of "synchronicity," a cornerstone of our current religio-magical age and a guiding central concept for those who adhere to the thinking of Carl Gustav Jung. My aim, as always, is to approach a striking religious, mystical, or paranormal phenomenon in a manner that discloses unmistakably its biological, naturalistic origins and significance from a specific psychological perspective.

Synchronicity: the term was coined, of course, by Jung,[21] and by it he means a coincidence so extraordinary that it supersedes mere chance to reveal what philosopher Gottfried Wilhelm Leibniz characterizes as the world's "preestablished harmony." The experiencer's participation in such an event causes him to "constellate the religious archetype," which is to say, causes him to feel the existence of the powerful, cohesive forces that reside both at the world's foundation and innately in his own being. As it turns out, Jung's favorite example of synchronicity derives from an incident that occurs in his consulting room. A patient with a Cartesian, rationalistic outlook (Jung presents her as "possessed" by rationalism) arrives for treatment shortly after having dreamed about an Egyptian scarab, or beetle. As she narrates the dream to Jung, a beetle flies into the office. Jung grabs the thing and shows it to the woman, who is, of course, flabbergasted. According to Jung, this wondrous event has the effect of breaking down his patient's rationalism and commencing her

spiritual rebirth. For Jungians generally, the beetle incident is surrounded by a "numinous," otherworldly glow; it is a supreme moment in
the history of Jungian psychotherapy and a witness to the accuracy of
Jung's synchronistic ruminations.

As we proceed to fashion our naturalistic approach to such events
we must remember that remarkable coincidences, even very remarkable
coincidences, are occurring all around us, all the time, and for no dis-
cernable higher or spiritual purpose. "I cannot stress too much," writes
Peter Watson in his definitive treatment of the subject, "that rare events
do happen. People do die in airplane crashes and get struck by lightning—they even make killings on the tables at Monte Carlo and Las
Vegas." Watson proceeds to describe a remarkable event that took place
in 1976 aboard the liner *Queen Elizabeth II*, during a crossing from
Southampton to New York. A young English gentleman tumbled over-
board while intoxicated and tossed about in the Atlantic for half an hour
before his absence was noted by his friends. The captain wheeled the
ship around and followed the traces of its wake. "Astounding as it may
seem," Watson informs us, "the Englishman was found thrashing about
in the water, his champagne glass still in his hand." Watson concludes
by observing that the "odds against finding someone in an ocean swell
like that must be enormous—but it happened."[22]

Once again, this time with the spiritual dimension implicitly in view:
"Improbable events *do* occur without the need to assume anything
supernatural to account for them."[23] The odds that you will be dealt a
royal flush during your next hand of poker, notes Watson, are 1 in
649,740; these are enormous odds, yet people on occasion are dealt a
royal flush. The odds that you will die during the course of a surgical
operation are 1 in 40,000; these are still extremely high odds, yet people
do die in surgical operations, rather frequently in fact.[24] Watson urges us
to remember that the world is a very large place, with trillions of living
creatures in it, including the rose-chafers, or beetles, of mountainous
Switzerland, where Jung's consulting room was located. Offering us a
brief history of his fascination with synchronous events, Jung writes that
certain of the coincidences he observed during the course of his life were
so remarkable "that their 'chance' concurrence would represent a degree

of improbability that would have to be expressed by an astronomical figure."[25] Well, as a preliminary reply to just this aspect of Jung's theory, would say simply that such things, involving just such astronomical odds, do in fact occur, and on a regular basis. "Events as rare as one in a million *do* happen," Watson instructs us again: "The truth is, in fact, that rare events are happening all the time. If that sounds paradoxical, remember it is a large world." He then writes, "Perhaps the most 'unlikely' gambling story that actually happened was when the 'even' [roulette] number came up at a Monte Carlo casino *28 times* in succession. . . . This configuration, it has been calculated, would occur by chance once every 286,435,456 times—*but it happened*. Mathematician Warren Weaver worked out, from the number of casinos and number of players each day, that, on average, this event should take place every 500 years at Monte Carlo. Rare events do happen."[26] Let me hasten to say here that I do not intend by all this to account for every remarkable coincidence in the history of the planet down to the present hour. Not only would that be impossible, it would also be superfluous. I mean, it is surely enough to observe that rare events do happen, everywhere, all the time, and without necessitating supernatural explanation, if our purpose is to demonstrate along naturalistic lines the way in which such rare events can trigger the emotional response that, for Jung, forms the synchronistic experience in its entirety. If we can perceive Jung's beetle in naturalistic terms, we can perceive enough to continue; we can perceive enough in the so-called objective realm to forge the empirical, psychological account of synchronicity that is our chief concern. We will have, on the one hand, the confident recognition that remarkable coincidences do happen in our world. We will not be "thrown" by them, or "spooked" by them. We will not be prone to go looking for the "paranormal" because something unlikely has occurred. On the other hand, we will have an entirely naturalistic explanation, rooted in personal, psychological factors, of the emotional response (including spiritual conviction) that may arise when a coincidence leads to a belief in synchronicity.

Of prime importance, then, is the individual's reaction to the "synchronistic" occurrence, his sense of something mysterious, divine, or "numinous," as Jung was fond of saying, having transpired, his conviction that a higher, guiding power must have brought such unconnected, distinct, disparate events together for his spiritual edification, his spiritual benefit, his inward, perceptual ascendance to an elevated plane of awareness. Jung informs us in his "Foreword to the *I Ching*" that "synchronicity takes coincidence of events in space and time as meaning something more than mere chance, namely, a peculiar interdependence of objective events among themselves as well as with the subjective (psychic) states of the observer."[27] For example, a quondam nonbeliever is gravitating toward a conversion to Catholicism. One day, as he sits pondering precisely this issue, the phone rings: it is a long-lost Catholic friend inviting him to attend an upcoming midnight mass. Surely a higher power is behind this, he realizes at once. Surely this is a "sign" directing him toward the change for which he has been preparing himself. Or again, an accountant at work in a bank is struggling to recall a brief, rather obscure article on financial matters that she recently perused. As she racks his brain, an assistant manager strolls by and drops a photocopy of the article on his desk. The two have never mentioned or discussed the paper. The accountant is stunned. How can this be? Surely such an event cannot be a mere coincidence. Surely unseen forces are working on her behalf. Or again, an artist dreams one night of an exotic, brightly colored, rarely seen bird. The next morning, upon awakening and looking out the bedroom window, he spies exactly such a creature in the treetops before him. Surely some divine, mysterious power has engendered this remarkable sequence. Surely the bird is a spiritual gift designed to enkindle his artistic imagination. As suggested, it is Jung's belief that such happenings attest to a "preestablished harmony" in the universe, to the existence of "elective affinities," to a congruous world, or *unus mundus*, rooted in transcendent "interconnections," in a single, overarching "soul," in "one common breathing"[28]—an especially vivid figure as we shall see very soon. The question for us is, of course, how might we regard all this "interconnection" and "preestablished harmony" from a purely naturalistic, biological angle? What is there in our development that might explain "synchronistic" occurrences—by which I mean both the coincidental event and the experiencer's subjective, "religious" reaction—in a perfectly straightforward manner, one that eschews Jung's metaphysical or perhaps mystical allusions? The answer emerges directly from the basic biological situation and the mnemonic feedback loops that commence their growth at the inception of our days.

Only during the course of the early period, when the caregiver and the child form the primary symbiotic unit, do we *actually experience*, actually and directly participate in, a single, whole world whose features are predominantly those found in Leibniz and Jung. Moreover, only during the course of the early period with its all-encompassing, core dyadic relationship do we *actually experience and internalize a whole world* in which *coincidence* or *concurrence* is a *central*, regular feature of the environment. Over and over again, dozens of times each day, hundreds of times each month, thousands of times each year, the care-giving parent, the mother, in the literal or generic sense of the term, fulfills the wishes and needs of the child—and not only fulfills them but does so in a *timely* fashion, *as* those wishes and needs emerge, *as* the child works to communicate his emotional and physical condition. The child is hungry; the child cries out. What happens then—not necessarily *at once* but often *at once* and very close to *at once* under normal, healthy circumstances? The caregiver appears to nourish and soothe. The child is wet and uncomfortable; the child cries out. What happens then? The caregiver appears with dry garments and ministering hands. The child is injured; the child cries out. What happens then? The caregiver appears to comfort and "make better." Consistently, diurnally, again and again and again, do we all *experience* these events directly, do we all participate in this "order," this "pattern," this "correspondence," this "regularity," this "meaning," this "interrelation of all things," for *in* this early "universe" the caregiver and the child *are* "all things" phenomenologically. Indeed, only during this period of our existence are *two* so powerfully united into *one* (dual unity); only during this period are "all things" so *concentrated* into one mutually devoted pair—a single "solar system" with twin stars revolving around each other. The first months and years of life, in fact, are *little else besides* an unending series of meaningful coincidences or meaningful concurrences or meaningful cross-connections, an unending series of physical and emotional *attunements*. Stephen Mitchell, following Winnicott, puts the matter this way: the key feature of the facilitating environment provided by the mother is her "effort to shape the environment around the child's wishes, to intuit what the child wants and provide it. The infant's experience is one of scarcely missing a beat between desire and satisfaction, between the wish for the breast and its appearance, for example. The infant naturally assumes that his wishes produce the object of desire, that the breast, his blanket, in effect his entire world, is the product of his creation. The mother's provision and accommodation to the infant's wish create what Winnicott terms 'the moment of illusion,' the foundation upon which a healthy self develops."[29] Thus the "preestablished harmony" of our *actual lives,* our *actual experiences*, is simply nature's creation of the integrated mother-child unit, through which the furtherance of the species' well-being, the furtherance of the species' *existence*, is more or less assured. It is adaptational necessity, biological, adaptational *cunning* in the service of the species' continuation that "preestablishes" the only perfect or nearly perfect interrelational "harmony" we ever *actually know* on the planet. The mother with the babe nestled in her arms is the unconscious source of Leibniz's philosophical-theological visions; the attunement of caregiver and child, and the endless concurrence that arises *from* that attunement, is the unconscious source of Jung's synchronicity: as the astounding, magical, uncanny coincidence transpires, as it is *registered*, one wishfully projects the internalized caregiver into the external world; one wishfully restores the original care-giving arrangement; some one, some thing, some presence is watching over me again. The environment and the self *remerge*. The uncanny coincidence, which "can't be figured out" and thus lulls the critical faculty to sleep, is one's *excuse* for rearranging the world in accordance with one's infantile wishes.

Just think about it for a moment. The notions of "preestablished harmony," "one common breathing," and *unus mundus* do not come out of the blue, nor do the emotions we attach to them. Some realistic source, some actual, natural source must in some measure give rise to these ideas and feelings. As it turns out, there is only one period in our lives during the course of which our experience *actually reflects*, actually approximates the kind of world that is suggested by the expressions preestablished harmony, one common breathing, *unus mundus*. Do we dare rule this period *out*? Do we dare ignore it as we strive to determine the significance of the Jungian-Leibnizean cosmos? No one would even dream of maintaining that the ideas and feelings we associate with marriage, divorce, separation, family, love, death, and so forth do not arise in some measure from our early interactional experience, our early psychological internalizations. Everyone understands that marriage, divorce, love, and death reach all the way down to our foundations as people, to the inner infant, the "inner child," as the popular usage has it. Why should preestablished harmony, *unus mundus*, and the related notion of synchronicity be exceptions? Why should the belief that God has created a perfectly "symmetrical" universe, in which miraculous coincidences continually occur for our potential benefit, be an exception? Surely when we emote over the idea that a supreme being is out there and guiding us, we are to some extent at least reexperiencing a time when *this was the case*. Surely that makes perfect, even obvious sense. And surely there is *in that* a perfectly obvious psychological *cause* for the occurrence of synchronicities, which, according to Jung, do not *have* a cause in the usual meaning of the term.[30] Allow me to approach the whole matter from another angle, one that focuses somewhat more closely on the individual who finds himself returning to the *unus mundus*.

The synchronistic event is rooted overwhelmingly in projection. Specifically, the subject projects the internalized caregiver back out into the environment where the caregiver originally resided during life's early stages. The ego boundaries that came to separate the parent and the child are, in the synchronistic moment, dissolved; the external world and the self are, once again, interlocked. The remarkable coincidence that triggers the projection (I am thinking here on Jung's beetle) is, to render it impressionistically, "not supposed to happen": the subject of the synchronistic event has already transferred to himself the object's care-giving function. *He* is now the one who watches over his existence. *He* is now the one who intervenes in a *timely* fashion on his own behalf. The synchronistic happening turns all this around. It suggests—and here is the magical, uncanny, "numinous" side of the business—that the caregiver is once more out there in the universe, that the caregiver has somehow *returned* to meet the subject's needs *when* they arise, in a *timely* manner, as was the case exactly during the foundational years. This is the unconscious *meaning* in the "meaningful coincidence," in the two events that are linked integrally by *time*. In this way, a synchronicity comprises a "return of the repressed," an *upheaval* that cannot be rationally or logically explained. If the subject is religious, if he has partially transferred the care-giving function to the deity, then a synchronistic event may be subsumed under the category of the miraculous, the category of divine intervention, or sign. The projective element will pass through the realm of the subject's illusory, transitional creations. Freud notes that traumatic incidents from the past can be reactivated by disturbing incidents in the present.[31] Slumbering mnemonic residues awaken. Accordingly, a remarkable coincidence is a kind of trauma. It strikes the subject as unbelievable, astonishing, weird. It shocks him or "shakes him up." Think of the jolt Jung's patient gets when he shows her the beetle. What the shock of synchronicity *predicates* is precisely the loss of ego boundaries to which I referred a moment ago. One has the sense of falling back into the early period, when the external world in the form of the object hovered over one and ministered to one's needs. Remember, during life's initial stages the parent *is* the entire universe to the child. In the midst of this wondrous, uncanny episode, one that is ultimately "inexplicable," the subject may also experience the symbiotic affect, indeed the gratitude and worship, that characterized his early interactions with the maternal figure upon whose love and care he entirely depended. As the subject projects all this into the world, the world undergoes a wishful transformation. Shedding its ordinary qualities, it becomes a place of intimacy, of bonding, of caring—a place of maternal holding and solicitude. In a word, the transformational, synchronistic moment offers the subject an opportunity to reattach himself to creation, to be "reborn" in a state of security and thankfulness. Synchronicity is an instance of transitional behavior, behavior that ultimately restores the early period, with the early period's "good object" as the centerpiece, of course. Synchronicity marks a regression to the stage when two were one in perfectly timed and attuned symbiotic exchange.

Throughout antiquity (and still in some primitive societies today) people sought for synchronicities from the gods through prayers and rituals. As parental projections fashioned unconsciously to account for natural events, the gods were the source of life and death, abundance and scarcity, creation and destruction. Moreover, their powers were directly associated with the element of *time*. One beseeched the gods for rain when rain was needed, for wind when wind was needed, for protection when protection was needed. And when the gods responded positively and thereby mirrored the good parent's behavior, one felt at home and secure in the world. Synchronicity is a partial, individualistic, small-scale version of such ancient spiritual belief and practice. One *registers* the coincidence of an external event with an inward aim of one's own, and one consequently believes "the gods" are on one's side. The unconscious, mnemonic reactivation of the early period and the good object's care give a boost to the ego, a boost to the will. One feels lucky as the gambler feels lucky when he is winning. One feels fortunate, blessed, in synch with creation. In the Jungian consulting room, it is the therapist who sits in the seat of the god. It is the therapist who "controls the climate" and who devises the "synchronicities," the "meaningful coincidences," that awaken the patient's capacity for wishful illusions, that convince the patient of the world's "numinous" involvement in his desires and activities. This is the goal of Jungian analysis: to cement the patient's spiritual attachment to the world.[32] Concomitantly, Jung's treatise "On Synchronicity" is his attempt to assure us, as members of the modern, materialistic order, not only that we are "wired for God" but that it takes only a jolt from a striking coincidence to establish His presence in our lives. By contrast, the sole, limited aim of the book the reader is now concluding has been from its inception to indicate in at least a preliminary way the naturalistic, psychological direction from which all such false, hallucinatory perceptions arise.

NOTES

1. Herbert Benson, *Timeless Healing: The Power and Biology of Belief* (New York: Scribner's, 1996), p. 195.

2. Virginia Demos, "Psychoanalysis and the Human Sciences," *American Imago* 58 (2001): 679.

3. Robert Plomin, *Development, Genetics, and Psychology* (Hillsdale, NJ: Erlbaum, 1986), p. 21.

4. Sharon Begley, "The Mind and the Brain," *Wall Street Journal*, October 11, 2002, p. B1.

5. Peggy La Cerra and Roger Bigelow, *The Origin of Minds: Evolution, Uniqueness, and the New Science of the Self* (New York: Harmony Books, 2002), p. 5.

6. Michael Shermer, "Challenging the Brain's Canon," *Los Angeles Times Book Review*, February 23, 2003, p. R1.

7. See D. W. Winnicott, *Playing and Reality* (London: Penguin, 1971).

8. See Romano Guardini, *Prayer in Practice*, trans. L. Loewenstein-Wertheim (London: Burns and Oates, 1957), p. 77.

9. Ole Hallesby, *Prayer*, trans. C. Carlsen (Leicester, UK: Intervarsity Press, 1957), p. 20.

10. Marvin Harris, *Our Kind* (New York: Harper and Row, 1989), pp. 399–400.

11. Robert Coles, *The Spiritual Life of Children* (Boston: Houghton Mifflin, 1990), pp. 249–75.

12. Ibid., pp. 225–48.

13. Ibid., pp. 203–24.

14. Ibid., p. 302.

15. Ibid., p. 40.

16. Winnicott, *Playing and Reality*, pp. 112, 114.

17. George A. Buttrick, ed., *The New Interpreter's Dictionary of the Bible* (New York: Abingdon Press, 1962), 2:221.

18. Frederick Faber, quoted in Tony Castle, ed., *The New Book of Christian Prayers* (New York: Crossroad, 1986), p. 20.

19. Michael Persinger, *The Neuropsychological Bases of God Belief* (Westport, CT: Praeger, 1987).

20. Eugene D'Aquili, Andrew Newberg, and Vince Rause, *Why God Won't Go Away: Brain Science and the Biology of Belief* (New York: Ballantine Books, 2002).

21. Carl Gustav Jung, "On Synchronicity: An Acausal Connecting Principle," in *The Structure and Dynamics of the Psyche*, trans. R. F. C. Hull, vol. 8 of *Collected Works* (Princeton, NJ: Princeton University Press), pp. 420–531.

22. Peter Watson, *Twins: An Uncanny Relationship* (New York: Viking Press, 1981), p. 135.

23. Ibid., p. 132.

24. Ibid., p. 105.

25. Jung, "On Synchronicity," p. 437.

26. Watson, *Twins*, p. 103.

27. Carl Gustav Jung, "Foreword to the *I Ching*," in *Psychology and the East*, trans. R. F. C. Hull (London: Routledge and Kegan Paul, 1986), pp. 192–93.

28. Jung, "On Synchronicity," pp. 490–94.

29. Stephen Mitchell, *Relational Concepts in Psychoanalysis* (Cambridge, MA: Harvard University Press, 1988), p. 31.

30. The full title of Jung's major work on synchronicity, cited earlier, is "On Synchronicity: An Acausal Connecting Principle." By "acausal" Jung suggests that "synchronicities" are engendered in ways that elude standard, objective methods of determination. He tries to explain these ways by alluding to quantum theory, the *I Ching*, metaphysics, and of course the spiritual literature of the world.

31. Sigmund Freud, *Inhibitions, Symptoms, and Anxiety*, trans. J. Strachey (1932; New York: W. W. Norton, 1959), p. 9.

32. It is worth noting here that Jung paid very little attention to children during the course of his career as a psychologist. He simply wasn't interested in human behavior from a developmental, clinical perspective. As F. X. Charet observes in his fine historical study, Spiritualism and the Foundation of C. G. Jung's Psychology (Albany: State University of New York Press, 1993), "There is ample evidence that Jung did not explore the life of childhood in order to establish the precise causes of later psychiatric and psychological disorders. . . . The bulk of Jung's writings are concerned with elucidating the archetypal background against which the experiences of adult life should be understood. . . . Jung idealized children. . . . [His] psychology has largely ignored childhood" (pp. 63, 83). Anthony Storr puts it this way in C. G. Jung (New York: Viking Books, 1973): "There is very little indeed to be found specifically upon the psychology of children throughout the Collected Works of Jung" (p. 66). The point is, had Jung turned to infancy and childhood, had he relied upon real human beings interacting with one another as opposed to his metaphysical

visions, he might have spied synchronicity's connection to the natural, biological order. In addition to the many points we've just made, think on the connection between synchronicity and the time sense, and on the origin of the time sense in the parent-child interaction, as explicitly described by Peter Harto-collis, "Origins of Time," *Psychoanalytic Quarterly* 43 (1974): 243–61, in our theoretical sections and implicitly by Mitchell, *Relational Concepts in Psycho-analysis*, earlier in this chapter.

Bibliography

Abrams, M. H., ed. *The Norton Anthology of English Literature.* Vol. 2. 4th ed. New York: W. W. Norton, 1979.

Alston, William P. *Perceiving God: The Epistemology of Religious Experience.* Ithaca, NY: Cornell University Press, 1991.

Anderson, Joan W. *Where Angels Walk.* New York: Ballantine Books, 1993.

Armstrong, Karen. *A History of God.* New York: Ballantine Books, 1993.

Bank, Rona. "Mythic Perspectives and Perspectives on Truth: Approaching Winnicott." *Psychoanalytic Review* 86 (1999): 109–36.

Basch, Michael. "Psychoanalytic Interpretation and Cognitive Transformation." *International Journal of Psychoanalysis* 62 (1981): 151–74.

Becker, Ernest. *The Denial of Death.* New York: Free Press, 1973.

Begley, Sharon. "The Mind and the Brain." *Wall Street Journal,* October 11, 2002, pp. B1, B4.

Benson, Herbert. *Timeless Healing: The Power and Biology of Belief.* New York: Scribner's, 1996.

Bleich, David. "New Considerations on the Infantile Acquisition of Language and Symbolic Thought." Paper presented to the Psychological Center for the Study of the Arts, State University of New York at Buffalo, March 16, 1990, pp. 1–28.

Blum, Harold. "The Conceptual Development of Regression." *Psychoanalytic Study of the Child* (Yale) 49 (1994): 60–76.

Bockian, Neil. *New Hope for People with Borderline Personality Disorders.* New York: Prima, 2002.

Bollas, Christopher. *The Shadow of the Object: Psychoanalysis of the Unthought-Known*. London: Free Association Books, 1987.

Browne, Sylvia. *Sylvia Browne's Book of Angels*. Carlsbad, CA: Hay House, 2003.

Browning, Robert. "The Guardian Angel." In *The Complete Works of Robert Browning*, ed. H. Scudder, pp. 194–95. Cambridge, MA: Houghton Mifflin, 1895.

Bruno, Frank. *Psychological Symptoms*. New York: John Wiley and Sons, 1993.

Burkert, Walter. *Creation of the Sacred: Tracks of Biology in Early Religion*. Cambridge, MA: Harvard University Press, 1996.

Buttrick, George A., ed. *The New Interpreter's Dictionary of the Bible*. Vol. 2. New York: Abingdon Press, 1962.

———. *So We Believe, So We Pray*. New York: Abingdon-Cokesbury, 1994.

Castle, Tony, ed. *The New Book of Christian Prayers*. New York: Crossroad, 1986.

Charet, F. X. *Spiritualism and the Foundation of C. G. Jung's Psychology*. Albany: State University of New York Press, 1993.

Coles, Robert. *The Spiritual Life of Children*. Boston: Houghton Mifflin, 1990.

Cotter, Patrick. *How to Pray: A Guide to Deeper Spiritual Fulfillment*. Boca Raton, FL: Globe Communications, 1999.

Crim, Keith, ed. *The Perennial Dictionary of World Religions*. New York: Harper and Row, 1989.

Cupitt, Don. *After God: The Future of Religion*. New York: Basic Books, 1997.

D'Aquili, Eugene, Andrew Newberg, and Vince Rause. *Why God Won't Go Away: Brain Science and the Biology of Belief*. New York: Ballantine Books, 2002.

Delgado, Jose. *Physical Control of the Mind*. New York: Harper and Row, 1971.

Demos, Virginia. "Psychoanalysis and the Human Sciences." *American Imago* 58 (2001): 649–84.

Dossey, Larry. *Healing Words: The Power of Prayer and the Practice of Medicine*. San Francisco: HarperSanFrancisco, 1993.

Douglas, Mary. *Natural Symbols: Explorations of Cosmology*. London: Routledge, 1996.

————. *Purity and Danger: An Analysis of the Concepts of Pollution and Taboo.* New York: Ark Paperbacks, 1984.

Edelman, Gerald M. *The Remembered Present: A Biological Theory of Consciousness.* New York: Basic Books, 1989.

Eigen, Michael. "Toward Bion's Starting Point." *International Journal of Psychoanalysis* 66 (1985): 321–30.

Elwell, Walter A., ed. *Evangelical Dictionary of Biblical Theology.* Grand Rapids, MI: Baker Books, 1996.

Erikson, Erik H. *Insight and Responsibility.* New York: W. W. Norton, 1964.

————. *Young Man Luther.* New York: W. W. Norton, 1958.

Feuerbach, Ludwig. *The Essence of Christianity.* 1841. Translated by G. Eliot. Amherst, NY: Prometheus Books, 1989.

Foster, Richard S. *Prayer: Finding the Heart's True Home.* New York: HarperCollins, 1992.

Frank, Leonard R., ed. *Quotationary.* New York: Random House, 1998.

Frazer, James. *The Golden Bough.* 1900. New York: Mentor Books, 1959.

Freeman, Eileen E. *Angelic Healing.* New York: Warner Books, 1995.

————. *Touched by Angels.* New York: Warner Books, 1994.

Freud, Sigmund. *Civilization and Its Discontents.* 1930. Translated by J. Strachey. New York: W. W. Norton, 1960.

————. *The Future of an Illusion.* 1927. Translated by J. Strachey. New York: W. W. Norton, 1964.

————. *Inhibitions, Symptoms, and Anxiety.* 1932. Translated by J. Strachey. New York: W. W. Norton, 1959.

Gallagher, Winifred. "Motherless Child." *Sciences* 32 (July 1992): 12–15.

George, Leonard. "To Err is Human, to Forgive Divine." *Georgia Straight* (Vancouver, BC), June 22, 2000, p. 7.

Gilligan, Carol. *In a Different Voice.* Cambridge, MA: Harvard University Press, 1982.

Godwin, Malcolm. *Angels: An Endangered Species.* New York: Simon and Schuster, 1990.

Goldman, Karen. *Angel Encounters: True Stories of Divine Intervention.* New York: Simon and Schuster, 1995.

Graham, Billy. *Angels: God's Secret Agents.* New York: Doubleday, 1954.

Greenacre, Phyllis. "The Transitional Object and the Fetish." *Psychoanalytic Quarterly* 40 (1971): 384–85.

Greenberg, Irving. *The Jewish Way.* New York: Simon and Schuster, 1993.

Guardini, Romano. *Prayer in Practice*. Translated by L. Loewenstein-Wertheim. London: Burns and Oates, 1957.

Hale, Nathan G., Jr. *The Rise and Crisis of Psychoanalysis in the United States: Freud and the Americans, 1917–1985*. Vol. 2. New York: Oxford University Press, 1995.

Hallesby, Ole. *Prayer*. 1948. Translated by C. Carlsen. Leicester, UK: Intervarsity Press, 1979.

Harris, Marvin. *Our Kind*. New York: Harper and Row, 1989.

Hartocollis, Peter. "Origins of Time." *Psychoanalytic Quarterly* 43 (1974): 243–61.

Hauck, Rex. *Angels: The Mysterious Messengers*. New York: Ballantine Books, 1994.

Heiler, Friedrich. *Prayer: A Study in the History and psychology of Religion*. 1932. Oxford: Oxford University Press, 1997.

Hinnells, John R., Jr., ed. *The Penguin Dictionary of Religions*. London: Penguin Books, 1995.

Horgan, John. "Why Freud Isn't Dead." *Scientific American* 282 (December 1996): 106–11.

Jacobs, Louis. *The Jewish Religion: A Companion*. New York: Oxford University Press, 1995.

James, William. *The Varieties of Religious Experience*. 1902. New York: Library of America, 1987.

Johnston, Elizabeth. *Investigating Minds*. Bronxville, NY: Sarah Lawrence College, 2001.

Jones, Timothy. *The Art of Prayer: A Simple Guide*. New York: Ballantine Books, 1997.

Jung, Carl Gustav. "Foreword to the *I Ching*." In *Psychology and the East*, translated by R. F. C. Hull, pp. 189–208. London: Routledge and Kegan Paul, 1986.

———. "On Synchronicity: An Acausal Connecting Principle." In *The Structure and Dynamics of the Psyche*, translated by R. F. C. Hull. Vol. 8 of *Collected Works*, pp. 420–531. Princeton, NJ: Princeton University Press, 1981.

Kirschner, Suzanne. *The Religious and Romantic Origins of Psychoanalysis: Individuation and Integration in Post-Freudian Theory*. Cambridge: Cambridge University Press, 1996.

La Cerra, Peggy, and Roger Bigelow. *The Origin of Minds: Evolution, Uniqueness, and the New Science of the Self*. New York: Harmony Books, 2002.

Le Doux, Joseph. *Synaptic Self: How Our Brains Become Who We Are.* New York: Viking, 2002.

Levy, Donald. *Freud among the Philosophers: The Psychoanalytic Unconscious and Its Philosophical Critics.* New Haven, CT: Yale University Press, 1996.

Lewis, James R., and Evelyn D. Oliver. *Angels, A to Z.* New York: Gale Research, 1996.

Liechty, Daniel. "Freud and the Question of Pseudoscience." *Ernest Becker Foundation Newsletter* 6 (1999): 6–7.

Lindsay, Gordon. *Prayer That Moves Mountains.* Dallas: Christ for the Nations, 1996.

Mahler, Margaret, and Manuel Furer. *On Human Symbiosis and the Vicissitudes of Individuation.* New York: International Universities Press, 1968.

Mahler, Margaret, Fred Pine, and Anni Bergman. *The Psychological Birth of the Human Infant.* New York: Basic Books, 1975.

Meissner, W. W. *Psychoanalysis and Religious Experience.* New Haven, CT: Yale University Press, 1984.

Milner, Marion. *The Suppressed Madness of Sane Men.* London: Tavistock, 1987.

Mitchell, Stephen A. *Relational Concepts in Psychoanalysis.* Cambridge, MA: Harvard University Press, 1988.

Myers, David G. *Intuition: Its Powers and Perils.* New Haven, CT: Yale University Press, 2002.

Neubauer, Peter. "Preoedipal Objects and Object Primacy." *Psychoanalytic Study of the Child* (Yale) 40 (1985): 163–82.

Neumann, Erich. *The Great Mother.* Translated by R. Manheim. Princeton, NJ: Princeton University Press, 1970.

Nietzsche, Friedrich. *The Gay Science.* 1882. New York: Vintage, 1974.

O'Neill, Kim. *How to Talk with Your Angels.* New York: Avon Books, 1995.

Parker, Rozsika. *Mother Love/Mother Hate.* New York: Basic Books, 1995.

Perakh, Mark. "A Presentation without Arguments." *Skeptical Inquirer* 26 (November 2002): 31–34.

Persinger, Michael. *The Neuropsychological Bases of God Belief.* Westport, CT: Praeger, 1987.

Person, Ethel. *Dreams of Love and Fateful Encounters.* London: Penguin, 1990.

Pine, Fred. "On the Psychology of the Separation-Individuation Crisis." *International Journal of Psychoanalysis* 60 (1979): 225–42.

Plomin, Robert. *Development, Genetics, and Psychology*. Hillsdale, NJ: Erlbaum, 1986.

Plotkin, Henry. *Evolution in Mind: An Introduction to Evolutionary Psychology*. London: Penguin, 1997.

Polkinghorne, John. *Belief in God in an Age of Science*. New Haven, CT: Yale University Press, 1998.

Prophet, Elizabeth Clare. *How to Work with Angels*. Corwin Springs, MT: Summit University Press, 1998.

Pruitt, James. *Healed by Prayer*. New York: Avon Books, 2000.

Rank, Otto. *Psychology and the Soul*. Translated by W. Turner. New York: A. S. Barnes, 1950.

Restak, Richard M. *The Infant Mind*. New York: Doubleday, 1986.

Rheingold, Joseph P. *The Fear of Being of Woman*. New York: Grune and Stratton, 1964.

Rizzuto, Ana-Marie. *The Birth of the Living God*. Chicago: University of Chicago Press, 1979.

Rogers, Robert. *Self and Other: Object Relations in Psychoanalysis and Literature*. New York: New York University Press, 1991.

Roheim, Geza. *Magic and Schizophrenia*. Bloomington: University of Indiana Press, 1955.

Roland, Paul. *Angels*. London: Judy Piatkus, 1999.

Roustang, François. *Dire Mastery: Discipleship from Freud to Lacan*. Baltimore: Johns Hopkins University Press, 1976.

Schachtel, Ernest. "On Memory and Childhood Amnesia." 1947. In *Memory Observed: Remembering in Natural Contexts*, edited by Ulric Neisser, pp. 189–200. New York: W. H. Freeman, 1982.

Schacter, Daniel L. *Searching for Memory: The Brain, the Mind, the Past*. New York: Basic Books, 1996.

Schlagel, Richard H. *The Vanquished Gods: Science, Religion, and the Nature of Belief*. Amherst, NY: Prometheus Books, 2001.

Schumaker, John F. *The Corruption of Reality: A Unified Theory of Religion, Hypnosis, and Psychopathology*. Amherst, NY: Prometheus Books, 1995.

Shaw, Mary. *Your Anxious Child*. New York: Birch Lane Press, 1995.

Sheldrake, Rupert, and Matthew Fox. *The Physics of Angels: Exploring the Realm Where Science and Spirit Meet*. San Francisco: HarperSanFrancisco, 1996.

Shermer, Michael. "Challenging the Brain's Canon." *Los Angeles Times Book Review*, February 23, 2003, p. R12.

Siegel, Daniel L. *The Developing Mind: Toward a Neurobiology of Interpersonal Experience.* New York: Guilford Press, 1999.

Smart, Ninian. *The Religious Experience of Mankind.* New York: Scribner's, 1969.

Solms, Mark. "Freud Returns." *Scientific American* 290 (May 2004): 82–89.

Southwood, H. M. "The Origin of Self-Awareness and Ego Behavior." *International Journal of Psychoanalysis* 66 (1973): 321–30.

Spitz, René. *The First Relationship.* New York: International Universities Press, 1965.

Steinzor, Bernard. "Death and the Construction of Reality." *Omega: Journal of Death and Dying* 9 (1979): 97–124.

Stern, Daniel. *The Interpersonal World of the Infant.* New York: Basic Books, 1985.

Stone, Joshua. *Soul Psychology: How to Clear Negative Emotions and Spiritualize Your Life.* New York: Ballantine Books, 1999.

Storr, Anthony. *C. G. Jung.* New York: Viking Books, 1973.

Taylor, Terry Lynn. *The Alchemy of Prayer: Rekindling Our Inner Life.* Tiburon, CA: H. J. Kramer, 1996.

———. *The Angel Experience.* San Raphael, CA: Amber-Allen, 1998.

Thompson, Keith. *Angels and Aliens: UFOs and the Mythic Imagination.* New York: Addison-Wesley, 1991.

Tomkins, Silvan S. *Affect, Imagery, Consciousness.* Vol. 1. New York: Springer, 1962.

Ullman, Chana. *The Transformed Self: The Psychology of Religious Conversion.* New York: Plenum Press, 1989.

Vygotsky, Lev. *Thought and Language.* 1934. Translated by E. Hanfman and G. Vakar. Cambridge, MA: MIT Press, 1979.

Watson, Peter. *Twins: An Uncanny Relationship.* New York: Viking Press, 1981.

Webb, C. C. J. *God and Personality.* New York: Kraus Reprint, 1971.

Webster, Richard. *Why Freud Was Wrong: Sin, Science, and Psychoanalysis.* New York: Basic Books, 1995.

Whitmer, Gary. "On the Nature of Dissociation." *Psychoanalytic Quarterly* 70 (2001): 807–37.

Wilson, Emmett, Jr. "The Object in Person." *Psychoanalytic Quarterly* 71 (2002): 381–96.

Winnicott, D. W. *Playing and Reality.* London: Penguin, 1971.

Winward, Stephen. *Teach Yourself How to Pray*. London: English Universities Press, 1961.

Wolf, Fred Alan. *The Dreaming Universe*. New York: Simon and Schuster, 1994.

Wood, Derek. "What Is a Hallucination?" *A Mood Journal*, May 2003, pp. 1–3.

Index